The Goddess on the Cross

George Young

The Goddess on the Cross

ISBN 186163 090 5

Cover design by Paul Mason
Cover painting by Dave Kendall

Published by:

Capall Bann Publishing
Freshfields
Chieveley
Berks
RG20 8TF

Contents

Preface

The Diana Cult

On the night of August the 31st 1997 the car in which Diana, Princess of Wales, was being driven crashed in an underpass in Paris. It had not long left the Ritz Hotel where Diana and her boyfriend, Dodi Fayed, had been besieged during the night by the international paparazzi. It was to evade these photographers on their mopeds that the driver had picked up speed on the way down into the underpass and thus precipitated the crash. In the collision the driver was killed, as was Dodi Fayed. Both appear to have died instantaneously. A bodyguard in the car survived but was badly injured. Diana was apparently conscious for a few moments as she lay twisted in the wreckage of the car. Her face was clearly visible to the huddle of photographers struggling to take their shots and hindering as they did so the efforts of a passing doctor to administer first aid. The sight of them staring in may have been her last vision of this world for, soon after, she lost consciousness and never regained it. Unbelted in the back of the car, she had sustained massive head and chest injuries. Those who reported seeing her in the hospital later spoke of the poignancy of this most singular casualty of the crash, remarking on the incredible blueness of her eyes and the beauty of a face which, though horribly contorted, was still recognisable as the one that had adorned a thousand magazines. There was also a sign of things to come when, as she finally expired, the nursing staff who had struggled frantically to save her life burst into tears, some sobbing uncontrollably.

Back in England the news of her death reached the Royal Family in its summer retreat at Balmoral in Scotland. As often happens at such times, first reactions set the tone. The attitude was to be one of stoical resolve. It was at the Queen's insistence, for example, that the young sons of Diana be allowed to sleep on and not be told of the news till they woke in the morning. Prince Charles appears to have been the only member of the Royal Family to grasp quite early on that extraordinary consequences might flow from this cataclysmic event, that this was one catastrophe that could indeed have catastrophic effects and, in particular, on the Royal Family and its standing with the nation.

When dawn broke over Balmoral that stoicism that had always served the Royal Family so well was already being forced to give ground. In fact, the royal establishment was in considerable disarray as to how collectively to respond. Diana had been an embarrassment to what the family liked to call 'the firm' almost from the start of her marriage to Charles. She had been an outsider, untrained for the part, who had signally failed to play the role tradition had allotted her as the wife of the heir apparent to the throne. Her at times bizarre alternation of the sex goddess role with that of the lady of mercy had made her a media personality of extraordinary pulling power, a highly marketable product the world's press and television greedily consumed but one the Royal Family found too eccentric and volatile to accommodate.

In the end the Queen and Prince Philip had been scandalised by the break-up of the royal marriage for the very public nature of which they held Diana more culpable than Charles. Now, in the manner of her departure from this world, the princess had left them, it seemed, with her final parting shot. Embarrassment was what she had always signified to them and embarrassment was what she had left them with at the end. It was at the heart of the heated debate that followed that morning. Charles wanted to go to Paris to collect Diana's body and bring it home. The Queen was against the idea. Perhaps she, too, sensed the storm that was about to break over them and wanted to distance herself. In the end she was overruled.

The plane that was to bring Diana back took off from Northolt near London at 10.00am that Sunday morning. Its first stop was in Rutland to pick up Diana's sisters then on to Aberdeen to collect Charles. In Paris Charles found Diana already laid out in her coffin. She had been embalmed but the effects of the crash were all too evident. Her head had been partly crushed and her face was badly twisted. A red-eyed Charles, though, was still sufficiently in control of himself to remember protocol. He shook hands with the doctors and nurses and thanked all of them for the work they had done. Back on the plane the destination of the body became an issue again. It was to have been taken to the mortuary in Fulham used by the Royal Coroner but at Charles' own insistence the plan was changed. The body was to be taken to a more august resting place, the Chapel Royal in St James' Palace. Already the news of Diana's death had been broadcast and there were intimations of the extraordinary events about to unfold. As the hearse made its way into London, the route was lined with people who had come quite spontaneously to express their grief as the coffin passed. Elsewhere flowers were starting to arrive outside various buildings with which Diana had been associated in the public mind.

In the days that followed, these gathering waves of public sentiment grew stronger and stronger, reaching at times crescendos of grief. Thousands came to the gates of Buckingham Palace to lay flowers. There were so many bouquets over the coming days that, viewed from the air, they looked like an incoming tide of flowers engulfing the gates, a great white foam of foliage getting larger by the day. Thousands more simply milled around, looking lost in their bereavement. Others just stood there staring, as if stunned by the spectacle of which they were a part. Later, with hindsight, many were to accuse the media of whipping up this mass affirmation of grief. If truth be told, the media were as surprised as any by the intensity of the response and followed public opinion, hurrying always behind it, trying desperately to keep up with the momentum of the mourning that afflicted the nation that week.

Within the Royal Family stoicism had gone and confusion reigned. Arguments broke out about how to respond but still questions of scale, procedure and precedence ruled the day. Such issues, after all, are not just emblematic in royal circles. They are the very currency of their trade. Was the princess to have a private family funeral or was she to be accorded a full state funeral at Westminster Abbey? If public it was to be, then how massive, on what kind of scale? Who was to walk behind the cortége and, once they were chosen, what was to be the role of other members of the family in all of this? How could royal protocol cope with a flood of public sentiment that threatened to wash all rules of precedence away?

The Queen herself was still working to distance her family from the outpouring of grief. It was largely at her insistence that the Royal Family refused stubbornly to leave their Scottish retreat. It was she who made sure that there was as little disturbance as possible to royal routines. The young princes were made to attend church with the rest of the family on the Sunday morning after their mother's death. Stoicism might have lost the day but convention was still to be defended every inch of the way. This desperate attempt to dam up the tide of grief by holding the line of protocol against it seemed heartless and cold to those many thousands who seem to have decided to give up their lives for the next few days to an act of mass mourning.

Soon grief turned to anger at the apparent intransigence of the royals, their refusal to bend to the popular will and, if they could not share it, at least to give some kind of affirmation of the feeling of sorrow being expressed. That anger soon found a symbolic focus. It was a tradition that the flag was never flown at the palace when the Queen was away. Elsewhere flags were flying at half-mast. Only at the palace was there no such flag. The naked pole became to many a symbol of the hollow formality of royal protocol and its reluctance to offer even the smallest hostage to the nation's grief. Then, suddenly, as if in a flash they had been struck by the enormity of what the death had unleashed, the royal establishment changed tack. The Queen relented on the question of the flag and then she and Prince Philip decided to head south and surrender their fate to the popular mood. There seems little doubt that a surrender is how they saw it and that privately they were astonished, even appalled, by what had befallen them.

Five days after Diana's death Prince Charles and his two sons could be seen outside the gates of Buckingham Palace examining the sea of bouquets and talking to onlookers. Even the Duke of Edinburgh was there, making a valiant show of his interest in the proceedings, picking up the odd bouquet, eyeing it rather quizzically then setting it down. The royal establishment, it seems, had decided to enter as fully as it could into the spirit of an event whose élan it could no longer ignore. The Queen was to go even further in compromising her original stand. The night before the funeral she gave a live television broadcast in which, strained though at times it seemed, she did her best to identify herself with the general grieving, even managing to give the impression that for her the death had been a deep personal loss.

On the day of the funeral Prince Charles, the Duke of Edinburgh, Earl Spencer and the two young princes walked alongside each other behind the hearse. As the cortége with its small cavalcade clattered through the streets there were those in the crowds lining the route who burst into sobs of uncontrollable grief. Millions more throughout the world watched on television and shared in the mourning. The funeral procession was a truly astonishing manifestation of mass feeling. There was nothing like it before; there has been nothing like it since. Later, during the actual service, the Royal Family had to sit through the public humili-ation of being criticised for their treatment of Diana by her brother in the pulpit. His funeral oration with its many barbs was loudly applauded by the crowds gathered on the green outside. To many in the establishment, not least the Queen and the Duke, it must have seemed as if they were victims of some kind of late century mock-up of the French Revolution of 1789 when the French king and queen and the young dauphin had been led by force to the capital by the Paris mob.

The ceremony over, the Royal Family retreated to the shadows, irritated yet at the same time relieved that they had at least managed to present themselves as willing participants in what had occurred. No longer did they seem like strangers to their own people. Outside, though, the public acclamation of Diana and her memory was still flowing strong. The hearse struggled to make its way through the crowded streets. At times so many flowers were thrown to the cortége the driver of the hearse could not see for the foliage mounting above the wipers on his window. Even out of the city and along the motorway to Northamptonshire there were crowds lining the route that swept forward in waves to hurl flowers and wave their goodbye as the car passed. Finally, in the Spencer family residence in the village of Althorp the extraordinary day came to an end. Diana was laid to rest in the midst of the countryside in which she had lived as a child, there on an island in the middle of a lake, alone, at peace, at last.

There had been great funerals before, of statesmen like Churchill and Kennedy, even of film stars like Valentino, that had provoked widespread outpouring of grief but nothing like this. The preoccupation with Diana's death had dominated not just the day of the funeral but almost the entire preceding week. On the day itself millions had watched on television throughout the world but it was in Britain where the impact was inevitably most felt. The cities and towns of this land were virtually deserted from when the funeral began till quite late in the afternoon. Many shops closed for the whole of the day. Even crime plummeted. It was as if there were no outsiders to this national cult, not even the criminal fraternity. It was truly a week when life seemed to slow and then come to a stop. Many reported being emotionally affected by the collective sense of loss not just in the following hours, but for days, in some cases weeks, after the event.

Naturally, in the months that ensued, as the nation returned to is workaday world and the memories of that week began to fade, a new mood of self-questioning started to emerge. Social commentators felt freer to think and talk more analytically about the strange, almost eerie miasma of grief that had settled on the nation that August month. 'Why?' was the question in so many minds. Why did it happen in the way that it did? Why was everyone, the media included, taken so by surprise? Why such an incomparable outburst of mourning and from a nation notorious for its reluctance usually to express its feelings? And, finally, why for her in particular? What was it about this people's princess that her death should have triggered such an extraordinary manifestation of the popular will?

Was it something about her and her alone that had caused it all from start to finish? Media celebrities had come and gone before. So had princesses and philanthropists. Was it just that she was not just one of these but all of them in turn? Perhaps her own special cocktail of glamour, glitz and charitable work was simply too powerfully addictive to release the people from its grip. It could be that they had drunk too deep of the cocktail and for too long to recover from its loss without the catharsis of a massive outpouring of grief. Or was it something deeper, much deeper than that? Certainly there were those who felt so at the time, who sensed that the seismic shock that rocked the nation must have come from tensions far below the surface of people's lives. Many pointed to the alienation and atomisation of modern urban life that seem to call out for occasional acts of mass bonding in sorrow, anger or joy. Yet even this analysis seemed too shallow to detect the source of such an unprecedented act of mourning.

It seems pointless to compare what happened with other mass expressions of emotion. No other death of a prominent figure has come anywhere near matching the grief felt for Diana. In her case the sorrow was so sudden, so intense, so widespread, the death that sparked it must have struck something deep, very deep, in the collective psyche of the nation. It was as if there was a call to the people, like a call to arms but in this case a call to mourning and not from the present but from the past. It was as if a voice called, a voice long forgotten for thousands of years but now suddenly heard, a voice that demanded obeisance, that would not allow this woman to die unmourned by all. It is the present authorís conviction that what Dianaís death unleashed was the power of an ancient archetype embedded deep in the collective unconscious and that the grief we witnessed that week was the explosion of that archetypal force. Furthermore, that what we heard in the sobs of the crowd as the cortége passed were the echoes of an ancient matriarchal rite, a rite of mourning not for a princess but for a goddess.

To some this might seem a heavy burden to place on the shoulders of a young woman relatively uneducated, whom many thought psychologically disturbed and whose behaviour at times bordered on the bizarre. It might also strike the casual reader as rather far-fetched but that is only because we have been conditioned by so many centuries of worshipping a male god in rites held under the tutelage of male priests. That god, too, is mourned and has been so for two thousand years. So deeply imprinted in our culture is the image of his bleeding corpse on the cross that we find it almost impossible to imagine that once a goddess was mourned in his place. It was that goddess who returned to merge with the memory of the dead princess in that fateful week and release psychic energies that had been kept in check by patriarchal culture for thousands of years.

It is significant that the princess bore one of the goddess's ancient names for it was she who that week became briefly the goddess that once died to be reborn and return to her divine mother in the after-life. What is more, this ancient goddess of death and resurrection was the central symbol of a religious cult that once embraced the whole of Eurasia from Iceland to the Indus Valley millennia before Christianity was ever heard of. Hence the extraordinary power of Diana's death. It was the power of an echo, the echo of a death cult in which the mass expression of grief had been central to the rite, way back in the remote past.

It seems significant, too, that men mourned Diana but women mourners far outnumbered them for that mirrored the ancient goddess cult. Among the servitors of the great goddess, among the practitioners of her cult, women also outnumbered men. This, then, was the conviction that led to the research and writing of this book: that in the remote past of pre-history there was a rite of death and resurrection of a goddess and it was the return of that goddess to merge with the memory of the dead Diana that led to that incredible, incomparable outburst of grief that in one fateful week almost brought the monarchy to its knees.

In her life-time Diana generated many myths. In this respect, too, she was the lineal descendant of the ancient divinity whose image she mirrored in her short, sad, life. Her myths were media creations. A myth has a kind of condensed, poetic truth and perhaps there was a flicker of a truth in the images of Diana the people greedily consumed. If so, then it, was a media creation that registered no more than subliminally on the threshold of consciousness. It was Diana herself who gave the images a greater truth for in the end she lived out her own myth to its tragic conclusion as if completing its narrative by her own death. It was her death itself that finally exposed the truth that had been slowly unfolding through her life. That truth was that Diana was a sacrificial victim to the voyeurism of the age.

In that sense, too, there was a link with the past. Diana was not the first maidenly offering. There were others before her in other times and to a divinity of a different kind. These were the maidens who figured in ancient rites that dramatised the myth of the dying and resurrecting goddess. Perhaps her forbears suffered for a more noble cause. Certainly there was nothing ennobling about the altar on which Diana died. What ennobled her at the last was the celebration of her funeral rite. It was that that joined her to the sacrificial offerings in the distant past. The paparazzi who hounded her to her death in the Paris underpass were, it seems, but the dogs of death, servitors of a goddess calling for her daughter from the after-life. It is an eerie thought. No wonder the kingdom shook that week and is reverberating still.

Chapter 1

The Goddess

High up on the Konya Plain of southern Anatolia in modern Turkey lies the remains of an ancient settlement. The modern name for it is Catal Hüyük. It is a large settlement covering some thirty two acres and much of it has yet to be excavated. At its prime several thousand people inhabited this site some six or seven millennia before the Gospels were written down. Who these people were we may never know for at some point in the sixth millennium they abandoned the site leaving their buildings and their buried dead behind them. From the evidence they have left us of their way of life we can tell at least that they were anything but uncivilised. They could work stone, weave and spin. They could make baskets. They could produce a rudimentary form of pottery as well as more sophisticated objets d'art such as obsidian mirrors, ceremonial daggers, metal trinkets. They used cosmetics. The leisure to produce these goods came from the surplus of wealth of the crops they gathered in the surrounding fields for, although these people hunted still, they understood the principle of field cultivation and had already domesticated the sheep, the goat and the hunting dog. Yet these were no isolated Neolithic farmers. They lived in a world of traded goods, with obsidian as a possible commercial product. Technologically too, they were ahead of their time. They still used wooden vessels around the home but the working of copper and lead on the site was well in advance of the general spread of this technology in the centuries to come. Already these metals were being made into beads, tubes, possibly a few small tools.[1]

The remains so far uncovered suggest a complex urban settlement with many houses and religious shrines. From the evidence these contain we can make certain tentative assumptions as to what might have been the structure of society at the site. The surplus of wealth that fostered the crafts was also enough to support a priestly class. The privileges of this class were as apparent in death as they were in life. Their burials in the shrines of the town were more richly equipped and accoutred than those of lesser mortals in the private houses. Curiously, the privileges of this wealthy exit from the world went mainly to women. To judge from the manner of their burial, if there was a ruling class in this town, then it was one of a group of prominent women. Given the multiplicity of shrines around, the rulers of this town may well have been a college of priestesses. The privileges of the priestesses only confirm what archaeologists have long felt about this site. Its ruling culture appears to have been matriarchal in the sense that the status of womanhood gave access to apparent privilege and power. There is further evidence of this in the interior of the domestic houses. They were entered from the roof and had a stepped floor structure leading up to a large raised platform. These raised platforms appear to have belonged to the women for it was they who were buried under them. With them were placed the children. The lower, more constricted, peripheral areas were allotted to the men.

The sheer number of obviously religious constructions on the site is testimony to the religiosity of its former inhabitants. About a third of the rooms so far uncovered are cult rooms or shrines. So far these indicate a ritual practice comparatively unstained by the blood of animal or human sacrifice. The dead appear to have been exposed to flocks of vultures for the purposes of skeletal excarnation but no evidence remains of provision for sacrifice. Sacrifice was to be a feature of almost all religions in the later Ancient World and its absence here is strange. We also search in vain for any representation of human genitalia. Again, in what might have been a fertility religion the omission strikes us as unusual. In fact, the images of the shrines reveal that it was not sexuality that was the central mystery for these people but the act of giving birth. A female figure is frequently depicted with her legs splayed in what looks like a stylised picture of the birth position. In one of these portrayals she seems to be giving birth to three bulls' heads placed one above the other beneath her.

The appearance of these bulls' heads is significant. Bulls' heads or bucrania and many other renderings of the bull can be found in many of the shrines. They appear to be a symbol of a male principle in the divine which can also be found in other forms, in a boy or in another instance, in a hunter with a leopard skin hat seated on a bull. In some cases, this male is clearly the consort of a female; in others her son, but always in a minor role. In a way that is bewildering to those conditioned by two millennia of Christianity to the inevitable predominance of a male god, what is female and divine is the central axis of the religious universe of these shrines, the axis on which all turns, including the smaller and more peripheral male. We are evidently in the realm of a Mother Goddess. She appears to us in three guises; as a young nubile woman, as an older woman giving birth, and finally as a crone, perhaps her deathly aspect for in one shrine she protrudes with vulture-beaked breasts. In any one of these aspects she can surface on the walls of the shrines but this privilege is denied to her consort and her images and statuettes also heavily outnumber those of the male god.

In the absence of a written script at the site there are few clues as to the mythology that might have figured in the rites celebrated in the shrines. Of all images other than those of the goddess that of the bull is predominant. In the abundance of bucrania it is tempting to link the goddess with a bull cult thereby bringing the male principle back to centre stage. Tempting though it might be to those used to the patriarchal flavour of the religions of the West, this elevation of the male runs counter to the other evidence at the site of his subordinate status. Given that evidence, it would be wiser to look for more exclusively feminine mythological relations. Such relations can, in fact, be inferred from some of the other images in the shrines. In shrine VI A.10 has been found a white marble figure of a dual goddess, with two heads, two pairs of breasts but only a single pair of arms. Twin goddess figures are also present in other shrines. In some of these portrayals one goddess is evidently older than the other, to judge from the presence of breasts for her alone and the greater maturity of her contours. Collectively the evidence of all these images would seem to point to a general representation of a mother goddess and her daughter or, as some would have it, 'mother' and 'maid'. Yet the question remains: what kind of mythical tradition could have sealed these goddesses together like Siamese twins? Why should a mother and daughter be joined together in a single image? What was the story behind their juxtaposition? To answer these questions we need to probe much deeper into the possible universe of meaning in which their worshippers lived.

Thousands of years before the community at Catal Hüyük began to farm the Konya plain their Stone Age predecessors scratched and daubed on the walls of caves the first enduring symbols known to man. The images on the walls are the earliest evidence we have of religious rites. What was celebrated in the flickering light of these caves is still a mystery. Some of the imagery is of the hunt. Arrows fleck the air. Bison tumble at the kill. Stick-like figures circle in what looks like an act of obeisance or adoration. A shaman hops about in imitation of a stag on its hind legs. These powerful and often quite eerie symbols on the walls are not, however, the only evidence of primitive religious ritual. Some time after the first etchings on the walls the earliest religious artifacts appeared. These are known as the Venus figurines and their meaning has troubled archaeologists ever since they were first discovered, buried in the soil or scattered on the cave floors. Carved in bone, ivory or stone, these figurines arrived in Europe among the implements of a people known as the Gravettian culture from the 'gravette' or blade tool they used. With heads unhewn and faces featureless but with breasts and buttocks enlarged to the point of grotesquerie, these figures look for all the world like a celebration of all that was fecund in the maternal principle.

The distorted lineaments of the Venus figurines are scarcely the stuff of which erotica are made. Their shape points rather to gestation and birth as the source of the mystery they celebrate. Archaeologists have been perhaps too willing to see in them a preoccupation with fertility in a utilitarian sense in which the figurines were used in rites of sympathetic magic for the hunt. There is no representation of such a figure on any cave wall close to the scene of a hunt. The artists that cut them into shape appear to have been captivated by the sheer mystery of the female body as a life source. It is easy to overlook the fact that in a hunting and gathering community the role of the male spermatozoa in reproduction is not readily apparent. The Australian aborigines had yet to discover it when the first European explorers arrived in their land. In such a community a life of promiscuous sexual intercourse begins before puberty and appears to be interrupted quite fortuitously by the onset of menstruation, gestation and birth, a cycle which it both precedes and finally outlasts in a seemingly unrelated fashion.

Birth remains a mystery of woman, an event which somehow she brings forth out of herself. By analogy, the event connects her to the earth which also by a mysterious process of parthenogenesis constantly renews the cycle of plant and animal life out of her womb. The mystery of women giving birth would thus have symbolised for the Palaeolithic artist something much more abstract than the size of the coming bison herd. It would have been a dramatic illustration in the life of the cave of how Nature managed to seed itself and in the process bring the latent into the world of the manifest. In a world in which the material was alive and in which to be was to shine with a numinous light the luminescent source of the divine would have been the vision of a goddess immanent in nature. It is no surprise, therefore, that no phallic figures have been found to match these early Venus figurines for if nature herself was matriarchal then women, surely, were her most transparent symbolic representatives on earth. In only one respect did the analogy between them fail to hold. Woman, unlike earth, could not take the dead back into herself.

The wide spread of Venus figurines would suggest that there once existed a shared symbolic system of religious thought across the whole of Eurasia. The figurines are not our only evidence for this. In addition to the hunting scenes depicted on the walls we find the first primitive motifs of what might have been the mythology, possibly the cosmology, of the goddess of the figurines. Some of these may represent the symbolic focus of the goddess cult, pictures of a variety of animals, of birds, of snakes, of crescent horns. Others imply more abstract thought: chevrons, meanders, spirals and labyrinths. Most intriguing of all these early markings, however, are the evident outlines of the moon and scratches in parallel that may represent the first attempt at some form of lunar notation.

It is not hard to imagine the awe in which the moon and the stars were held by Palaeolithic man. In an age in which the flickering torch was the only form of artificial lighting, the world was much more than it is today a world of darkness. The day began and ended in night. The rising sun, welcome though it must have been, would not have appeared self-evidently the primal source of terrestrial light. After all, it was still light when the sky was overcast and dark and the sun had gone. Moreover, the idea that the light of the moon was merely a reflection of solar light would not have been obvious to those who put their trust in the evidence of their eyes. Unaware of the vastness of space, they would not have interpreted the relation of the moon's shape to the position of the sun as the effect of the angle of reflection.

Total solar eclipses might have provided a clue as to the real significance of the light of the sun but they are a rare occurrence, too rare perhaps for a society without records to accommodate and, when they did occur, would have inspired terror not contemplation at the brief but unnerving return of night. It was at night that the sky itself would have seemed most awesome in the splendour of its stars. The sun, so powerful a symbol for us, would have looked like the ruler of a far less regal land. A faint trace of this ancient pre-eminence of night still remains. Our own solar day of hours begins in darkness, in the middle of the night.

It must surely have been the moon not the sun that first caught the primitive imagination. The moon could be seen with the sun in the day-time sky. This privilege was not reversed. Unlike the sun it did not weaken and grow faint as the winter solstice approached. As a luminary it had an energy and volatility that the sun lacked. There was an elation, almost an exaltation in its movements which followed the direction of the sun but over a different time scale and in a much more complex and dramatic pattern. As it rose and set, it swung across great arcs over the horizon just as the sun did but in a more vivid and turbulent way.

Even more extraordinary would have been the occasional shock of a lunar eclipse. An eclipse of the moon happens whenever its mass is cut off from the light of the sun by its passage through the shadow of the earth. Lunar eclipses conform to a pattern of periodicity but for that to be mapped required observation of the heavens over hundreds of years. That degree of measurement was almost certainly beyond the capacity of Palaeolithic man. In its absence lunar eclipses would have seemed a terrifyingly destabilising phenomenon to the dwellers in the caves.

If the eclipse seemed a sinister episode in the lunar cycle, more reassuring to primitive man was the endless capacity of the moon for frequent renewal. In a cyclical universe the moon was the messenger of eternal recurrence.[2] It was born in the crescent, grew to fulfilment in the full moon, waned and then disappeared only to be re-born in another crescent. The passage through this cycle of growth and decay may have been the first cyclical phenomenon perceived and then numbered in separate segments. That the moon was the first chronometer is evident from those first crude endeavours at lunar notation in the caves. The relevance of such notation would have been reaffirmed by the synchronicity of lunar with terrestrial cycles.[4] By association with the moon's changing shape all life on earth would have been seen to participate in a drama of eternal return in harmony with the lunar phases, a drama that embraced the rise and fall of the tides, the velocity of plant growth, the earliest folklore about the weather.

In the minds of the Palaeolithic peoples these correlates of the lunar cycle were not simply a chronometrical phenomenon. They were aspects of an organic universe the constant renewal of whose life force was dramatised by the recurrent movements of the moon, filling and saturating bodies as it waxed and emptying them as it waned. Each night, moreover, brought an additional decanting which was to be seen in the morning in the fallen dew. Even as late as classical times the idea lingered on that dew was a fertilising force, further evidence, if that were needed, of the power of the moon to make things grow. As the whole of fertility was conceived as a feminine force the metaphor of fecundation could be extended from moon to woman and then to the entire natural world. The metaphorical thread that linked them together was the association of all three with the symbol of menstruation. Like the waning moon, women were seen to decant their life blood in the course of the menstrual cycle.[14]

Memory traces of this mythical association survived in the folklore of the Ancient World. Ishtar, the moon goddess of the Babylonians, was thought to menstruate when the full moon began to wane. By historical times the menstrual cycle was already heavily tabooed. The day of the full moon was thought to be a nefarious time when a general malevolence descended like a miasma on Babylonian villages and towns. No work was done, no journey made, no food consumed that had been cooked. The taboo was the mirror image in reverse of the numinous significance of menstrual blood in earlier times for it was out of the coagulation of this blood in the womb that the foetus was once thought to have come.4 Earth too had her effluents. Full of sap like seeping blood, her trees and plants were a reservoir of rich associations with the menstrual cycle. Many of these can still be traced in the primitive botany of the Ancient World. We find them in the work of the botanist Theophrastus who claimed, for example, that the resin of the silver fir was the menses of Eileithyia, the goddess of childbirth.

From the vestiges left in ancient myths we can attempt to recreate how the analogy between earth, moon and woman might have been worked out in detail to form the structure of a primitive mythology in Palaeolithic times. The three phases of the moon would have symbolised the life cycle of woman from the maiden at the crescent through the matron at the full moon to the crone on the wane. The lunar phases of maiden, matron and crone would then have provided by analogy a form of calibration for the solar and terrestrial cycles.[3]

In Ancient Greek mythology the moon goddess, Euryphaessa, was the mother of the sun whose annual circuit of the sky was timed to the feminine cycle of the earth, in spring a maiden, in summer a matron, in winter a crone. The seasons were only one of a series of triads in which the changing face of the earth mirrored the fluctuating phases of the goddess of the moon. Her offshoots in the fields were the green stalks, the ripe ear and the cut corn. Their upward thrust, efflorescence and collapse into detritus fostered yet another triadic notion: of the maiden of the upper air, the matron of the earth and the underworld crone.[7] The imprint of this mystical analogy can be seen in the many female triads that still prevailed in the myths of the Greeks: the three Furies, the three Fates, the three Muses, three Graces and so on.

The moon rises like the sun in the east and describes a westward arc of varying height each night before setting like the sun in the west. The impression to the naked eye is of a circle half visible, half of it submerged beneath the earth. That pattern too would have been divided by analogy with the phases and in a way which united the moon directly with the earth. The rising arc would have been the maiden, the matron the point of culmination, and the whole circumference from the waning to the passage under the earth, the darkening segment of the cycle, the world of the crone. As ruler of this underworld the crone face of the moon goddess was thus also an aspect of the goddess of the earth. In an age that knew not the role of the male in procreation mothers and daughters would have formed a closed loop of fertility which constantly reproduced itself. It would have been but a short step therefore to complete the mythic triad of earth, moon and woman by making the moon the daughter of earth eternally returning to her mother to be re-born just as the weakening of the life force at the menopause was renewed by the wombs of the next generation of women on earth. The relation of mother to daughter may in this way have been the first human propinquity to be projected onto the natural world.[11]

The triad of earth, moon and woman would have formed a matrix of meanings, a semantic field that would have supplied its adherents with an endless source of simile and metaphor, a fertile bed of significances that encompassed all the phenomena of the natural world and returned them to the ever-recurring cycle, the harmonic at its root. Yet the paradigm must surely have found expression in a syntagm, a myth, a cosmogony in fact, projected onto space and time that explained the origins of such a universe, how it all began. In search of evidence for such a myth we need to go back in time to the earliest literary evidence.

The task we are engaged on is one of intuitive reconstruction similar to that of the archaeologist who tries to piece together the few scattered slivers of an ancient bowl by first imagining its original shape. In myth so complete has been the metamorphosis to the male that unlike the archaeologist we are left as investigators with only the shadows of the once pre-eminent goddess myth to conjure with. Sadly, the shadows are thrown up by the setting light of a matriarchal culture that was already dying before the first inscriptional evidence of myth appears. That evidence is from the two peoples who have left us the earliest literary testaments to their myths, the Sumerians and the Egyptians. The Sumerians were the first literate inhabitants of Mesopotamia and the decipherment of their texts has enabled us to trace the beliefs of their temple priests back to the third millennium BC. About the same time appear the first Egyptian expressions of myth. These are contained in a collection of hieroglyphic texts inscribed on the interior walls of certain pharaohs of the Fifth and Sixth Dynasties. These dynasties were in power between 2,480 and 2,137 B.C.[4]

These early peoples were haunted by the spectre of a primal state of chaos. In their mind's eye they saw a dark ocean. No wind moved the watery waste. 'Nun' the Egyptians called it. The hieroglyph they used to represent it contained signs for both the water and the sky for this ocean was the sky and, in a world without a horizon, curved over the void, encircling it above and below with its inky translucence. Memories of this watery surround lingered on in Egyptian conceptions of the body of their goddess Nut as the vault of heaven, a dome of blue oceanic light, through whom coursed the sun and the luminaries of the night.

To Nut as upper vault corresponded Naunet, the lower vault, Nut's image mirrored beneath the earth, the sea through which the sun sailed after dusk. Thus Naunet was Nut, her watery belly through which the sun barque, swallowed in the west, passed back to the day-time rising in the east for Nut was no less than the celestial sea whose encircling shell turned night into day as it revolved around the earth.[6] Decipherment of Sumerian tablets has revealed a similar vastness in an ancient goddess of Mesopotamia. Her name was Nammu and was written with the ideogram for 'sea'. She was the mother who gave birth to heaven and earth, according to her epithet.[13]

Older than Nammu even may have been An, a Sumerian sky goddess. To the temple scribes she was a celestial cow. Rain was the milk of her udders, the billowing clouds. Her power to lactate in this way she shared with the Egyptian Nut depicted as a great cow or a heavenly sow suckling her offspring, the stars. The milk spilt from the breasts of these goddesses is still there in the sky today in the image of 'the Milky Way'. The cow-like character of these deities was a memory trace from a time long before the temple scribes when fertility was a feminine principle exclusively and ubiquitous in nature. In the vision of the world to which these goddesses belonged the conception of male gods could scarcely have been other than erotic in nature. We can imagine the goddess surrounded by smaller phallic titans, servitors not fecund but ecstatic, the titillating ancestors of the later Priapus and Pan. Could these be the ithyphallic men we find occasionally drawn suggestively on the walls of caves?

Immanent in nature, the goddess had the power, visible everywhere in the natural world, to recreate herself out of the vitality of her own tumescence. It was thus that she emerged as earth out of her own celestial sea in the shape of the primeval hill. That it was the goddess who rose from the waters had long been forgotten by the time the various Egyptian temples were competing with each other as the site for the location of the hill. There is no set form for its symbolisation in the pyramid texts. Among the oldest hieroglyphs we often find it engraved as a hill slope like the mounds the priests must have seen in the Nile bed when the floods receded. More formally in later texts it is converted to a rectangle with rising steps on either side, perhaps the origin of the pyramids. Whatever its shape or location, the hill was to the Egyptians the centre of the earth. Once it had been the navel of the belly of the goddess swelling up from its submergence beneath the sea. The idea that earth had a navel was an enduring one. The supposed place was marked in many cultures by an obelisk or stone. Such a stone at Delphi was thought by the priests to be the centre of the earth. A stone similar in shape at the Druid sanctuary of Uisnech in Ireland was believed likewise to be the navel of the land. As earth took back the dead into her womb, these sacred spots became by association burial plots, symbols of death and re-birth at the centre of the world.[8]

From the primal mound rose the first tree. Akin to the sacred navel stone, the world tree, the 'axis mundi', shared its umbilical connection with the womb of the earth.[16] Tall enough full grown to spread its foliage in the heavens, the trunk of this tree ran down through the bowels of the earth like a mirror image branching to the vault of the counterheaven in the underworld beneath. The sacred tree partook of the generative power of earth. As the tree of life it could give birth and also like the earth take the dead back into itself. As a receptacle for the souls of the dead it has left us an enduring image in the cross and gallows. Traditionally, whoever died by the tree received the gift of immortality from it. In Egyptian texts we find the goddess Hathor among its leaves handing its sacred fruit to the passing dead as the food of immor-tality.[34] A more primitive form it took was the suckling of the pharaoh by the tree goddess as a mark of his journey to eternal life. In the tomb of Thutmosis III in the Valley of the Kings the dead ruler can be seen sucking the tit of the goddess in the tree of life. The tree of the dead was also the soul tree of re-birth with the dead returning as the stars twinkling at night among its branches, a distant memory of which is still reflected in the candles of the Christmas tree. In a world still innocently unaware of the need for individual redemption the dead souls returned in shoals by clan and tribe identity.[9] Hence the status of sacred trees as tribal centres. On their journey to the underworld the dead took their wisdom with them to the earth. The tree of eternal life was thus also the tree of knowledge. It shared with the navel stones the power to indicate the fate of the living. The Viking world tree was depicted on a mound in the centre of the ocean. Beneath lay the Spring of Fate. By it lay the well of Mimir into which the Viking god Odin cast his eye in return for a vision of the future.

Candidates for the role of sacred tree were many and varied. Among some peoples an apple tree was chosen. Among others a special holiness attached to the ash, oak, yew, fig, mulberry or sycamore tree. In the north it was the silver fir that was often felt to be most numinous. In the south the palm tree was preferred. A candidate for sacred status in the Eastern Mediterranean was the 'ficus sicomorus', the black mulberry or sycamore fig.[2] The Egyptian goddess of this tree was Hathor, 'Lady of the Sycamore', like the goddess Nut the ruler and body of the sky, like her too, a cow goddess, the giver of the milk of immortality to the king. Her name 'Hat-hor' meant 'mansion of Horus', the Egyptian sun god symbolised by a falcon. This god was thought to have been born in the top most branches of her sacred tree. Sacred trees were often later formalised as pillars. The tree pillar of Hathor was in her temple at Denderah. It was here that the New Year ceremony was performed in a ritual that went back to a time long before the pharaohs. At its culminating point the rays of the sun lit up the face of her statue borne up from her sanctuary to unite with the sun's disc.[10]

Pillars aligned to catch and, as it were, give birth to the rising sun, often at the winter solstice, were common throughout the ancient world. Yet there is evidence in myth that the original offspring of these pillars was another luminary. An illustration of this can be seen in the sacred marriage of Hathor and Horus. In her temple at Denderah this goddess of the sycamore had been reduced to the status of the wife of the triumphant god of light whom the Greeks identified with Apollo. At first sight the marriage between them appears to unite Hathor with the sun. It is only when we look at the calendrical phasing of the ceremony that we realise that the solar myth that underpinned it concealed another, older one.

The marriage took place each year in the temple of Horus at Edfu during the third month of summer but, significantly, on the night of the new moon.[12] On the fourteenth day before the new moon rose the state barge with a flotilla of boats in tow carrying priests and notables set out from Denderah on the first stage of the journey up the Nile to the temple at Edfu. In the barge stood resplendent the statue of the bride, the goddess Hathor. On reaching Edfu it was met at the quayside by the statue of Horus with his priests in attendance. Together the bride and bride-groom were led to the Birth House where they spent their wedding night.

On the day of the full moon after her conception Hathor sailed home to give birth in her temple at Denderah. The lunar calendar betrays the original meaning of this ceremony and, in doing so, reveals the once subordinate status of this all-conquering god of the sun. Hathor's lover, he was also once her son. As such, it was he who had gone to her not her to him. Only that way could he have been re-born from her celestial branches. Yet even that re-birth was a patriarchal act of obfuscation for in origin it was not the sun but the more powerful moon that first rose out of the topmost branches of the lady of the sycamore tree.

The association of a goddess with the world tree is apparent also in an ancient Sumerian hymn from the region of Eridu. It tells of the great tree whose roots reach down into the very depths of the earth. All world trees had an umbilical connection and this one too, says the creator of the hymn, stood at the very centre. Its foliage, he goes on, was the couch of the primal mother. He compares it to a leafy temple into whose spreading shade no man had ever entered. It was the home of the great mother who transited the heavens.[15]

It was from this tree the moon first rose on the night the sky was filled with the light of the constellations. On this endless circuit she passed each night and once a month for three whole nights into the womb of her mother to rest in the foliage of the world tree in the counterheaven beneath the earth before continuing her journey to the next moonrise. At each rise her immortality was confirmed together with that of the dead who travelled with her in the stars across the night sky.

So too was re-affirmed the propinquity of women to the earth for what happened in the sky each night was merely the lunar aspect of the cycle in which mothers gave birth to daughters who mothered in their turn before following them like the moon back into the earth. What the eye of the ancients saw played out in the night sky was thus a primal myth of parthenogenesis. Moonrise was the sign that the mound had once more risen from the celestial waters with above it the world tree from which the lunar goddess now visible had ascended to begin her procession across the sky. In the west her transit ended as she dipped beneath the horizon on her descent to the world tree beneath in the womb of Mother Earth there to be resurrected eastwards towards the opposing horizon the following night.

A cyclical myth of this encompassing scope must have been a great source of reassurance to believers, a harmonising force in all their lives but it could not in itself have answered to those all-too-human aspirations which we know from their earliest burials they entertained about the after-life. There must surely have been a secondary and connected myth that dramatised the role of mankind or, perhaps more centrally, womankind in this cosmic scenario and in a way that calmed those fears of enveloping chaos that come from the daily vicissitudes of life and offered some promise of eternal life. Even in a world so much more harmonious than our own there must have been an allegory that redeemed the consciousness of tragedy in life with some notion of hope. A myth of this kind would have been celebrated in rites that preserved the identity of the clan or tribe and tied its desperate urge to survive to the ever-recurring cycle visible everywhere around it in the universe.

What we are searching for, in fact, is the central cultic myth of the ancient matriarchate, the myth that figured in rites held by priestesses in communities throughout Eurasia and the Middle East. If those rites were truly a dramatisation of the role of the community in the cosmogony described that linked it to human aspirations for an after-life then the lunar cycle would surely have supplied the dramatis personae of their motivating myth. The lunar drama that unfolded in the night sky was one of eternal return that united terrestrial cycles with a cyclicality in the after-life. Each night the souls of the dead travelled the heavens with the goddess at the helm of her crescent boat to rest like her in the world tree beneath the earth only to rise again in the celestial sea the following night. The image of the after-life was thus not, as in many modern religions, an inversion, a transvaluation of life on earth but its metaphorical extension. What was seen in the night sky was not an act of transcendence, a triumph over death but its accommodation in the cosmic cycle that held both heaven and earth in its embrace. The central accommodating symbol in all of this was the death and resurrection of the moon itself as each month it waxed, waned and then vanished for three nights before rising again with the souls of the dead in the after-life.

Yet the death of the moon each month took an uncanny form. The waxing and waning moon was also a metaphor for the life cycle of the goddess in her development from maiden to matron and crone. Tragically, however, the lunar maiden began to die at her menarche. At the point at which she began to menstruate in the course of her transformation to a nubile matron death set in. The first menstrual flow was for the full moon the harbinger of her eventual demise as gradually she began each night to waste away to a slender crescent in the sky. When finally the crescent vanished it was to leave the sky bereft of her light for three whole nights. In the minds of her worshippers this would have been the time it took for her to complete her journey through the labyrinthine passage of the underworld that led to the sacred tree before emerging from the womb of mother earth at moonrise on the fourth night. This lunar odyssey had a parallel on earth in the rites of passage of the menarche when girls at puberty were conceived to die symbolically to be re-born as the matrons of the tribe.[17]

As in many other aspects of the lunar cycle the monthly death and resurrection of the moon would thus have harmonised with a cyclicality in the lives of her servitors but there would have been times also when chaos flooded in to threaten this primal harmony. These were those rare occasions when the two cycles of death and re-birth, of girl to woman and moon to earth, were dramatised by a third cycle, far more awesome and unpredictable, in the heavens, the cycle of the lunar eclipse. Eclipses occur only when the moon is full. It was thus at the untimely moment of its exaltation that the lunar cycle would suffer this arrest.

At the full moon, her menarche, and about to decant her blood on the wane, the goddess daughter of earth would be slowly swallowed by a circling shadow before the horrified gaze of her worshippers. To them it must have seemed as if the fearsome crone aspect of the goddess below had reared up like a thief in the night to steal the maiden at her menarche and drag her down before her time beneath the earth. Seen in human terms a grieving earth would set off at such times in search of her missing daughter who was but the vanished part of herself, a hostage now of that other darker part of the goddess triad, herself as crone. What the eclipse presented was the endless lunar cycle of death and regeneration but in a more sudden and traumatic form.[18]

Where the trauma required a sympathetic ritual of death and resurrection on earth the natural candidate for the dramatic role would have been a maiden of the tribe at her menarche. In the drama of the rite the maiden, or her surrogate, would hang from the tribal sacred tree while her spirit was conveyed through the labyrinth of the underworld. In the shade of the underworld tree in the counter-heaven beneath the earth she would be proffered an apple or a pomegranate, the fruit of wisdom from its branches, a gift of the crone full of significance, for it was both her passport to eternal life and her contract to return. With the first taste of the fruit she was doomed, for only with the payment of a forfeit could she could she be ransomed back and restored to earth. Above, an effigy of the dead goddess would have been carried processionally to the tribal sanctuary amid loud lamentations. Only when the bargain had been struck with the crone would grief give way to joy.[19]

So much we presume for the descending goddess remains a hypothesis. Soon we shall see evidence accumulate but at the moment we must handle our hypothesis with a delicate touch as if, to quote Whitehead's admirable phrase, it were as light as gossamer. As to the aspirations of these early worshippers we are compelled to acknowledge that the symbols that have survived so far from the goddess cult in the Neolithic Age give us only the vaguest idea of the hopes it extended to its believers. Two of the most common, the snake and butterfly motifs, are symbols of transformation. The snake sloughs its skin; the butterfly emerges full-winged from the chrysalis. In their different ways they both represent a release from one phase to another, perhaps higher phase of what is, nevertheless, the same eternal cycle. Like the waxing moon they are images of exaltation.

To the exalted among her worshippers the hand of the goddess might well have stretched forth to point the way for them to follow in their turn the path of her daughter on her descent through the passageways to the underworld beneath the earth. Such may have been the message of the many labyrinths, spirals and meanders that decorate the walls of caves and the shrines of the Neolithic age and which have so baffled historians and archaeologists. At the end of this lunar journey to the earth would have lain the wisdom of the crone aspect of the goddess proffered to all believers in the fruit of the tree of knowledge. Not redemption, then, as in the Christian story of the resurrection, but ecstasy would have been the precious gift of the goddess to her celebrants, the ecstasy that flows from the intuitive grasp that the universe is a sustaining harmony that resonates in cycles and holds both the throbbing heart of earth and all the mysteries of the after-life in its maternal embrace.

The eclipses of the moon might have provided the drama with its inspirational motif but certainly in the Palaeolithic and early Neolithic Ages they would have been too unpredictable to furnish the rite with a calendrical base. Eclipses occur when the tracks or 'ecliptics' of sun and moon cross, placing both luminaries in line with the earth. When the earth is between the sun and the moon, it stops the sunlight falling on the moon and we get an eclipse of the moon in the earth's shadow. When the moon occupies the middle position, it blocks sunlight coming to the earth, and from the earth in the shadow of the moon we witness an eclipse of the sun.

When the ecliptics cross in this way we can get either an eclipse of the sun or one of the moon but, of course, never both. It takes generations of lunar observation to find a periodicity that can predict when one or other luminary is at risk to an eclipse but as the eclipse may be either full or partial and above or below the horizon as seen from a particular point on earth, visually, even after many years of observation, the phenomenon is not easy to anticipate. Rather easier to predict would have been another frightening celestial phenomenon whose co-occurrence would have compounded the anxiety of an eclipse and may therefore eventually have provided the ritual of death and resurrection with a firmer calendrical base. This second pattern is the tendency for each luminary to rise and set lower and lower in the sky each day until it reaches its nadir and then begins to come up again. In the case of the sun the pattern is transparent and is the chronometer of the seasons. Where the moon is concerned, however, the volatility and time-span of descent renders the pattern obscure. The lowest moonset occurs in a cycle every 18 or 19 years but in a pattern of extremes in which gathering lows can be interspersed with sudden periods of elevation. Furthermore, the cycle may alternate by 18 or 19 years but these alternations are not necessarily in regular or immediate succession. In fact, they cycle gets more predictable once it locks into a 56 year recurrence pattern which can last for as long as 300 years at a time.

Even before any patterning had been plotted the extremes of this lunar cycle would have impressed themselves as a visual phenomenon on the ancient mind. At its height in the sky the moon is very bright particularly on the full. At its lows it may have looked to the primitive eye as if it was about to vacate its role and leave the sky, an anxiety presumably increased when it was also on the wane. More menacing still would have been the prospect of the two most feared cycles, the eclipse and the lows, co-occurring, in other words, an eclipse of the moon close to one of its periodic lows. Such a dire conjunction might well have provided in time a periodicity for the rites of the goddess descend-ing to the underworld if only it could have been predicted. In fact, there is evidence that this very conjunction was studied with intent towards the end of the Neolithic Age. The students in question were the builders of the Megaliths.

These massive stone circles began to appear among the late Neolithic farming communities of Western Europe somewhere around the middle of the fourth millennium. Their construction must have come close to exhausting the physical resources of the tribes that built them. It was for these small, dispersed communities a Herculean task, an act of collective will surely driven by religious zeal. Work began on the most famous of them, Stonehenge, around 2,800 BC. A start was made at the more extensive Avebury complex three centuries later. This is about the time that work began on the pyramid at Giza although there is no evidence to link the two constructional developments.

The sites appear to have functioned as both temples and observatories and the general consensus today is that, at least in their earliest form, they probably had a lunar alignment, that is, they were physically constructed to illustrate or dramatise a critical position of the moon in the night sky. We can tell from the position of the stones, for example, that whoever built Stonehenge was interested in the moon's highs and lows.

We also know that they may have plotted their pattern of recurrence with success from the number of the famous Aubrey post holes. These were used to locate the positions of the moon and add up, intriguingly, to the critical 56. In addition, it has been suggested, they were interested in predicting a lunar eclipse and not only that but its patterning with the cycle of the highs and lows. Certainly, whoever aligned the renowned 'healstone' at Stonehenge knew that, when the winter full moon rose over it every nine or ten years at the mid-point of the lunar cycle, there was danger of an eclipse. As we would expect, later building work reveals a growing preoccupation with a solar alignment at these sites but it is at least conceivable that in their earliest lunar form they offer us our first tentative archaeological evidence of the goddess cult and myth.

The evidence of the Megaliths is not only remote in time but involves us in an extended chain of inference. More powerful would be literary or inscriptional evidence but in pursuing it we confront the same problem we came up against when trying to reconstruct the matriarchal cosmogony. By the time writing had been invented the old matriarchy had already been submerged by the rising patriarchal order throughout most of Eurasia and the Middle East. Whatever had been the text of the women's mysteries had already been subjected to centuries of re-editing and re-interpretation by male mythographers and priests.

In most cases the best we can hope for is to peel back the obfuscating layers of later myths until we reach what might have been the kernel of the underlying myth. This work of literary excavation is no less a work of inference than that of the archaeologist. If it were all we had to go on the picture would be bleak but, surprisingly, some literary evidence has survived that has been relatively untampered with. It comes in fact from a single myth complete in itself but from it we can pick up the trail of an entire tradition of descending goddesses that somehow survived into late Classical times. How it survived, why it survived is itself a mystery but one we must now investigate.

In the course of our investigations we will find ourselves unravelling a thread that connects a line of goddesses to the very origins of the Christian Church. To begin our investigative work we must return once more to the Sumerians, and the evidence of their strange cuneiform script.

We have already encountered the Sumerians as the first literate inhabitants of Mesopotamia whose cultural achievements were on a par with those of Ancient Egypt. Sadly, their cities had been destroyed by the end of the third millennium. From then on they ceased to be active players in the Middle East but, like the Romans in the Dark Ages that followed the collapse of their empire, they left behind a rich literature to be copied by succeeding generations. The greatest collector of their myths was a later conqueror, Assurbanipal. A brutal but reflective king, he built a great library to house the records from the past in the city of Nineveh. The records were kept in a cuneiform script produced by pressing a wedge-shaped instrument into tablets of clay. Assurbanipal eventually went the way of all conquerors with his library reduced to a buried mound of broken shards. It was the fractured tablets left behind that a young Englishman, Austin Henry Layard, began to find when the first excavations started at the site in 1839.

From the tablets deciphered since then we have been able to recreate how the Sumerians imagined the world beyond the grave. To them it was a dark and gloomy place, airless, dusty and inhabited by fearful flitting shades. Its ruler was a grim goddess, full of foreboding, whose very name was chilling to the living, the Queen of the Underworld, Ereshkigal. Originally perhaps a celestial goddess, she had been taken down by force into the underworld by an entity even more primeval than herself, a deity by the name of Kur. The etymology of her abductor is quite instructive. The sign for Kur was a pictograph of a hill or mound.

In time it came to refer to the earth. Sumer itself was called 'kur-gal', 'great land'. The root lies in the name of Ereshkigal itself, but with the meaning of the earth below. 'Ki-gal', in fact, meant the 'great below'[20] 'Kur' was often used by itself to mean the 'other world', envisioned as the empty space between the earth's crust and the primal sea.[24]

A serpent dwelt at the bottom of this chasm, half-submerged in the dark sea. The name of this monstrous being was also 'Kur'. Was this Kur of the deep a shadowy folk memory of our goddess of the celestial sea from whom the primal mound emerged? If so, then her crone aspect beneath the earth looks very much like the stern, forbidding Ereshkigal. Gloomily enthroned in her chthonic realm, the freedom she may once have had to roam the skies was still the privilege of her younger sister in Sumerian myth. This was Inanna, later to become the Semitic Ishtar, daughter of the moon, indeed a lunar goddess in her own right and ruler also of the planet Venus. A powerful goddess still, she figures in many myths but one above all intrigues us for it represents a strange departure from an otherwise patriarchal Sumerian tradition. In this tale Inanna, the lunar goddess, for some obscure reason decides to go down alone to the Sumerian Hades to see her sister.

Inanna embarks on her journey in a manner befitting to a goddess, bedecked with jewels, her raiment shining. At the gateway to the underworld she halts ominously to instruct her servant Ninshubur on what it is that must be done if she fails to return. Neti, the gatekeeper of Hades, is at first confused by this unexpected visitor, the daughter of the moon, the goddess of the morning star that appears in the sky before the rising sun. Why, he asks, has Inanna of the sunrise come to the land of no return.[21] She has come, she replies, to see Lord Gugalanna 'the great bull of heaven', husband of her elder sister, the queen of the underworld who has recently deceased. It is only right and proper that she see him commemorated in his statue and grace his funerary libations with her divine presence. Inside the seven-fold walls of her kingdom her sister is at first unwilling to countenance such an unusual request. Inanna is finally given the signal to proceed but in a manner that acknowledges her submission to the powers of the underworld. She is to follow Neti on bended knee through the seven gates of her sister's realm. At each gate a functionary strips her of part of her regalia. When ultimately she finds herself before her sister's throne, it is in an attitude of naked abasement. A celestial goddess she may be but her writ does not run in the world of the dead. Undismayed, however, and in apparent disregard for the original purpose of her visit, she struggles to topple her sister from her eminence and replace her on the throne herself. The commotion does not pass unnoticed by the seven judges of the dead who, witnessing the act of lèse-majesté, condemn her to death. Bizarre though it seems, the goddess is killed in the kingdom of the dead. Her decomposing body is left hanging on a stake.

When three nights had passed, the tablets tell us, Ninshubur knew for certain that something was wrong. It was time to set in motion what the goddess had decreed should be done if she failed to return. The decree was for a general mourning and lament-ation for the fate of the goddess. The grieving Ninshubur in turn calls on each of the gods to draw their attention to what has happened. In the land of Nippur lives the god Enlil by one mythical tradition himself the father of Inanna. How can he, asks Ninshubur, let his daughter languish in the underworld? The god, however, is powerless to intervene. No more powerful is Inanna's father by another account, Nanna, the moon god of Ur.

The last hope for salvation for the lunar goddess is Enki, the sweet water god of Eridu. A resourceful god, he plots a cunning stratagem. From the dirt encrusted in his fingernails he fashions two mourners whom he then despatches to the underworld with the water and the grass of life. Arriving in the dark kingdom, they find Ereshkigal herself in mourning, not for the dead Inanna indeed, but for children who have died and have had to descend to the underworld before their time. The ambassadors ingratiate themselves by echoing her pitiful cries. Touched by their seeming tenderness, the Queen of the Dead offers them a blessing. Their eyes flit towards the hanging body of Inanna. The goddess is loath to grant their silent request. She offers instead the swollen river and the field full of grain but, having agreed to grant their wish, she is forced to relent and hand the body of Inanna over. At once they throw upon it the revivifying grass and water. In an instant, life returns to the goddess who stands now before them in all her splendour.[22]

Release, however, is conditional. Inanna must find a substitute to take her place among the dead and with this in mind she roams the world in search of one with a retinue of functionaries from the kingdom of the dead. It is an eerie procession of the shades that seeks this special favour from those the goddess visits on her rounds. Victim after victim sprawl in the dust at their feet in a desperate plea to be allowed to remain in the world of the living. Each time Inanna's heart melts until, that is, she arrives at a gnarled and twisted apple tree in the desert of Kullab. In its shade lolls her husband, Dumuzi, dressed to kill and intent on his pleasures, in total disregard for her predicament. Cut to the quick by his evident unconcern, Inanna this time accepts the request of the men from Hades and allows them to drag her errant husband down into the underworld. On the way down a frantic Dumuzi appeals to the sun god to be changed into a snake to evade his captors. At this intriguing point the main version of the tale breaks off although in these last few lines there is a twist suggestive of developments to come. Another version of Inanna's descent from Ur leads us to believe that Dumuzi's prayer was finally granted.[23]

What is most surprising in this text is the sheer number of thematic features that have survived from the originating myth. The sacred tree is still intact in the shape of the apple tree in the desert of Kullab although its mirror-image beneath the earth has shrunk to the proportions of a wooden stake. Hanging from it we find the lunar goddess on the three nights of moonlessness that follow her descent to the underworld crone. The tree has lost its guardian snake which now pops up incongruously at the end though its link with immortality is still confirmed.

Elsewhere we find what were once perhaps more ritualistic elements of the myth embedded in the text: the lamentation, the appeals, the forfeit and the quest for a surrogate on earth, who, in descending, will allow the moon to rise again. We are fortunate to have so much of a goddess text. Whoever committed it to the tablets inadvertently preserved it for us. The act of writing freezes the symbol written at a point in time, creating thereby an ineluctable facticity, the basis for an evidential claim that a hostile reader must either re-interpret or destroy. Why, otherwise, have the pogroms of our century been heralded first by 'the burning of the books'?

In the case of the Inanna text the process of re-writing has already begun. Actors have started to be removed, to be replaced by patriarchal players. The maiden hanging from the sacred tree has become the sybaritic Dumuzi lolling in its shade. Alien motives have been incongruously interpolated in the text. Shorn of her original motive for descending, Inanna is forced, absurdly, to go down for the obsequies of her sister's brother, a motive which she soon forgets.

What remains still retains, however, much of the flavour of the uncontaminated text. The impression is of a religious narrative used for recitation in a ritual perhaps over a number of days. Much more than this it is difficult to say for the coherence of theme and motive that would have invested the text with significance has already fallen victim to the first fumbling patriarchal gerrymandering with the body of the narrative. In fact, had the narrative not been written down at this early stage we can imagine how it would finally have ended up, barbarised as an adventure story, with masculine actors, themes and motives increasingly intruded until the entire tale had altered shape, perhaps in the form of some kind of male heroic underworld quest. What the rites signified for believers it would thus be pointless to seek in the extant text. The divorce of the two has already occurred and is too far gone for the ritual to be inferred from the myth. Yet some of the original meaning of the rites can still be grasped not from this text but from fragments of its myth that survived among the later Greeks and in a context that connected it to a living ritual.

At first the survival looks unpromising for by the time the Greeks came to tell the tale it had clearly been subjected to much more ruthless re-editing. The theme of the descent still remains but with new themes and actors inserted in and motives almost unrecognisable from the earlier text. Not all is lost, however, for, curiously, there are matriarchal features, possibly from another source, that were missing from the more ancient work.

The story the Greeks told explained how Kore, the maid, the daughter of the goddess Demeter, became co-ruler of the underworld, the Queen of the dead. It opens with a warm Spring day. Kore is gathering flowers with her companions. Strolling with her basket, she catches sight of a beautiful narcissus. As she stretches forth to snap the stem a great cavern opens in the earth. Out of the dark gorge comes a rumbling. Into the sunlight thunder jet-black horses. A chariot wheels into the meadow grass. At the reins is a shade whose face is invisible. With a scream Kore is gone, back with the chariot into the earth. The meadow rolls back and the cavern is gone leaving, of all the divinities, only Hecate, the moon goddess, as a witness to the deed that has been done. Aware thus of the peril her daughter could be in, Demeter sets out on her search. In the guise of a crone she roams the earth. At night she continues her quest by the light of her torches. She takes no food and can enjoy no rest so frantic is her pursuit of her Kore. In the course of her travels she arrives at Eleusis where in ignorance of her real identity the ruler and his wife assign to her the care of their newborn heir, Demophoön.

Eleusis is a happy place and a brief interlude of hilarity there lightens her quest. Her spirits lift at the antics of their lame daughter, Iambe, and the old nurse, Baubo, who act out at an improvised comedy together. In return for the hospitality she has received at the court she resolves to give the child Demophoön the greatest gift of all. Unhappily, that night she is surprised in the act of holding him in a fire to burn away his mortal self. Her spell is broken and he dies in the flames. Only misery, it seems, can she bring to others in her great distress. It will soon be the lot of all humankind to experience the truth of this. Informed at last, by Helius, the all-seeing sun, of the identity of the abductor she seeks, she determines to withhold fertility from all the crops of the earth until the arch-villain of the piece agrees to return her daughter to her. Such now is the hardness in her heart that she stands her ground stone-faced against the urgent requests to relent that come from Zeus and all the other gods.

Deep in the bowels of the earth Kore has taken the name Persephone, innocently unaware of the chaos her departure has caused in the world above. Hades, the god of the underworld, is attentiveness itself and naturally reluctant to forego his prize. Eventually, however, he succumbs to the constant pressure of his brother, Zeus. With some ill grace he agrees to release her. The maiden is allowed to ascend. Great are the celebrations when finally she sinks into the exultant embrace of her mother.

The joy does not last long, however. Under the anxious interrogation of her mother she reveals that she has done what Demeter had feared all along and eaten the food of the dead. Just seven seeds from a pomegranate tree in the orchard of Hades but enough, her mother knows, to consign her to the underworld forever. Having tasted of that fruit, she can never again enjoy the prospect of a full sojourn on earth. Yet all is not lost. For the benefit of all, a compromise is reached. To the god who raped her she will return for a third of each year, re-ascending annually to rejoin her mother.

So ends the tale told by the poet Homer in his *Hymn to Demeter*. To the Greeks there always remained an element of the uncanny about the legend. A grieving goddess fitted ill with their conception of the happily, playful world of the gods on Mount Olympus. Nor did the sorrowful descent accord well with images of gods of light who, like the Greeks themselves, feared to trespass on the dark regions beneath the surface of life. There were few shrines to the underworld gods, who were deaf to all but the curses hammered by the fists of outraged men into the earth above. The point of the myth, the Greeks believed, was to explain how the Queen of the Dead first came to join her husband in the underworld. Why Hades needed a consort in the first place was never explained. After all, there was no issue from his act of rape. Kore the maid became the barren goddess of the underworld.

Of course, much would have been explained had the Ancient Greeks had the benefit of modern etymology. The name Persephone, we now know, is not Indo-European. A goddess by this name must therefore have been worshipped by the indigenous inhabitants before the arrival of the Indo-European Greeks.

In contrast, the name of Demeter and Kore are genuinely Indo-European at root. The inference seems clear. These two later goddesses arrived with the Greeks and their legend merged with that of a pre-existing Persephone. In other words, the underworld goddess was always there seated on her throne and if there was a maiden that descended then her descent would not have required the 'dens ex machina' of the act of rape. Indeed, the rapist himself may not have been there.

Persephone, we could hazard a guess, was the Sumerian Ereshkigal, at least in the shape of what Kore became, Queen of the Dead. Kore herself was Inanna no longer descending voluntarily but under duress. Her stooping posture in descent has become the lameness of the daughter of the ruler of Eleusis. The Ereshkigal she meets has long since lost her kingdom and with it the aspect of the crone which has been comically transposed to the old nurse Baubo. The ancient themes still keep a tenuous hold on parts of the narrative.

The refusal of the underworld powers to relinquish the dead that sent Inanna searching for her substitute is manifest in the annual return of Persephone. A portion of this tragedy has been transposed to the infant Demophoön dying in the flames. Ereshkigal, we recall, was weeping for children who had died before their time. Lunar fragments also still cling stubbornly to the tale. Hecate, the moon goddess, now merely witnesses a descent that may once have been hers. Demeter wandering the night by torchlight looks like a lunar aspect of Mother Earth. Mother Earth, 'Da Meter' is exactly what she was and her presence suggests that the Greeks may have derived their story from a source even older than what we have uncovered at Nineveh. A grieving Mother Earth was surely there before she was forced to abandon her role to the servant Ninshubur of the earlier Mesopotamian myth.

Further evidence of the age of the Greek myth can be seen in the role played in it by the underworld tree. We noted how in the Sumerian tablets the tree had already been foreshortened to a stake. However, not only has the tree survived in the story of Persephone but it has kept intact its symbolic function. It is by eating the fruit of it, in this case the pomegranate, that Persephone is condemned to return for a third or, in some versions, three months of the year. This annual return was interpreted by the Greeks and in fact by commentators ever since as symbolising the return of fertility to the fields. The preoccupation with fertility was no doubt very old.

Returning for a moment to the Sumerian version we recall that Ereshkigal offered the envoys sent to her fields full of grain. The tradition continued with Demeter who was the tutelary guardian of the crops, the goddess of fertility in the earth. Her daughter Kore, it has been suggested, was a symbol of the seed corn deposited in underground silos for later planting.[25] This interpretation would be more impressive if a third of the year or three months for that matter were a span of significance in the life of the grain.[29] No grain seed lies anywhere in the agricultural calendar for that period of time. Homer, in fact, placed the return of Kore in the spring, a season in which flowers blossom but not one of decisive significance in the life of the grain apart from the fact that it shares in the general efflorescence at that time of the year.

The significance of the return of Kore is probably much older than the fertility symbolism that coalesced around it and can perhaps best be explained by exploring the special meaning of the tree to which it is linked. A good authority on this was the traveller Pausanias. On one of his many journeys he records seeing a pomegranate in the hand of the statue of Hera at Argos. He evidently knew what it meant but he warns the reader that he cannot speak of it for fear of breaking an injunction of silence.

Elsewhere he unwittingly betrays his secret. He makes mention of a certain pomegranate tree that grew from the grave of Menoikeus outside one of the gates of Thebes. Menoikeus suffered a martyr's death. During a siege of Thebes he saved the city by hurling himself from its walls to appease Aries, the god of war, who had nursed a grudge against its people ever since its founder had killed his sacred snake. Menoikeus actually fell to his death in the chasm that had been the haunt of the snake. What the tree signified that grew upon his grave was the commemoration of a heroic death on behalf of the community. The pomegranate was thus a symbol linked to death but Menoikeus was unusual.

Elsewhere it was women that were more often the objects of grief. In Boeotia the pomegranate was called 'side'. In myth Side was the boastful wife of Orion the hunter. In her arrogance she compared herself in beauty to the goddess Hera. For that she suffered an untimely death. The curse of the goddess led her to destroy herself in a way that seems uncannily appropriate in the light of our myth. She committed suicide on her mother's grave. From the blood that trickled forth Earth caused the pomegranate to grow. In fact, Side was the name of a number of towns and the mythological women after whom they were named. Was the reddish juice of this fruit, as one author has proposed, the menstrual blood of Kore as she left the earth.[26] Was this first blood the reason why in myth it was so easy to replace maidenly descent with an act of violent rape.[31]

Is the whole fertility aspect of the myth a patriarchal imposition? After all, no farmer ever prayed to Persephone for the sustenance of his crops. Nor was Demeter always so closely associated with the grain. In the Homeric Hymn it was the goddess Rhea who first persuaded her to give mankind this gift. One account even made Rhea the mother of Persephone.[27] What is more, some have found the root of her name etymologically in 'rhoa', the pomegranate tree.[33] In the minds of the Greeks her daughter remained for ever, a death goddess, the negation of earthly life. As for the pomegranate, we now see it in a new light. It was the food of the dead not the living, a symbol not of fertility but of acceptance in the after-life. Acceptance for whom, we might ask? Not for the individual herself but for the community at large.

The nature of this acceptance we can gauge more easily from the Greek than from the Sumerian evidence for the Greek myth was attached to rites known throughout the whole of Greece. The rites involved a series of initiations into what were called the Eleusinian Mysteries. Eleusis, where the mysteries were held, we have already had mention of in the Homeric Hymn. The name means 'the place of happy arrival'. It shares a root with 'Elysium', 'the realm of the blessed' in the after-life. In origin Elysium meant 'apple land'. The apple image connects it to Arthur's 'Avalon' and the Latin 'Avernus'. A composite picture begins to build of an orchard in the after-life. According to the sacred history of Eleusis the first to 'arrive' in this happy land was Demeter pursuing her daughter in the Homeric Hymn. In her delight at finding her we are told she returned to mankind the grain she had withdrawn in her distress. But the most precious gift she gave, said her tutelary priests, was the commemorative cult at Eleusis.

The Mysteries were the most talked-about in all of Greece but, unfortunately for our purposes, the actual rites themselves were protected by a vow of silence. So fiercely was this rule maintained that two uninvited guests who inadvertently blew their cover by asking too many questions were summarily executed in 200 BC. Only later Christian writers felt free from this constraint and their testimony is inevitably open to suspicion. At the heart of the Mysteries, we know, was some act of initiation, 'myesis', conducted 'en masse', although whether or not to participate in this was a matter of individual choice.

The privilege, it seems, was limited to the citizens of Athens most of whom were, at some time in their life, initiated. There were two ceremonies in fact, the Lesser Mysteries held at Agrai and the Greater Mysteries at Eleusis. After admission to the Lesser Mysteries candidates were termed 'Mystae' and were allowed to take a limited part in the next celebration of the Greater Mysteries that followed these. They had to wait for full initiation till the Greater Mysteries that in turn succeeded those. After full initiation they were called 'epoptae' or seers. The Greater Eleusinia were held in September every five years so the period of initiation was quite prolonged.

On the first day the youths of Athens would go to Eleusis to bring the sacred objects there back to the city to be housed temporarily in the Eleusinion at the foot of the Acropolis. The next day the cry went up 'Initiates into the sea!' and the 'mystae' began to bathe to purify themselves. Under their arms they carried young pigs to wash in the sea and sacrifice. On the appointed day the initiates gathered for their long day's walk along the Sacred Road to Eleusis. The procession they made was the most famous in Greece. According to Herodotus the noise and dust it raised as it moved across the plain was witnessed from a distance in spectral form at a time when the festivals themselves were under interdict during the Persian invasion. The legend, if such it was, is testimony to the strength of feelings the Mysteries evoked.

The procession ended at the Telesterion or House of Initiation at Eleusis late in the evening. The following nights saw a number of celebrations in different parts of Eleusis that had a particular sanctity in myth. At some point in these proceedings the actual mysteries were performed. The drama unfolded under the cover of darkness. What it involved for the participants is itself a mystery. All we know for certain is that something quite dramatic was 'seen'. The crowd of initiates were marshalled together in the Hall of Mysteries and in the hot press of bodies witnessed a series of disturbing spectacles. At the climax of these a great light burst forth from a furnace hitherto concealed in the dark interior of the Hall. With his throne protected by a screen from the heat of the flames the Chief Priest cried out: 'The Mistress has given birth to a sacred boy! Brimo has given birth to Brimos!': that is the strong one to the strong. Now Brimo was one of the names of the Queen of the Dead and it was at this very point, it was said, that the onlookers held their breath for out of the bowels of the earth came a vision of Kore rising conjured up by the priest to the strokes of a gong. As the spectre shimmered and faded abject terror gave way to awe and then ultimately to wave upon wave of trance-like joy. In the deathly silence of the Hall as all these feelings gathered force the priest held out to all an ear of corn pressed tight between his finger and his thumb. In his other hand he held a knife. In one great flourish the corn was cut.

Did the mystes really witness a divine epiphany or were they victims of a theatrically induced hallucination encouraged by their extensive fast before the festival began? As to the symbols the received wisdom is that they referred to the gifts bestowed by Demeter on man: material plenty resuscitated in the earth. The ceremony was often related to the sowing on the land. Demeter was no doubt a symbol of fertility. In myth she once coupled with her lover in a ploughed field. There was no denying the nature of what she bestowed. Yet there remains the problem of the asymmetricality with the agricultural year. The ceremony was held too early to be linked to the sowing. As with the myth of Kore no point in the farmer's calendar can be made to fit. In fact, the fertility symbols have all the appearance of an overlay that conceals more than it reveals.

It is not only the fertility symbolism which looks suspiciously like a later addition. In the form in which it has come down to us, imprecise though it is, the rite contains at least one massive contradiction which went curiously unnoticed in the Ancient World. At the critical moment when the priest calls out 'To Brimos a boy is born' there appears from below a vision of Kore rising. What conceivable connection, we might ask, can exist between these two events? Kore as Persephone in the underworld was a barren goddess. The child Brimo could not therefore have been hers. If Brimo is indeed an old name for the Queen of the Dead then it must refer to a goddess much older than her. A predecessor did exist, we have suggested, in a pre-existing Persephone, a pre-Greek Ereshkigal, but such a goddess, as we saw in the Sumerian myth, is a most unlikely candidate to give birth. As for the cutting of the ear of corn, this clearly ties in the rite to Demeter, the corn goddess, but has no resonance in the Homeric Kore myth where the symbol of the maiden's fate is not the corn but the pomegranate.

The ritual, however, does begin to make some sense once we trace it back to our reconstructed goddess myth, removing along the way not only the birth of Brimos but also the male priest with his ear of corn. Then the initiates huddling forward in the darkness look like participants of a much older drama, one of a voyage to the underworld. The host they seek is not the priest but his predecessor, at least in myth, Persephone or Ereshkigal. The path they take towards her is the one trodden by the lunar maiden on her moonless nights beneath the earth. The burst of fire from the furnace too makes sense when we realise that the ancients, unaware until the Classical Age, of the moon's reflected solar light, believed the luminary was lit by its own inner flame.

The symbolism is complete within the rite when the moon, long since thought dead, rises from the underworld ablaze with the light from the soul of the maiden who has died on the sacred tree. It is the spirit of this maiden that the celebrants see in the silver crescent of the new moon but the metaphor conveys much more. Kore rises for all. Her promise is not just of the new moon but of re-assurance of an after-life in the embrace of Mother Earth. As she returned to Demeter so would all souls find their way through the labyrinth to the light.

Some such reassurance must have been at the heart of the emotional experience of the Eleusinian initiates. Immortality was never mentioned in connection with the mysteries at least not an immortality that transcends the earth. What took the terror from death for the initiates was what had come down to them, despite all the patriarchal editing, from the ancient lunar myth, the perception that beneath all the apparent chaos of their lives there lay a divine harmony which they would finally come to know when they too at death returned to the earth.

Kore descends thus, like Inanna before her, for the sake of the community and the benefit of all. It was the distant folk memory of this that lit the darkness at Eleusis and fired the imagination of the initiates. Sadly for them, unforgettable though the experience was, much of the explanatory myth had already gone, corroded away by hundreds of years of patriarchal re-editing. The aspirations the myth had in the fullness of its power once engendered might still have been inferred, if only the initiates at Eleusis had grasped its significance, in the annual retirement of Kore to the underworld and her subsequent resurrection. What that annual return once re-affirmed was a vision of the after-life quite different from our own, a vision in which the world beyond the grave was not a transcendence or an inversion of the world of the living but an extension of its cyclicality, no more than another returning spiral in a web of eternal recurrence.

It is hard for us to imagine the worlds of the living and the dead sharing a resonance in their mutual embrace by Mother Earth but for the ancient matriarchs their commonality would have been palpable and visible to all for could not the dead be seen in this life in the sky each night voyaging to the underworld with the goddess in her lunar barque?

The death of the maiden on the sacred tree, the umbilicus of Mother Earth, returned the community to the primal myth of parthenogenesis for when the moon rose with her wandering spirit from the underworld image of that tree beneath the earth it did so as it had done on the very first night when the primal mound rose from the waters of the celestial sea. Yet the maiden hanging from the tree remains still the most enigmatic element of the ancient rite. The symbol of the tree itself we have seen preserved in isolated fragments. In the story of Inanna it is reduced to little more than a wooden spike beneath the earth while above it has the stunted shape of an old and twisted apple tree in the shadow of which the maiden herself has been displaced by the sybarite Dumuzi. By the time Kore descends to the earth the tree has all but vanished. Only the fruit remains, once the passport to eternal life, in the form of the deathly pomegranate. Kore still descends but, apart from the pomegranate, her link with the tree has gone. Inanna still hangs from what remains of the tree but only in the underworld and in the guise of a rotting corpse. Slender though it is, Inanna's body hanging on the stake would seem to be the sole surviving fragment of what must have been the key connecting symbol in the originating myth. We might be tempted to bring the investigation to a close at this point were it not for the fact that there does exist elsewhere in myth evidence that there once was a cult of a hanging maiden. In search of it we need to turn to the source of the Eleusinian mysteries on the island of Crete.

According to the Homeric 'Hymn to Demeter' it was by way of Crete that Demeter reached mainland Greece and there was a strong tradition that the island was the original home not only of the Eleusinian Mysteries but of much of the later Olympian religion of Greece. Our best authority for this is Diodorus Siculus. A Sicilian who was writing at the time of the Roman emperor Augustus, his observations were based on a detailed knowledge of ancient myth replenished by his own researches on his travels. It was his considered view that what happened at Eleusis did indeed derive from Crete but in a form quite different from the later ceremonies. By the Cretans themselves he was told that the Mysteries so resolutely concealed by the Eleusinian priests were once upon a time a public ceremony open for all to enjoy in Ancient Crete. Now if, as seems possible, the Mysteries were the vestigial relic of our lunar rite, then such a change in the conduct of their observance would be what we might expect. In the face of the growing power of the patriarchate old matriarchal cults would probably have gone underground to preserve themselves only later re-emerging in a more respectable but concealed form and under the tutelage of male priests.

In another sense, a Cretan origin also fits our theory. The culture of Crete before the arrival of the Mycenean Greeks was very definitely matriarchal. Archaeological digs throughout the island have produced widespread evidence for the cultic predominance of women. Seals, statuettes and gems unearthed generally depict priestesses or goddess figures and the few representations we find of men in early Crete clearly relegate them to inferior positions as servants, cup-bearers, musicians, sailors, field hands and labourers in general.[28]

Early Cretan culture named 'the Minoan Civilisation' by the English archaeologist Sir Arthur Evans (after Minos, the legendary ruler of Crete) was once dominant throughout the Aegean. Although its matriarchal features were apparent from the earliest excavations, it was not until its script, known as Linear B, was deciphered that we first began to get some idea of the pantheon of Minoan religion. Not only were many of the later divinities of Greece already evident in the script but, more interesting for the thesis presented here, there was an intriguing reference to a mother and maiden.

Mention of this duo naturally brings to mind the twin goddess figures noted at Catal Hüyük. The settlement there preceded Minoan culture by at least three, perhaps four, thousand years. Could there have been a Persephone cult of mother and maiden stretching back so many years? Compelling evidence for such a view has been found elsewhere in twin goddess artifacts made during the intervening years further west in Malta and Sicily. Conceivably such finds are evidence for an unbroken religious tradition linking the Neolithic settlement at Catal Hüyük to the land that gave the Eleusinian Mysteries to Greece. If such is the case and our hanging maiden really did exist, then we would expect to find at least a trace of her in what the later Greeks remembered of the ancient Cretan myths. In fact, such a trace does exist. It can be found in a mysterious reference in Linear B, the Minoan script, to a certain 'Labyrinthoio potnia', 'the Lady of the Labyrinth'.[30]

The lady in question appears in a story told by the Greeks. It begins with Poseidon, god of the seas. Angered, it was said, by an affront to him by Minos of Crete, he resolved to punish that unfortunate king by causing his wife to fall wildly in love with a great white bull. The wife, Pasiphae, disclosed her predicament to the inventor Daedalus. A man of resource, he achieved the seemingly impossible by constructing a perfect representation of a cow in wood. By lying inside it with her legs splayed, the besotted queen was finally free to satisfy her lust.

The offspring of this strange copulation was the Minotaur, humanoid in body but with a bovine head. Asterius was the name she gave to this unlovely child. In shame and grief the king made Daedalus tunnel an underground maze, the Labyrinth, in the dismal depths of which he hid his errant wife and her son. To survive, however, Asterius required a barbarous diet. Human food was most to his taste and the bodies he ate were paid in tribute by the Cretans' underlings, the Greeks. Every ninth year a ship left Athens for Crete with on board a living larder of seven youths and seven maidens.

When the tribute was due for the third time the Athenian hero, Theseus, offered himself as a victim under subterfuge with the aim of killing the monster in his lair. The ship sailed in the spring with Aphrodite hovering at the helm. It was not long before this goddess of love took a hand in these events. It was no doubt by a stratagem of hers that Ariadne, the daughter of the king, felt her heart melt at the sight of the flaxen-haired Theseus coming ashore. For the hero the infatuation was a lucky stroke. Ariadne agreed to help him murder her half-brother in his den. She alone, she told him, could get him to the centre of the labyrinth and back again. From Daedalus she had received a magic ball of thread which, with one end tied to the lintel, would roll before Theseus of its own accord until it stopped outside the room where the monster slept. From there, the deed done, the killer could return through the maze by following the line of the unrolled thread. The plan worked. The Minotaur was despatched in his sleep and hero and lover left Crete with the maidenly victims they had released.

The tale reads like a barbarisation of an earlier myth. Much ink has been spilt on the meaning of the labyrinth. Some have seen in it a child-like rendering by the primitive Greeks of the Minoan palace at Knossos with its many rooms and passages. Its real significance may be more mythical than this. Its name is linked to 'labrys', the double-headed axe found on Cretan sites, a symbol perhaps of the waxing and the waning lunar crescents. In myth its occupant was Asterius. A monster in the tale but, etymologically, a masculinisation of Asteria. That name means 'starry'. Was this a Cretan goddess at the centre of the maze? Was she the original denizen of these depths whom the Minotaur displaced? We recall Inanna first descended for the obsequies of the 'bull of heaven'. Was the Minotaur the bull of heaven now permanently in residence? Have we here yet another example of patriarchal displacement? Is it too esoteric to proceed, then, to suggest that the unravelling ball of thread is the waning moon on its voyage to the underworld? Remarkably, at least one coin from Knossos depicts a new moon at the centre of the maze.

The sequel to this story is more remarkable still. Ariadne received scant reward for helping Theseus who proved a somewhat insubstantial lover. As to the exact nature of her fate, accounts differ. One theme alone is paramount. She was deserted by her lover and her desertion ended in a violent death. By one tradition, she was abandoned pregnant in Cyprus where she eventually died giving birth at Amathos. Amathos was a notable site of goddess worship. Death in childbirth was always at the hands of the virgin goddess Artemis.

The association with that goddess must have been widely known for Homer, too, has her slain by Artemis but closer to Crete on the island of Dia. Dia was in turn another name for the island of Naxos. There, it was said, she was left by Theseus asleep on the beach. Waking up, she was about to kill herself in despair when the god Dionysus appeared and took her as his wife. Dionysus was the son of Semele, the moon goddess, providing yet another lunar connection. Other accounts forsake her in despair. Stricken with grief or fearful of the avenging Artemis, she hangs herself.

Whether from the darts of Artemis or by her own hand, no other heroine, it has been said, suffered death in so many ways. Even more noteworthy than the details of her death was the fact of its celebration. This consisted of two festivals on the island of Naxos. One was of mourning for the woman abandoned by Theseus who died on the island. The other was of joy and exaltation for the risen bridge of the god Dionysus. The two rites, it has been suggested, are but two halves of a single cult, of lamentation at an untimely death followed by the celebration of a resurrection. Normally, in the Ancient World male gods were the objects of such rites. Uniquely, the rites on the island of Naxos featured a heroine. 'Ariadne' means 'very holy maid'. Her tomb was the centre of a cult in Cyprus. Have we here, at last, the missing fragment of our lunar rite, the hanging maiden?

Curiously, the killer of Ariadne in many tales, the goddess Artemis, was herself hanged in at least one cult. The evidence for this is from the traveller Pausanias. On one of his many journeys he arrived at a place called Kondylea in Arcadia. There he came upon a small grove of Artemis and a temple to her near by. Shrines to this goddess he had witnessed many times but this one had a legend to it so bizarre he felt compelled to tell it. Once it had been called the temple of Kondylean Artemis but since then, said the local inhabitants, its name had changed. The cause of the change harked back to a tragedy that had once afflicted the region and filled all those who remembered it with shame. The local children, so the story went, had taken to playing round the sanctuary. In the course of their games they had tied a rope around the neck of the statue of the goddess. When this childish act of desecration came to light, the locals, fearful of the vengeance of the goddess, reacted hysterically and stoned their children to death. Sadly for mortals, the attitudes of the gods to such things are not so easily divined. The wrath of the goddess was not long in coming but it was on their heads that it fell and for their own crime. Throughout the region the women began to contract a strange, cancerous disease of the womb. Babies were stillborn. Suspecting the goddess of childbirth at the root of this, the people sought oracular advice. The judgement of the oracle was that the children had died unjustly. Atonement would have to be made by giving them their proper burial rites and, forever after, an annual offering in commemoration of their suffering. The incident had left a scar on the memory of the community which is probably why they had changed the name. The name they chose to give the shrine must have left Pausanias even more bewildered and perplexed. The dedication they had given it was to 'the Hanged Artemis'.[32]

The garbled story Pausanias heard looks like yet another patriarchal rendering of an ancient matriarchal cult. Our suspicions of this are confirmed by the nature of the goddess herself. Artemis had powerful lunar connections. A virgin goddess of the waxing moon, her silver bow symbolised its crescent. In the shrine of Artemis Hegemone near Acacesium the cult statue showed the goddess with torches in her hands. The goddess as light-bearer was an emissary of the moon and a giver of immortality by virtue of its fire. It was the same fire in which Demeter bathed the infant Demophoön.

Artemis too had her links with Demeter. Deeper into the shrine near Acacesium was the sanctuary of Despoena, daughter of Demeter by Poseidon, a name often used for Persephone herself. In the sanctuary Demeter also had her shrine. Beside her throne was a statue of Artemis the huntress. In one hand she held two snakes; in the other a torch, her lunar symbol. Her presence seems incongruous at first until we discover that, according to one cult legend, Artemis was Demeter's daughter. The legend is confirmed by Herodotus who learnt of it from Egyptian priests. If Herodotus can be believed we may have the last missing fragment of our lunar myth. Artemis or Kore, either way Demeter's daughter, was hanged not raped on her journey to the underworld.

Yet the task of reconstruction is not quite complete. There is still a missing element in our myth. Whether goddesses or heroines, our hanging maidens appear to have lost their attachment to the sacred tree. We know from the archaeological evidence that a tree cult was prominent in Crete and there are goddesses from that island with powerful arboreal links. A sacrificial hanging, however, does not figure in their myths. Nowhere on Crete does the connection exist. In search of it we must leave the island and cross the Aegean to Rhodes where yet another lunar heroine met her death. For an account of it in myth we are once more indebted to the traveller Pausanias.

His story is of Helen over whom the Trojan War was fought. The face that launched a thousand ships has excited mythographers ever since but the tale Pausanias was told was remarkable in one respect. It ended for Helen in violent death. Late in life, so the story went, after the death of her husband Menalaus, Helen was driven from her home in Sparta by a family feud. In search of a haven she fled to Rhodes to her friend Polyxo. The two had once been very close but Polyxo had been widowed by the Trojan War and, unknown to Helen, held her indirectly the cause of her husband's death. The opportunity for vengeance came one day when Helen was at her morning ablutions by a stream under a large overhanging tree. Disguised as the Erinnyes, the divinities of retribution for blood spilt, some of Polyxo's serving women crept up on Helen and then hanged her from the tree.

This curious version of events was no doubt puzzling to Pausanias. It was related to him, he said, to account for the cult on Rhodes of 'Helena Dendritis'. 'Helen of the Tree', the tree cult of a hanged heroine. The Rhodians were said to have atoned for their crime by dedicating a temple to it. Again, it seems, Pausanias has revealed the corruption of an ancient myth to explain a cult that had lost all meaning. For a clue as to what its original significance might have been we need only refer to the nature of its heroine, Helen herself. She was in fact the name of the Spartan moon-goddess. The moon figured greatly in Sparta's worship. Indeed, reluctance to fight when it was unfavourably aspected delayed the arrival of her troops at the field of Marathon and might have lost that battle for the whole of Greece.

The actual world 'helene' meant 'torch' and reminds us that the ancients thought of the moon as having fire in its light. In her lunar aspect, Helen was often tied to Artemis although the union looks incongruous at first sight. They were merely two different aspects of the lunar goddess. On Rhodes this goddess returned to her sacred tree. There her maidenly surrogate hung while the priestesses of the Death Goddess looked on. In the story Pausanias was told the washing in the stream was placed in ignorance out of sequence. It would have happened after the hanging not before and to cleanse not Helen but her priestesses of ritual blood pollution.

With Helen our search for the vestiges of a matriarchal cult is temporarily suspended. Temporarily because later in the text we will have occasion to meet Helen again. So far we have managed to unearth a number of interesting fragments of our lunar rite and primal myth. Helen can for the moment be placed alongside Ariadne, Artemis and Kore as survivors from a tale of maidenly descent to the underworld and resurrection there. If such was the case then the composite of their different starring versions of the tale may once have supplied the myth the dramatisation of which invoked the rise of the goddess from the depths at Eleusis. Who knows how far back in time those ceremonies of initiation stretched? To Inanna of the Sumerians? Perhaps even to the twin goddesses we saw at Catal Hüyük? In all cultures initiation of this kind affirms some intuitive understanding of how the life cycle of the individual in the collective is patterned with the cosmic order. In the ancient matriarchal culture that understanding found its embodiment in the primal myth of parthenogenesis. In the vision of that myth the Great Mother gave birth out of her own inner self in the shape of the mound that rose from her celestial sea.

The life force that emerged was a manifestation of her primordial being that returned eternally to its source. All beings shared in the harmony of this cyclical return to her embrace. The patterning was plain for all to see as each night the moon daughter sank into the womb of her mother to be re-born eternally from her umbilical, the world tree. Like the moon, woman also died to rise again. This was the wisdom of the first initiates. She alone had the privilege of return with the moon to the underworld tree. Only those she chose to accompany her could share with her this passport to Elysium for she alone knew the path through the labyrinth to the sacred tree. This was the wisdom the goddess gave her as she hung from the boughs of the sacred tree.

1 Mellaart J. *Cattail Hüyük: A Neolithic Town in Anatolia* Thames and Hudson. London 1967.
2 Young G. M. *The Dying Goddess*. Dorrance. Pittsburgh 1993.
3 Young G. M. ibid.
4 Young G. M. ibid.
5 Young G. M. ibid.
6 Young G. M. ibid.
7 Graves R. *Greek Myths* Vol. 1 Penguin Books, Harmondsworth 1955 p. 14.
8 cf. Young G. M. *The Dying Goddess*. Dorrance. Pitsburgh 1993.
9 Brandon S. G. F. *Creation Legends of the Ancient Near East*. Hodder and Stoughton London 1963 p. 15.
10 Neumann E. *The Great Mother: An Analysis of the Archetype*. Princeton University Press, Princeton, New Jersey 1955 p. 222.
11 Brandon ibid p. 68.
12 Young G. M. ibid.
13 Young G. M. ibid.
14 Young G. M. ibid.
15 Young G. M. ibid.
16 Stone M. *The Paradise Papers*. Virago London 1976 p. 232.
17 Watterson B. Gods of Ancient Egypt. Batsford. London 1984 p. 131.
18 Watterson B. ibid p. 132.
19 Baring A and Cashford J. *The Myth of the Goddess: Evolution of an Image*. BCA Lonon 1991 p. 208.
20 cf. Young G. M. ibid.
21 cf. Young G. M. ibid.
22 cf. Young G. M. ibid.
23 Kramer S. N. *Sumerian Mythology*. Harper and Row, New York. 1961 p. 76.
24 Kramer ibid p. 76

25 Jakobson T. *The Treasures of Darkness: A History of Mesopotamian Religion.* Yale University Press New Haven. Connecticut 1976 p.56.

26 cf. Young G. M. ibid.

27 cf. Young G. M. ibid.

28 Cornford, F. M. *'The Aparchai and the Eleusinian Mysteries'* in *'Essays and Studies Presented to W. M. Ridgeway.* Cambridge University Press 1913 p. 153.

29 Kerenyi C. *'Eleusis'* (trans. by R Mannheim) Routledge and Kegan Paul London 1967 p. 44

30 Kerenyi *Eleusis* ibid p. 139.

31 Young G. M. *The Dying Goddess* ibid.

32 Kerenyi ibid 1967 p. 133.

33 Kerenyi ibid 1967 p. 135.

34 Kerenyi ibid 1967 p. 23.

35 Richardson D. A. *'The Mother Goddess in Minoan Crete and Vestiges in the Contemporary Greek Orthodox Church,* unpubl. Phd dissertation, New York University p. 164.

36 Marry J. D. *History, Society and Religion in the Minoan-Mycenean Era.* Unpubl. Phd Stanford University 1973 p. 219.

37 Levi P. (ed.) *Pausanias 8 k VIII* Penguin. Harmondsworth, 10971 p. 426.

Chapter 2

The Lover of the Goddess

The goddess cult is no more. Its celebrants are long since dead. All they have left us are a few physical remains and whatever of their myths and rites was too potent for male mythographers to change. Our work of reconstruction has had to depend heavily upon inference from these. In the absence of firm data historians in other fields frequently resort to arguing by analogy, often plundering disciplines like anthropology in search of evidential claims. In our case, the argument by analogy necessarily fails. There are no matriarchal cultures still existing that have managed to avoid the probing tentacles of the patriarchal West.

Some evidence has been preserved of cultures with at least some retentive features of what may once have been a pre-existing matriarchate but nowhere is there enough for us to conjure up the world of Catal Hüyük. Few historians would still deny that a matriarchate was once pre-eminent and that at the heart of it was a goddess cult. What it was, however, will probably always remain shadowy and obscure. Too much of what might have illuminated it has been lost. That has been one of the prices we have been forced to pay for the interminable advance of our patriarchy. Yet, thin though the evidence is for historical debate, one bedevilling question remains to be confronted. How did that patriarchy come to power in the first place? In other words, how did the goddess's erstwhile servitors become our gods?

To answer this question we must turn once more to contemplate the as yet ill-defined outline of the matriarchy it once displaced. As to the nature of this matriarchy modern anthropology warns us against too sweeping a generalisation. It is in horticultural societies that women are more likely to be dominant or at least influential and then often only at the fringes of forests where herds of domesticated animals are less likely to be found.[1] As for the hunters and gatherers of Palaeolithic times all we have to go on are the images on the cave walls and the artifacts, notably the Venus figurines. These cult objects, if that is what they were, are clearly matrifocal but cannot be used as evidence that the women whose attributes they idealise enjoyed a preponderance of tribal wealth and status. No-one would suggest, for example, that the innumerable paintings and statues of the Blessed Virgin are prima facie evidence for the exalted status of women in Medieval Europe.

The issue raises an important definitional distinction. What passes for matriarchy has many strands. A culture may indeed be matrifocal in its imagery foregrounding the female as the femininely divine. Of this the Venus figures seem, as far as we can tell, a good example. Equally, a culture may lack this matriarchal attribute while having others. It may, for instance, be matriarchal in its marriage system, with the newly-wed husband living with the family of his wife. As a correlate of this it may also be matrilineal in its property relations with inheritance only through the female line. It may be all of these or one or two or none. Clearly if all of these once obtained, as may have happened at Catal Hüyük, then we would have a matriarchy in that case on its strongest ground. The evidence for matriarchy this strong as late as Catal Hüyük remains faint, however.

Old though it seems to us, the settlement at Catal Hüyük appeared comparatively late on the scene. By the time the community came to settle there a goddess cult may already have been in existence for thousands of years, in fact throughout most of the Palaeolithic and into the Neolithic Age. We are talking of a time span here of perhaps fifty or sixty millennia. During the whole of that period it would have had to accommodate progressive changes in the material culture surrounding it. Beginning as a cult among small matriarchal clan of gatherers, it would sooner or later have had to adapt to the arrival of a hunting economy and with it the ritualised violence of the fraternity of hunters. Some have seen in the blood-letting of the hunt the first traumatic shock to the psychic harmony of the cult. Others have sought in the dynamics of this development justification for the existence of a Palaeolithic male deity more savage than the goddess, the ancestor of the later horned god of the witches.[2]

Paintings in caves of male cultic figures adduced as evidence of this, however, look less like deities than tribal shamans. Even if merely shamanistic, these paintings could still be a sign of the increasing involvement in ritual of men. The point is debatable. Hunting does add a powerful asset to the role of men but that does not mean that Palaeolithic man was socially dominant in other ways. Excluded from this growing male preserve, women might still have retained their rights in the more mysterious matters of theology and ritual. The two worlds might simply have failed to inter-penetrate. Intriguingly, no image of a goddess has yet been found close to the depiction of a hunt. There is an obvious inference we can draw from this. The goddess lived in a separate world.

More likely is it, though, that the goddess cult itself would have had to metamorphose to help contain the violent psychology of the hunter. Her capacity for this may have been greater than we think. The goddess who gave life also dealt in death for she took the dead back into herself often before their prime, a benevolent embrace presumably extendible to the stricken and the slain. That some such adaptation did occur is apparent from the wealth of imagery from Catal Hüyük and elsewhere of a goddess flanked by wild animals, often portrayed alone with them on distant mountain peaks. Her inheritor in the later Ancient World was surely the Artemis of the Greeks, goddess of the moon but also of the hunt and of all that was wild and inaccessible in nature. Like her forbear she was both giver of life and bringer of death, protector of women in childbirth who also struck them down in that state in which they were closest to her own untamed nature. If warfare was originally an extension of the hunt, then from the same process of differentiation might have come the later goddesses who made both love and war. It may be the shadow of this darker face of the goddess of the caves that we see in the shape of Ishtar, the Syrian Aphrodite, goddess of the brothel and the battlefield, stamping in blood.

How far the goddess cult changed to incorporate the image of the hunter it is difficult to say. In any case by the time greater historical evidence begins to accumulate things were already moving in a direction that would lead eventually to patriarchy. Somewhere around 11,000 BC, what is called the early Neolithic Age, in an area from the Balkans through central Anatolia to the Middle East, the hunters and gatherers of late Palaeolithic times turned to a more settled exploitation of animal and plant life. We can imagine them passing through a first stage of orchard cultivation in which the food supply from the hunt was supplemented by small cultivated plots in forest clearings. Once the principle of cultivation had been learned, it would not have been long before gardens were transformed into fields. In orchard cultivation women are more likely to retain some predominance but with field agriculture men come more to the fore as garden gives way to field tillage and then to stockbreeding on a large scale. The process that ended in the cattle-drawn plough would have triggered a considerable extension in the roles of men which would have laid the foundation for the patriarchy to come.

This sequence of events was by no means universal. Some Palaeolithic hunters in the desert and on the steppes appear to have moved from hunting and gathering to cattle herding while remaining constantly on the move. Nonetheless, a shift towards a more sedentary pattern of agriculture was characteristic of what we call the Neolithic Age. By the second half of the second millennium our community at Catal Hüyük already had cattle under full domestication. By the time the settlement was abandoned in 5400 BC farming villages with cattle and grain were becoming commonplace throughout the Anatolian region.

These primitive agrarian developments may well at first have triggered a second proliferation in the goddess cult. Agriculture is in many ways less arduous than hunting. Ploughing, sowing and harvesting take up less than a couple of months leaving much of the year free for other things. Contrary to popular belief, the life of the Neolithic peasant was not a laborious one but it did run to the rhythms of a schedule that the hunter lacked. Forward planning elevates the principle of utility in the affairs of men. Now the appeal to the goddess had never been utilitarian in this narrow sense. There had been no crops around for her to oversee when her cult first emerged in the Palaeolithic period. Wisdom and ecstasy were her gifts to her worshippers. This may have changed with the coming of the crops. It was then perhaps that the earth goddess and her daughter began to be seen as having tasks to do on earth as guardians of fertility with an appropriate concern for the proper rituals of sowing and harvesting. Then, too, that their festivals began to move into closer alignment with the agricultural calendar although as we saw at Eleusis, even by Classical times this process was by no means complete. The adjustment would not have been so difficult to make for the fertility of women and earth had always been linked. Both, it was believed, were affected by the phases of the moon, its light and its fertilising dew.

Whatever the immediate effect on the goddess's role, at a certain threshold one cultural discovery would certainly have been made. With the arrival of systematic stockbreeding, if not before, would have been revealed the role of the male in procreation. The discovery was to be of truly Copernican proportions in its impact upon all aspects of social and religious thought. The revelation would have broken the closed loop of earth, moon and women that previously had held all things together. Gone forever was the idea that women gave birth mysteriously out of themselves. With that went much of the seductiveness of their hold over man. A role now had to be found in the overall scheme of things for the male spermatozoa. More than this, however, an entire way of thinking symbolically about the universe had to change. The feminine, whether terrestrial or divine, would soon cease to be so potent an explanatory metaphor.

Yet it would be easy to exaggerate the immediate effects. There is unlikely to have been an instant paradigm shift. We can imagine a cultural lag of many generations in which primitive mythologers were compelled to grope around in the dark for alternatives to fill the gap. At this early stage we are still a long way from the ultimate reduction of the womb to a mere passive receptacle, little more than a hothouse for the sperm, a degrading of the female role that eventually took hold throughout the Ancient World.

The revolutionary concept of fatherhood may have remained obscure for longer than we think. The kind of confusion and inconsistency that marked the process of transition to more patriarchal symbolic systems is evident in the story of Jacob in Genesis. After leaving home under a cloud of suspicion, Jacob ends up working at the homestead of his mother's brother. The uncle is a critical male role in matriarchal cultures and Jacob, we are told, is helping out with an eye on Rachel, his uncle Laban's youngest daughter, by marriage to whom he clearly hopes to inherit by the common matrilineal principle of ultimogeniture. When finally he gets his hands on her, however, she proves at first unable to bear a child. In his anger at this Jacob reveals an ignorance of human biology that somehow survived editorial re-working and exposes the whole story as a relic of some very old Neolithic folk-tale. 'Am I in God's stead', he says, 'who hath withheld from thee the fruit of thy womb.'[3] In other words, although a stock breeder, Jacob regards whatever is going amiss in Rachel's womb as very much a matter between her and her presiding deity. That he has not truly grasped the scope of his own role in this is apparent some time later when, after Rachel does eventually give birth, he decides to separate off from Laban and return to his own place.

The two men agree to divide off part of the flocks for Jacob on the basis of their different colours and markings. Once the criteria for separation have been decided in this way, Jacob is not above cheating his father-in-law by boosting the fertility of the cattle with his own markings. His subterfuge however, tells us a great deal about the biological assumptions behind this primitive attempt at eugenic breeding. To force the stronger cattle with his own markings to conceive, he places cut rods of green poplar, hazel and chestnut in their watering troughs.[4] So successful is this ruse, we are told, that it arouses the ire of Laban's sons. A worried Jacob decides to stake all on one final desperate throw and flees with both the cattle and Rachel with 'the images that were her father's' in her saddlebag.[5] In doing so, of course, he was challenging the matrilocal principle of marriage by taking his wife to his father's house. The stolen images were probably the icons of the goddess cult.

What the strange tale of Jacob tells us is that, long after the pillars of the old matriarchal system had begun to crumble, the old folk ways still retained some power over the Neolithic imagination. It is as if the male principle had yet fully to emerge from the shadowy womb of Mother Earth. We can see the incongruity of this in the androgynous goddess figures of Neolithic Europe which appear at the end of the eighth millennium with an egg-shaped body, often bird-like in shape, but with a phallus for a neck. What this phallic extension of the womb suggests is that the male principle had yet fully to detach itself as a separate source of fertilising power in Neolithic art. In some curious way the male sperm was regarded as belonging to the woman. It was her life fluid that men returned to the womb to pass back to her.

Still trapped in the coil that for millennia had been thought to circulate the life force between mothers and their daughters, the concept of the sperm took time to wriggle free. Initially it may have been identified symbolically with the waters of mountains, lakes and streams. In Sumeria, for example, one word stood for both water and semen.[6] The analogy with the inland waters would have fitted well the inchoate status of the sperm at this time for they were thought, like the veins of her body, to be very much the possession of earth. The fertilising power of water was never far from the minds of farmers in a parched land and, as every midwife knew, it was present in the womb too, the herald of the coming birth.

The separation of this aqueous force as an embodiment of increasing male power can be charted in the rise of the sweet water gods of the Sumerian pantheon. The creative force within this pantheon was conceived first in the form of the goddess Nammu. Her identity was with the salt waters. In this respect, we have seen, she looks very much like our primal goddess of the celestial sea. By the time the Sumerians had learned to cut her name on their cuneiform tablets she had acquired a male consort, Apsu, who personified the sweet waters. From among a succession of descendants the two eventually produced the offspring that would eventually bring them down. This was Enki, another deity of the sweet waters, who led a revolt against them of the younger male gods.

A persistent adversary of this young water god was Ninhursaga, 'lady of the stony ground.'[7] Transparently, an early earth goddess, possibly in origin the primal mound, she was also 'the lady of the womb', a symbol of the power in the womb that made the embryo grow, and the mother, therefore, of both gods and men. An old myth linking her to Enki reveals by what primitive reasoning her power was first subtracted and then added to men. From her coupling with Enki was produced the goddess Ninsar herself the producer by her father of Nin-kurra 'lady of the mountains'[8] who by the same process became mother in her turn of Uttu,[9] the spidery goddess of weaving. She too would have mothered in the same fashion if Ninhursaga had not removed the semen of Enki from her body. From the sperm eight plants grew, each of them eaten by Enki who earned thereby the curse of Ninhursaga.[3] The curse of an earth goddess was not to be dismissed but for the water god there was something far more morbid still in store. Inside him the plants began to grow. Unable to give birth, the troubled god had to be taken into the vagina of Ninhursaga where he could finally give birth to the eight children his semen had produced.[11]

As the sweet waters of rivers and streams had always been considered to be the veins of the earth, the rise of the sweet water gods naturally led to a closer relationship between the male as a divine principle and a goddess who had always been thought of as the power immanent in nature. It was now that a most important development took place. Under the pressurising logic of this new principle of procreation the goddess of the earth was forced to take a son to her bosom to complement her daughter. For millennia mother and daughter had embraced each other in a cyclical relationship that symbolised the eternal return of the regenerative powers of nature. Now the cyclicality of their myth had to alter shape to harmonise with the dynamic of the intrusive male.

Men could not, like women, replicate the unfolding fertility of earth but they could claim to fertilise her with their blood and sperm. The metaphor of penetration, in fact, meant that they could be said to return twice to the womb, first to the womb of the daughters of the goddess in the act of impregnation and then to the womb of the goddess herself for entombment in the earth. This different rhythm of the male constrained the age-old cycle of daughter returning to earth to convolute into a double loop. In this new mythic pattern the son was seen to come back twice to Mother Earth. On his first return he gave her back her due, returning her own sperm to its rightful place in the womb. On the second he fertilised her with himself, with the blood and detritus of his body after death.

For millennia women too had descended to the bowels of the earth but in ritual as personifications of the moon. Their lunar rite was one of death and resurrection in which their spirits returned from their journey to the underworld in the shape of the rising moon. Thus they re-affirmed their propinquity to Mother Earth. This symbiotic link was sanguinary at root. Its sanction was the menstrual cycle which shared the time span of the lunar transit and seemed to bless women with earth's capacity to be an autonomous source of life. Out of the analogical extension of this consanguinity to men emerged a radically new conception. In some ways, it mirrored the age-old sanctification of women's blood. The reasoning went thus. If men's sperm had the potency to fertilise the earth then surely the blood from which it came was equally sacred. And just as women were most fecund in their menses and lost their fecundity when the cycle ceased so men's blood was most equivalently powerful at their sexual peak. We are a long way yet from the reduction of women to a mere hothouse for the sperm and the tabooing of her menstrual power but the idea must soon have emerged that if men too were to enjoy the status of a sacrifice then it would be better for them to be despatched in their prime so that only their freshest, their most invigorating blood could fertilise the earth.

The arrival in the picture of the male sperm would probably have added a new dramatic significance to the fertility implications of the old rites although the consequent rise in status of the male god would have taken many centuries. No doubt he remained for long an underling, a symbol merely of the flourishing mortality of the buried seed, the representative of the discontinuous and concealed in what was manifestly more fixed and constant, the vegetation cycle of the earth. High above, his wistful glance caught sight of his wandering sister in her lunar barque crossing the sky with the souls of the dead on her nightly descent to Mother Earth. Inevitably, therefore, wherever the figure of the young male god makes an appearance at this early stage we find him in the act of adoration of the goddess.

Before the revelation of the role of the sperm the contract the moon daughter renewed in the underworld must have seemed her genetic inheritance. In holding her for the three moonless nights beneath the earth the goddess merely took back a power of reproduction that was rightfully hers and which in due course she returned in the confirmation of the lunar cycle. When the young male god took on a duplicate cycle of disappearance and return he naturally entered the inclusivity of the originating cult. What compelled his entry was the still encompassing vision of the power of Mother Earth. His sperm was as much hers as the corn in the fields. His equation with fertility at this stage thus only served to confirm his subjection to the divinely feminine immanent in the earth. The symbol of the young vegetation god dying in the amorous embrace of the mother that had suckled him earthed the male principle and contained it in a way that has never happened since. The bipolarity, the contrariety even, of this relationship had yet to be discovered.

Interestingly, we have more evidence of the dying son/lover of the goddess than of any preceding and, indeed, of many succeeding phases of patriarchal development. Of all the stages in the historical shift between the matriarchal and patriarchal extremes of the religious continuum this one proved by far the most retentive. Other cults were to supersede it along the continuum, many of them far more grandiloquent in their claims for the male, but surpassed though it may have been and in many cases diminished by them, it stubbornly survived into the Classical World. It could even be said that this god survived in Christian form although, as we shall see, much abstracted, shorn of the sensuality, the lush lasciviousness, the unashamed fleshliness of the seminal cult.

It was these very characteristics which probably ensured its survival at a cultural level beneath more transcendent forms of masculine deity. Woman has never, until today at least, been in danger of losing her nurturing role and the sexual power of her pheromones has always caught the imagination of the male. The conjunction of these two biological prerogatives represents a powerful potion, at times even terrifying, to the male psyche, a power witnessed by images such as the 'vagina destata' and the near-universality of incest taboos In the shape of Freud's Oedipus complex it has risen yet again in this century to trouble man.

Doubtless for some of its celebrants an attractive feature of the dying son/lover cult was the still remaining complementarity of the roles of the sexes in its rites. Inevitably perhaps, in a cult that foregrounded the sexual potency of the male, these rites were orgiastic. Their sexual promiscuity was a celebration not only of the fertility of the fields which by the logic of sympathetic magic it was intended to achieve but also of ecstatic union with the image of the goddess. For these express purposes 'hierodules' were at hand, somewhat unfairly labelled 'sacred prostitutes' today, for their role was in no way as venal or meretricious as this makes them sound.

These women were more or less permanently in residence at the goddess's shrine. Dedications have been found that attest the status they enjoyed - some were high-born, the 'gifts' of noble families keen to ingratiate themselves with the cult. So salient was their sexual role as representatives of the goddess that, when men were eventually introduced as permanent officiants in the rites, they were forced to mimic it in sodomitic intercourse with worshippers. These were the 'dog priests' that aroused such apoplectic rage among Old Testament prophets. With the spread of patriarchal values the anger the promiscuity aroused became general throughout the Ancient World. In 186 BC it led the Roman senate to lay a total ban on one dying god cult, that of the Greek Dionysos.

Complementarity between the sexes there may have been but it was still on matriarchal terms. In many respects the worship of the dying god was still a women's cult. When finally it replaced the dying maiden cult, women appear to have transferred to it the affections they had felt for the older cult. The worship of this god was probably the last phase in religious development when women still played a dominant role as officiants in a cult celebrated by men. It was a phase when powerful goddess archetypes still ruled the masculine imagination. Goddesses like Artemis, Anath, Cybele, Astarte, Asherah, Ishtar, Isis and Aphrodite had not lost the power to mesmerise, even to terrorise their male worshippers. So powerful were these goddess archetypes that men frequently strove to cut themselves free from the stem of their masculinity and merge with them. At the great festivals of the goddess at centres like Ephesus, Pessinus and Syrian Hierapolis whirling crowds of men, the ancestors of the modern dervishes, would gyrate to such a point of ecstatic union with the goddess that they could hack off their genitals in their frenzy. To hurl the severed testicles at the feet of the goddess was only, after all, to give back what was rightly hers, the emblem of her own life force. The goddess in turn extended the hand of welcome to these unsexed men in the cold light of dawn that followed their night of suffering for thus she swelled the ranks of her eunuch priests.

Strongly though the young male god figured in these rites he always remained something of an intruder interpolated in an older myth. The incongruity of the intrusion is apparent in the status of the phallus once this, as time passed, began to separate out into an important polarity in itself. Modelled in clay and borne in baskets by the priestesses of the cult, its replicas were a symbol of its rootlessness once it was detached from Mother Earth. There had been a time, perhaps, when the erect phallus had provided the royal road to ecstasy for male participants in the old goddess cult.

What else do we make of those circles of ithyphallic males on the walls of Palaeolithic caves? Sexual union and ecstatic trance had always been the gift of the goddess to her male worshippers but the prerogative of giving had been granted to her female servitors. Unlike women, however, men were precluded by the determinants of gender from ever achieving this supreme act of total identification with the goddess. In their sodomitic rites the temple priests could only ape the act of grace tendered by the hierodules. They might also lead the way, as in Rome they did in the cult of Attis, in the procession of the icon of the goddess through the streets but for all their cavorting never could these perfumed half-men ever truly match the blissful rapport of the priestesses with their goddess. The closeness of that relationship harked back to a time far more remote than they could possibly imagine when woman, moon and earth were but different aspects of a darker goddess whose gorgon stare could freeze the blood of trespassing men.

It is possible that for some years the two cults, one of a dying maiden the other of a dying god, remained alongside each other in uneasy co-existence. There is evidence for such a pattern later in Greece where mysteries reserved for women could be found along with male mysteries and those in which the sexes were mixed. Cults have their own peculiar will to power, however, and sooner or later there would have been a tendency for the dying god to displace his sister and achieve thereby pre-eminence in the arms of Mother Earth. The residue of this we will examine later. It is apparent, above all, in the derivative symbolism of the dying son/lover cults. Wherever such derivatives pile up, we can guess we have a lineal descendant in masculine form of the old goddess cult. We also have fortuitously to hand in an ancient Mesopotamian text evidence of the actual process of inheritance. The inheritor is our old friend Dumuzi whom we last saw being dragged down into the underworld as a substitute for Inanna's own descent.

The appearance of Dumuzi on the scene is full of foreboding for the old goddess myth. The repercussion is already apparent in a later text. The direct descendant in myth of Inanna was the Syrian goddess Ishtar. Her story too figured a descent which is described in an Akkadian version from the end of the second millennium from Ashur, the old religious centre of Assyria. The details of the descent to the underworld mirror that of Inanna the earlier goddess, as we might expect. The ascent, however, contains a significant elaboration of the Dumuzi sequel. The text begins to close with an account of the ransom Ishtar must pay to avoid a return to the world of the dead when, all of a sudden at this point and unrelated to the earlier story, mention is made of the revival from the dead of Tammuz, her lover. As his name suggests, Tammuz was a derivation from Dumuzi. He was also to become, as we shall later see, perhaps the most famous dying and resurrecting vegetation god in Mesopotamia. The abruptness of his arrival on the scene is suspicious. It looks as if his revival has been inserted by mythographers in an attempt to alter the significance of the tale. A development already implicit in the descent of the earlier Dumuzi has been made manifest in the text. The male actor with a walk-on part has shifted now to centre-stage. Soon the spotlight will shift from the heroine. Ishtar will lose her role to her lover who will go down in place of her to a redemptive death.

Tammuz was only one of many dying vegetation gods that survived throughout the Ancient World. To their many worshippers these gods were known by different names but, wherever they were worshipped, there were certain common features in their cults that never changed. They were always the husbands or lovers of a goddess. She too was known by many names. She might also be their sister, more usually their mother, but, whatever the relationship between them, one fact remained. They were passive variables. She was the fixed, constant and always the more powerful participant in the tale. Her fixity and power she derived from the pre-eminence she had once enjoyed as the giver of all life and the creator of the universe. Her lover, as we have seen, was essentially an interloper inserted late into the mythic texts of her cult. His variability betrayed the time when this occurred. That variability, we might almost call it season-ality, in his career was a metaphor, his own defining metaphor, for the role of the grain in the agricultural cycle. This was a patriarchal farmer's god.

There is constant reference in all the variants of his myth to the winnowing, pounding and planting of his body in the ploughed fields. Such a god formed in the image of the corn must first have appeared in the Neolithic Age when field agriculture had been established, when arable farmers and stockbreeders had grasped the role of the male in procreation but before they had begun to express this in images of transcendence. Like his mother this male god was still immanent in the earth. He belonged to her to whom he returned with the buried seed each year. At his most primitive he was still little more than the evanescent spirit manifest in the corn of her fields. One of his titles was 'the reaped ear of corn'[12] and he was often invoked in the fan used to winnow the wheat from the chaff. His exaltation was experienced by his worshippers at the sight of the waves borne by the warm wind through the proud ranks of yellowing corn at the climacteric of the growing season. His death came whenever the land was bare and parched.

In Mesopotamia this sterile time was under the late summer sun when the fields had been harvested. In Egypt it was in late November when the level of the fertilising Nile was at its lowest. Resurrection for one who had once himself been a water god came naturally with the rains, either directly from the skies above or, in the shape of their overflow, the inundations of the rivers. It was then that the grain cut and saved for sowing sent forth its first few green shoots in the succulent mud and the word passed from mouth to mouth that the god had risen and had been found.

Once we begin to examine the dying god cults in detail we begin to realise just how much they owed to their matriarchal predecessor in narrative and imagery. Let us take first their narratives as these were the mythic justification for their rites. It was with the death of the young god that the narratives began. Cut down in the full vigour of his youth his death sent the goddess lover into mourning. In the course of her travail she began to search for his corpse in the wilds. Unable to find it, she was compelled often to descend beneath the earth to ransom it from the powers of the underworld.

In such versions of the story the underworld goddess or god usually only agreed reluctantly to release the body, often exacting a forfeit as a price. The forfeit generally took the form of an agreement by the goddess to return the god to the underworld each year for a definite period. On this understanding the re-animated lover of the goddess could be resurrected and returned at least temporarily to join her fellow gods and goddesses in the world above. These were the central features of the myth dramatised by annual rites in which women acted out the part of the goddess in rituals of lamentation followed by rejoicing when the god was found. There were many versions of this myth and just as many local variations in the rites but the succession of moods induced remained the same throughout. The pattern was always one of despair followed by elation.

In Mesopotamia it was Tammuz who was mourned, the lover of Ishtar. Like all the corn gods he died in the fullness of life. His rites were celebrated in the month that bore his name when the sun was at its height and the land was barren. At such times women chanted dirges over effigies of the dead god which they washed and anointed as they waited for the goddess to complete her bargaining with the goddess of the underworld. When on the third day the goddess returned with the body of her lover the death shrouds were thrown off and the women gave way to an ecstasy of loud rejoicing. Tammuz was the Syrian Eshmur. The Greeks learnt of this cult from the Phoenicians with whom they traded on the coast. Not knowing the correct appellation of the god, which was one of the mysteries of the cult, they mistook his title for his name. 'Adoni' was how the women of Phoenicia addressed him in their grief. It meant 'my lord, my master' but it entered Greek religion in the person of the god Adonis.

As Greek influence spread, the new name replaced the old in many centres. Chief among these were Byblos on the coast, the Mecca of the Phoenicians, and Paphos in Cyprus although there were thriving centres of the cult as far south as Alexandria. In Alexandria the rites were celebrated in late summer; in Greece they tended to occur in mid-summer; but in Phoenicia the celebration was in the spring. The Phoenician rites took place around the time the river Adonis near Byblos was said to turn red with the blood of its eponymous god. Like most of the vegetation gods Adonis died a violent death.

The reasons for the death of Tammuz had remained obscure in myth, an obscurity which failed to satisfy the inventive Greeks. They had him gored by a boar, possibly the incarnation of Aries their god of war jealous of the esteem in which the youth was held by the goddess they equated with Mesopotamian Ishtar and Syrian Astarte, their own amorous goddess Aphrodite. The redness of the river that symbolised his blood was palpable enough but the actual cause of the colouring was the iron oxide washed down from the banks as the swollen river rose in the hills. Wherever the cult was honoured it took one of two forms. In the so-called 'Adonia' images of the god or his coffin in terracotta or wax were borne through the streets by wailing women or deposited in commemoration outside their doors. A more delicate rite involved the cultivation of 'Gardens of Adonis'. These were shallow baskets of earth filled with fast-growing vegetables and flowers, sown, then tended by women for a period of eight days. Without roots the plants sprouted but then soon withered under the summer sun. The withered shoots were then consigned to rivers and springs or taken down to the sea where they sank along with images of Adonis.

Often identified with Adonis was the figure of Attis. He was yet another corn god. One of his symbols was the ear of corn and throughout the period of mourning in his rites his worshippers abstained from bread. The goddess with whom his death was linked was Cybele, the great earth mother of Asia Minor, worshipped in caves and on certain sacred mountain-tops. Myth had it that it was when Attis was a young shepherd that she first fell in love with him. His prize, as the recipient of her favours, was to assume the mantle of her chief priest. Sadly for Attis, as it turned out, a commitment to life-long chastity was a prerequisite for continuing in his post. When the vigorous youth finally felt compelled to break his vow, the goddess struck him with a frenzy that drove him mad. In his delirium he chopped off the tumescent source of his misery beneath the branches of a spreading pine. From the stream of blood flowing down his thighs brightly coloured violets sprang, a garland for the overhanging tree that immediately received the spirit of the dying man.

The tomb and cult centre of the god were at the town of Pessinus in Asia Minor. There the most numinous symbol of his goddess lover was a solitary black stone, perhaps in origin a meteorite. In 204 BC the Roman senate asked the local ruler, a client king of theirs, if they might take possession of the stone in the hope that its talismanic power might help them in their war with Carthage, which was going badly at the time. A request from such a power-ful source was not easily denied and a deputation was soon despatched to fetch the stone. The return of their ship with the stone was awaited by a long chain of Roman matrons who had been assembled to pass the stone from hand to hand all the way from the Tiber banks to the city gates. The symbolism reflected the way the goddess was perceived by the Roman senate, who never truly took to the establishment of her cult. In their eyes it always remained a women's cult. Nevertheless, men did figure prominently in her rites in the shape of the Galloi, her eunuch priests. They were there in great numbers whenever her festivals were celebrated.

The most acclaimed of these occurred at the beginning of Spring. It began with the traditional day of mourning when a sacred fir garlanded with violets and wound with woollen bands was borne processionally through the streets amid a general atmosphere of gloom and despair. The following day was a day of frenzy when the priests whirled and leapt to the savage rhythms of their flutes and cymbals. The third day was the Day of Blood when the priests, now at a fever pitch, began to cut themselves and splatter the tree and altar with their blood. On the fourth day all spirits rose from this sanguinary abyss when the shout went up that Attis had risen. At Rome the celebration took the form of a carnival, the Hilaria, the Festival of Joy. There is some evidence that this carnival was added later. At all events, the final day was a day of rest.

Attis was not the only dying god associated with Adonis. There were strong resemblances to the Egyptian image of Osiris and, in fact, the city of Byblos figured in the myths of both cults. Where Adonis, however, was merely the corn spirit manifest, the myth of Osiris took the concept beyond this passive form, elevating the god to the more active role of a culture bearer, a civilising force, wandering the earth and spreading the cultivation of the grain. In his absence on these forays his mythical kingdom was governed by his queen, who also happened to be his sister, the powerful goddess Isis. However, the fame his travels brought him sparked the jealousy of his brother Set who, with the help of a number of conspirators, buried him alive in a coffin which they dumped in the Nile.

The coffin, with Osiris by now dead inside, floated down to the sea and was carried on the waves as far as Byblos. It was there that the grieving Isis recovered it in circumstances the peculiarity of which we will leave for later. Suffice it to say, she made good her return and hid the corpse from the prying eyes of Set in the swamps of Buto. As luck would have it, Set stumbled upon the body of his brother while out hunting. To make doubly sure this time there would be no mistake, he cut the flesh and bones into fourteen parts and scattered them over the realm of Egypt. Nothing if not persistent, Isis, nevertheless managed to recover the fourteen parts, all, that is, except the phallus which she was forced to replace with a new member created in its image. With the corpse more or less a composite again, she buried it in Upper Egypt although not without first uniting herself to its re-animated image.

Horus, the posthumous offspring of this final act of love, grew up to take vengeance upon Set for his murderous act. Osiris did not return to earth. Instead, he became the ruler of the underworld. As his cult spread, the rites provided the motif for the funerary rituals for all deceased. From the Middle Kingdom onwards they were addressed as Osiris on the eve of their journey to the nether world. As with the other dying gods his festivals were marked by lamentation and rejoicing.

It was as god of the dead that Osiris enjoyed his greatest esteem but his story is very much that of a fertility myth. His murder by the barren Set has been interpreted by historians of myth as a symbol of the threat to the fertile sown posed by the desert and its hot, parching winds. The theme of passion and resurrection, so central to this tale, was mimed in celebrations throughout the length and breadth of Egypt. The main cult centre was at Abydos in Upper Egypt. Here an ancient festival was held that involved the discovery, burying and eventual re-animation of the god. From the evidence of inscriptions we know that on the second day of the feast a funeral procession featuring the dead Osiris proceeded to the tomb in an ancient royal necropolis and that his death was then avenged in some kind of pantomime display. The drama was resolved by the destruction of his enemies and the triumphal return of the god to his temple at Abydos. From about

1500 BC the identification of Osiris with the grain became stronger in ritual. The ceremonies celebrating the resurrection of the grain Osiris took place in the late autumn when the waters of the Nile started to recede. Moon-shaped images of moist clay mixed with incense and spices were used as sprouting symbols of the god's resurrection. We are reminded of the gardens of Adonis. Indeed, at Busiris the parallel was even clearer. There, water was poured onto the so-called gardens of Osiris, pots containing seeds of barley and compost. The first green shoots to appear were the insignia of the risen god, the sure sign that he had once more come to life again.

The god the Greeks equated with Osiris was their own Dionysus. Like his Egyptian cousin, Dionysus was a culture-bearing god, wandering the earth, teaching the arts of cultivation. In his case the crop most popularly associated with his name was that of the grape. Known in myth as the twice-born, his original mother was Semele, whose name was a variant of Selene, a lunar goddess. Unfortunately she was destroyed by the lightning of her lover Zeus before the nine months of her pregnancy were up. Naturally concerned for the fate of his unborn son, Zeus sowed his foetus in his thigh till it was ripe for birth. However, the offshoot of this murky extra-marital affair aroused the jealousy of the wife of Zeus. At her command the boy was seized and torn to pieces by the Titans, traditional enemies of Zeus. The shredded limbs were consigned to a cauldron where they simmered until rescued and reconstituted by the goddess Rhea, the grandmother of this long-suffering god. Under the spell of her dark arts he came to life again and was soon off on his wanderings with a wild army of satyrs and maenads in his wake.

The story of Dionysus recalls the death of the corn god Osiris at the hands of Set and it is only fitting, therefore, that in this aspect of the god he was like others of his kin invoked in the form of a winnowing fan. Like them, too, his absence brought sterility to the earth. The death of vegetation in winter was represented as the flight of Dionysus or his temporary extinction. But every third year, after a sojourn in the underworld he was born anew. It was then that images of the new-born god were cradled in winnowing baskets on the slopes of Mount Parnassus. These rites of resurrection of the god generally took place somewhere around the shortest day. They became proverbial throughout Greece for their emotional excesses. The orgiastic nature of the worship of this god was particularly frightening to men for this most effeminate of deities, bisexual, hermaphroditic almost, was, paradoxically, very much the women's god. It was on him that all the passion once felt for the dying maiden was most obviously displaced.

It is worth noting in this respect that, of all the dying gods, Dionysus was the most disconnected from his female lovers. Perhaps in his image the divinely masculine first emerged as a challenging potency in itself, and that was the source of his attraction. Yet his phallus was still thought by his female worshippers to be their own sacred property, the source of their ecstatic possession. It still remained an appendage of the old female powers of the earth. In the savagery of their mood swings his women celebrants reminded the Greeks of a dark past they would otherwise have chosen to forget. We recorded earlier how, when the rites first reached Italy, they were proscribed by the Roman senate. This was only one of many attempts by the cities of the West to stem the turbulent flow. Eventually the Greeks gave in. The symbol of their surrender was preserved in the inner sanctum of the temple of Apollo at Delphi. There in the very heart of the most famous shrine in all of Greece, the home of their masculine god of reason and light, lay the tomb of Dionysus.

With Dionysus we come to the end of our catalogue of the narratives of the dying gods. As actors in these narratives they all, Dionysus, Tammuz, Adonis, Attis and Osiris, shared one important characteristic in common. They were all dying vegetation gods who suffered an agonising end and then came back to life again in some form under the aegis of their divine lover, sister or mother, the goddess. The life force symbolised by these youthful gods was the vegetation cycle of the earth. The value of its fecundity saturates their myths. Even their resurrection was embodied in the seeds germinating in the soil. They might, like Tammuz and Osiris, ascend to the world of gods after their return but they could not, like the resurrected Christ, walk the earth. Once entombed in the earth, they could not return as incarnate gods to the sensual enjoyment of terrestrial life.

Although sharing much of the divinity of the gods, their fate, at least in the passion at the heart of their myth, was that of all mortals. They could rise again like all the deceased did in the earth, coming up like them in the brightening sheen that spread through the green on the burial mounds after the autumnal rains. They could thus fructify the earth but their sojourn thereafter could only be in the world of the spirits or the divine. Suffering like mortals, their death could not, any more than their life, be interpreted as an act of transcendence, a victory over the finite. That boundedness, that entrapment marks them out as survivals of an earlier age, indicators of a more primitive phase of the masculinisation of myth when the male principle was still tightly embraced by mother earth. There was thus no sense of final liberation in their death and resurrection nor even of redemption except in so far as with their blood and sperm they redeemed the failing fertility of earth.

The narratives of the dying god myths are what we would have expected from derivatives of the dying maiden. When we turn to their imagery we find this too draws heavily from the same source. Mythic images, mostly metaphor and simile, convey poetic truth. No more than myth itself can they be taken literally. They function, rather, as archetypes, nodes, if you like, in a network of associations that give them an emotional resonance, itself a mnemonic source of strength, that ensures their survival. Translated into the flow of a narrative, they additionally provide those essential props to any tale, the sensuous detail of circumstance that prevents its collapse into abstraction.

Such props generally survive the insertion of fresh actors in the story. As a rule, they do not survive entirely unscathed. They are often re-interpreted by narrators who have long since lost the significance of their inclusion in the text. Radical re-editing of this sort must have occurred when the son/lover was first inserted by patriarchal mythographers in the goddess myth. Nevertheless, the archetypes remain, the clue to the origin of the text, half-buried in the surrounding myth, fragments still visible in its landscape, incongruous at times, even grotesque, but recognisable nonetheless.

In fact, wherever we look in the tales of the dying gods we find the imprint of the older matriarchal myth and behind the god the shadow of the dying maiden. To begin with, the navel stone survived in many of the dying god cults as the emblematic symbol of the lover of the god. In the cult of Adonis in Cyprus and Phoenicia it took the form of a large white cone-shaped stone or pyramid. In the worship of Attis it was the famous black stone of the goddess Cybele at Pessinus. The emblem survived, too, in the religion of the Greeks. Earlier we noted in the temple of Apollo at Delphi the tomb of Dionysus. To the Greeks it seemed remarkable not only that the tomb of one god should exist in the temple of another but also that such a wild and turbulent god should be remembered thus in the inner sanctum of their diaphanous god of light. Unknown to them, the key to the conundrum lay alongside the tomb in the shape of a stone like a large cone wrapped in woollen cords. Delphi was a centre of prophecy. As such it was unusual in another respect. It had a woman as its prophet. Tradition had it that only with a strand in her hand from the cords round the stone was she fully empowered to pronounce on the fate of men.

With her other hand the Pythia, as she was called, shook the branches of a sacred laurel tree. A laurel tree that grew inside the inner recesses of a temple was equally a novelty to the Greeks. Some inkling of what the tree once signified can be gained from the name of the Pythia herself. It was from the same root as 'pythein', the sloughed skin of a snake. The snake in question was Python, who had once, so the story went, been the guardian of the sanctuary in the name of Mother Earth. The snake, as symbol of chthonic wisdom, is an unsurprising denizen of the site. In association with a sacred tree it recalls our primal myth. By historical times the laurel tree had been sequestered by the masculine god of light but the more primitive association was with Dionysus. This god had far stronger arboreal connections. One of his titles was 'Dendrites', 'tree-youth'. In Boeotia he was known as 'Dionysus in the tree'. The pine was sacred to him, as was the fig, and his symbol was often a post or tree.

When we turn from Dionysus to the other dying gods, it is remarkable how many of them were either born or suffered death in a tree. The tree-borne origins of Tammuz are betrayed by the name of his father Ningishzida 'lord of the wood of life' and his death is foreshadowed by that of his predecessor Dumuzi, hauled from the shade of an apple tree by the attendants of Inanna. His Greco-Syrian descendant Adonis tumbled into life out of a myrrh tree.

According to a popular version of Adonis' life his mother was Smyrna, a victim of child abuse in mythic time. When her father discovered she was pregnant with own child, he tried to put her to the sword. Witnessing her plight, the goddess Aphrodite changed her into a full-grown myrrh which the blade of her father split in half. From the severed trunk the infant Adonis came to life. The myth of the birth of Attis is yet more primitive than this. His mother, Nana, conceived by eating a pomegranate sprung from the severed genitals of a monster called Agdistis. Now Agdistis was another name for the great earth goddess of Asia Minor, from a rock called Agdus on Mount Dindymus. With its rock, moon goddess and pomegranate tree the birth story of this god is replete with the symbolism of our matriarchal myth. The tree associations pursued him to his death. When in his delirium Attis unmanned himself it was into a fir tree that he changed. The event was remembered in his rites in which an effigy of the god was tied to the garlanded trunk of the fir tree carried through the streets. The trunk of a conifer was also once the symbol of Osiris. Later it was formalised in the shape of the famous djed pillar. So close was the identification that many believed the pillar to be the vertebral column of the god. When raised to the vertical in his rites the cry went up: 'Osiris is risen'. At Busiris his rites took place in the presence of a cow of gilt sycamore wood with a human effigy inside it. Could there be an image more evocative than this of our primal myth?

The Egyptians tried to explain the link between tree and pillar in the peculiar circumstances of his death. We have seen how he was nailed into a coffin by his brother Set and floated on the tide to Byblos. There the coffin was miraculously enclasped by a tamarisk tree. So enormous did the tree become in encircling the coffin with its spreading trunk that it was cut down and made into a pillar for the palace of the local king. It was to this king that Isis came finally in search of her lover and in his palace that she cut the coffin free. Translate the coffin back into a tree and we hear the echo of the earlier myth, the journey of a dying god from tree to tree.

The myth of Osiris is illuminating from another perspective. More than the other dying god sagas it retained most of its lunar connections. These can be traced in the numerical symbolism in the text. In the Ancient World certain numbers, either descriptive of the lunar cycle or derived from attempts to map it calendrically, were known and recognised as 'lunar' numbers. Twenty eight was an obvious one, roughly the length of the monthly cycle. When fractioned by a half and a quarter it produced in turn fourteen and seven. Seventeen was a less transparent number. It marked the beginning of the period when the full moon was over. Still more obscure was seventy two. According to Egyptian texts their god Thoth won from the moon in a game of draughts a seventy-second part of every day which he then accumulated until he had a sum of five whole days. These he proceeded to add to the old lunar year of 360 days, thirteen times a fraction either way of twenty eight (the lunar cycle is in fact, fractionally less than twenty eight). This was the origin of the five intercalary days the Egyptians added to the lunar year to harmonise it with the solar cycle.[13]

Now numbers in the Ancient World were not the neutral cyphers of today. Their significance was also magical and sacred. Ancient historians and mythographers would have been alert to their sacred lunar aspects whenever they surfaced in the text of a myth. Plutarch was no exception to this general rule. He had the advantage of being both a historian and a Delphic priest and he was quick to spot the implication of the numbers in the Osiris myth.[14] His assistance, however, we do not require at this point. Knowing the meaning of the numbers we can ourselves decode the myth. Osiris, we find, was murdered in the twenty eighth year of his reign and on the seventeenth day of The moon when the sun was starting on the wane. To inveigle him into his coffin, his killer Set needed the help of confederates. As a band they just happened to number seventy two. After Isis had hidden the body of Osiris in the marshes, it was discovered by Set, out hunting, by an intriguing coincidence, under the full moon. When at that moment he resolved to put paid to his brother for the last time, he divided his corpse into fourteen parts.

None of this was lost on Plutarch who saw Osiris as the lunar, Set the solar principle. Extending the analysis, he saw Set, further, as a possible symbolisation of earth's shadow devouring the moon. The interpretation reveals the growing rationality and scientific sophistication of the West. Plutarch was writing in the second century of our era and was more of a rationalist than he realised. What he could not know, because undocumented, was the origin of these numbers in an earlier myth. Osiris was once a dying lunar goddess not a god. Isis was his mother (to the Greeks she was always the Egyptian Demeter) and his coffin was not just the tree of death but the moon-boat on its way across the celestial sea to moor under the cool shade of a tamarisk tree.

The dying vegetation god was in origin a Neolithic farmer's god. His resurrection in the growing season re-affirmed the most important symbolic relationship of the early patriarchate. That relationship was of the earth mother with the son who would one day dislodge her from her throne. In fact, the introduction of her eventual supplanter as her lover in the text of the myth had already broken the most important symbolic bond of the preceding matriarchate. That bond was of the mother with her daughter. We have seen how, once begun, the dying god narrative survived in a modified form throughout the Ancient World.

Even today we see its images in silhouette behind those many paintings of the Virgin nursing her child or with his later crippled corpse spread-eagled across her lap. The Virgin and her Christ child are but a pale reflection of the early version of the dying god myth bereft of the phallus and its fecundity. The dying god still dies in an orgy of sensuous detail, reeking of blood on the cross, but his mother is no more than a faint, abstracted after-image of his old lascivious lover. The outlines have been lost that once so traumatised his rites. They have been obscured through centuries in the course of which layer upon layer of masculinisation has been laid upon this and beneath it the dying maiden myth. The process of obfuscation has, in fact, lasted for thousands of years. Behind it, its constant impulse and driving momentum, has been the restless male principle, seeking that ultimate transcendence, release from the thrall of the goddess.

1 Lerner G. The Creation of Patriarchy. Oxford Univ. Press 1986 P. 30.
2 Murray M. A. The God of the Witches Oxford Univ. Press Oxford 1952.
3 Genesis ch 30-2
4 Genesis ch 30 v 37-43
5 Genesis ch 31 v 19
6 Jakobsen T. The Treasures of Darkness: A History of Mesopotamian
        Religion. Yale Univ. Press. New Haven and London 1976 p. 111.
7 Jakobsen ibid 1976 p. 104.
8 Jakobsen ibid 1976 p. 112.
9 Jakobsen ibid 1976 p. 113.
10 Jakobsen ibid 1976 p. 113.
11 Jakobsen ibid 1976 p. 113.
12 Frazer, Sir James The Golden Bough: A Study in Magic and Religion.
        Macmillan London 1954 p. 353.
13 Frazer ibid. The Golden Bough p. 363.
14 Plutarch Isis and Osiris Vol V in Plutarch's Moralia Ed. and
        translated by F C Babbit. Loeb Classical Library London, 1936.

Chapter 3

The Transcendent Rise of the God

Whether a maiden actually died on a tree or a mere surrogate was hanged in an act of mime we may never know. It may be that her agony was but a symbol, a ritual motif, a saga proclaimed at her rites. The same qualification can be applied to her successor, the dying god. It used to be fashionable to believe that the god of the corn or the vine was impersonated by a youth, a male priest or priest king who, enjoying the good things of life for the fullness of a year, was then whipped to a bleeding erection and cut down in his prime, his separated genitalia returning to the earth. The evidence for the more lurid depictions was never strong. Some have gone so far as to cast doubt on the entire thesis of a ritual death such as this.[1] After all, Christ does not require an annual impersonation to re-affirm the emotional significance of the crucifixion. Against that, of course, it could be said that Christ died in an alleged historical time whereas his predecessors died beyond space and time, in the world of myth. Whatever the reality of the dying god's death in the lives of his worshippers, the manner of it had an irrevocable effect on his symbolic status. Christ died to join his father in the heavens. The vegetation god returned to Mother Earth. His blood and sperm went back to her. How could it be otherwise when she was the fertility latent in the earth? Certainly his spirit could not rise above the earth.

To overcome the latency of the female principle, its ubiquity in nature, the male principle had first to surpass and then transcend it. The womb was the centre of the goddess cult. It was the dark hinterland of woman, the mysterious condominium she shared with the earth. To eclipse the power of this mystery, the male principle had somehow to soar above its earthly clinging hold and create an enigma of its own in the world of the spirit. This was not easy for the earliest male gods, the gods of sweet waters, for the rivers and streams they inspirited were veins of Mother Earth. Nor were the first primitive vegetation gods they sired any more likely to be liberated for dying vegetation collapsed into the earth. Only a more spirited embodiment could raise man above the earth. In their search for it patriarchal mythographers turned to an element, evanescent, invisible yet essential to life on earth: the air. It was a happy find. In the mind of ancient man spirit wove with air like two streams of smoke coiling together.

The conception survived among the Greeks who had the same word for breath and spirit. Not surprisingly then, we soon find the male principle emerging as a god of the air. Gods of the air begin to rise in status in the pantheons. In Sumeria we find Enlil, Lord of the Air, of the hurricane and the deluge. Soon he would have 'Enlil's Way', his own promenade in the heavens. According to Egyptian priests, their supreme god Atum created Shu, their own air god first, and it was he who with his bride, Tefnut, gave men the earth and sky.

From water to earth and then to the wind was a more natural progression for the upward embodiment of the divine in the male than would seem the case today. The wind that moved the clouds and, to the naive imagination, the constellations further up was more powerfully conceived in the mind of the ancient. It was in many cases a metaphor for fate. The metaphor is preserved in folk-lore to this very day. 'It is an ill wind', we say, 'that blows no-one any good'. We are not surprised, therefore, to find that Enlil, Sumerian Lord of the Air, was also the master of men's fates. Air was even once thought to have had a fertilising power for there are stories that have come down to us from different cultures of women impregnated by the wind. Potent though it was, however, it could never be more than a half-way stage in the elevation of the male. True dominance could only come in the heavens with the capture of the one element of transcendence in the goddess myth, the moon barque of the lunar summit of the cycle before its nightly descent to earth.

The eventual male assault on the moon is thus not difficult to predict. If the male principle was to be projected onto the heavens then the extrapolation could only succeed within the terms of prevailing beliefs, that is, within a mythic universe in which the moon was still considered more powerful than the sun.

Predictably, the 'man in the moon' appeared in the Sumerian heavens before the incarnation of the male in the sun. His name was Nanna, the moon god, and we are not surprised to find that he was the first-born son of the wind god Enlil. A well-known Sumerian hymn depicts him moving in state across the sky in the very moon boat from which, presumably, he had earlier dislodged the goddess. As its occupant he enjoys all the privileges that once were hers, lighting the night, measuring time on the lunar calendar and dispensing fertility to life on earth. When the moon is dark, he copies her descent into the earth. There he holds court with other male gods to decide the shape of human destiny.[2] His work done, this busy god leaves the underworld and, as the new moon, ascends once more to heaven. Only one vestigial trace in lunar ritual recalled the identity of the victim of this interloper. As late as the Third Dynasty of the Sumerian city of Ur, offerings of supplication in the dark time when the moon was beneath the earth were the province still of the reigning queen.[3]

Here and elsewhere the rising male priesthood of the late Neolithic and early Bronze Age would have become the inheritors of the priestesses' lunar powers but the inheritance, nonetheless, presented them with a serious dilemma. The descent of the moon daughter to earth had been an act of obeisance, of submission almost, to the power of the cyclical maternal principle. Only by freeing itself from the taint of this subservience in its descent beneath the earth, could the male lunar principle finally emancipate itself.

Curiously, we have evidence of just such an attempt to free itself in a very old Sumerian myth. It tells how Enlil, the wind god, was banished from the city of Nippur for raping the young goddess Ninlil. In the course of his exile he entered the underworld. Pregnant with his child, the future moon god Nanna, Ninlil followed him at a discrete distance.[4] On the way Enlil took the shape of the functionaries he met at the successive stages of his descent. At the end of his journey, however, he suddenly turned to confront the pursuing Ninlil and used all his persuasive powers to get her to lie with him again. His intention was made very plain. It was to engender another child to take the place of the future moon god Nanna in the underworld and thus save him for the world above.[5] The moon god would then not have to descend to the underworld. He would already be there in a separate form.

Freeing the lunar son from the embrace of Mother Earth would have allowed the budding concept of fatherhood in to the lunar cycle. From moon son to moon father would have been the next step. Evidence of this can be found in myth throughout the Mesopotamian region. The Sumerians, who were dominant in this region in the third millennium, eventually succumbed to the more warlike people from the deserts and the steppes. Their cultural descendants were the Assyrians and Babylonians. The Nanna they had worshipped became the Babylonian moon god Sin. In the change of identity he had aged considerably. He was now an old man with a long beard the colour of lapis-lazuli who traversed the sky at night in his crescent-shaped boat. He was by far the most venerable of an astral triad of gods the two other occupants of which he himself had fathered.

These two lesser luminaries were Ishtar, the planet Venus, and Shamash, god of the Sun. The sun had already been masculinised by the Sumerians and, conditioned as we are by our own modern solar myths, it is hard to imagine a time when the sun was not only the lesser luminary but also a feminine one at that. Yet fragments of a lesser, female sun survived in the myths of many peoples. Among the many gods of the pre-Islamic Arabs was Atthar, the sun, a female divinity. Far away to the east, a similar sun goddess, Amaterasu, came to dominate the Japanese pantheon. It is in Mesopotamia, again, that the sun goddess can be found in her original splendour riding on her sacred animal, the lion in a relief from the Hittite rock shrine of Yazilikaya.

In the beginning no more than the eye of the primordial goddess in the day-time sky, later perhaps her younger daughter inferior to the moon, the sun goddess lost her ancient tenancy of the sky in the shift of myth to the solar paradigm. In the solar paradigm of myth solar images took precedence over lunar ones as sacred metaphors. The goddess, in fact all goddesses, suffered greatly under the new solar dispensation for it occurred under the momentum of a general patriarchal re-interpretation of myth which, after the capture of the moon, had the mythic colonisation of the sun next on its agenda.

The rise of the sun under patriarchal auspices was in part a development in thought indigenous to the Neolithic farming folk. To the extent that it was indigenous it would have harmonised with trends which we now know to have been occurring quite early on in Neolithic societies. The harmony lay in the symmetricality of these trends with the character of the solar cycle. The movements of the sun are to the naked eye more regular, more linear, indeed more foreseeable, more predictable and planable than those of the moon. As regular as clockwork, the sun follows its track or ecliptic across the sky. The only variation apparent to the primitive observer is its tendency to fall slightly lower each day in its circuit until a low is reached at the winter solstice or stand-still when it starts to rise. This up-and-down motion is the source of the regularity of the seasons. In contrast, as we have already noted, the moon swings about the sky from night to night in a more turbulent pattern.

The source of the developing harmony between the apparent regularity of the sun and the patterning of Neolithic life lay in the seasonal, in other words the solar, rhythm of the farming calendar of field cultivation. The working world of the fields has to be rationally planned. Fields have to be ploughed, sown or left fallow, then harvested at the seasonal points determined by the position of the sun. At its height the sun can desiccate the crops. At its low come winter and autumnal rain. Drainage and irrigation have to be engineered to compensate. Grain has to be stored in silos for sowing or for consumption in lean years when crops fail.

In such a world the sun replaces the moon as the power over fertility that must be appeased. So we find gods of sunlight like the later Greek Apollo guardians of the fields. As an embodiment of this light Apollo had his festivals in spring and summer. His spring feast, the Delphinia at Athens in April, commemorated the coming of calm after the equinoctial gales. His Thargelia the following month honoured him as the god of summer. So that the crops might ripen, he was given the first fruits of them and at the same time propitiatory gifts to induce him to release the land from parching heat. At the height of his power, at the sun's greatest altitude in July and August, his gift from the Greeks was a sacrifice of slaughter, a hecatomb. Not only was he seen as the protector from the sun's heat. Blight and mildew that rotted the crops and vermin like the mice that fed upon them were all an annual cause of supplication to the god of light.

The farming calendar is only one aspect of the convergence between the perceived regularity of the solar cycle and the increasing linearity of social organisation. The concept of the field itself as a linear plot sectioned off by title of ownership, a resource potential conceived in time and space, carries within it a notion of containment, of constraint that is alien to the mere gatherer and hunter. It is the product of a rational enterprise and presupposes much else about the nature of the relationships between the community of growers. Once above subsistence level, rational planning of growth can soon generate a surplus. The life of the cultivator is more leisurely than that of the hunter. There is time to spare between ploughing, sowing and the more hectic harvesting. With a surplus, a leisured class soon emerges from the accumulation of entitlements to ownership. Power comes to lie with the distributors of the stored grain. On the strength of the surplus hierarchies build.

The first drones in these rising hives were probably the priests. They were to perpetuate their rule through the written symbol. It is significant that the first experiments in writing were on tabs attached to sacks of grain. It is as if the rationality of the distributive process triggered the linearity, the disembodiment, the conceptual hierarchies of the future symbol on the page. A large surplus was a stimulus to population growth. The linearity of the field was extended to the urban landscape. Towns developed within perimeters still defined in historical times by the scope of a single ploughing. The agglutinative structures of settlements like Catal Hüyük now separated out into residential streets. In this new urban world the meaning of wisdom underwent a change. It ceased to be so intuitive, so latent, so circular and involuted, so obscure and deceptive. It became more rational, more analytical, more linear, lighter and transparent, more male. Its god was the new sun god, god of enlightenment as well as of the fields.

In the shift from the lunar to the solar paradigm we can imagine a transposition of symbols proceeding over many years and in different cultures at variable speeds. As the incumbent system, the encasing shell, as it were, the disintegrating lunar cult would still have retained the power to mould, to leave its imprint on the new solar cult as it flowed like molten lava into the recesses of the old lunar mythological positions. In the course of the change ancient lunar images would have simultaneously been both masculinised and solarised. The case of Apollo is instructive. The Dorian Greeks claimed him as their solar god from remote antiquity. Yet, at base, his calendar was a lunar one. Not only the seventh day of the month, his birthday, but also the first day of each month, that is, of each new moon, was sacred to him, a characteristic he shared with Janus, the Roman god of light. The story of Apollo's birth in myth confirms his lunar origins. He was born to dark-robed Leto, undoubtedly a divinity of the night, under a palm tree on the floating island of Ortygia. The place of birth recalls our primal myth of the tree on the first mound. It was from that tree the moon first rose. Sure enough, the memory is enshrined in the myth. Tradition had it that Apollo's birth was preceded by a day by that of his sister, the moon goddess Artemis. Not only that but his lunar twin, miraculously full-grown, then set to to help his mother through the long travail of his birth. We could not wish for a more transparent illustration of her age-old pre-eminence over him in myth.

The Artemis of the Greeks was a virgin goddess, a huntress, swift and inviolable. At Ephesus in Asia Minor, however, she was a mother goddess of a more familiar type, festooned in a cluster of breasts or testicles as some would have it. The contrast was puzzling to the later Greeks who did not know that the shrine at

Ephesus had once been dedicated to her mother Leto. In historical times this dark goddess was still represented by a wooden image reputedly found in the local swamps. This was hung on a sacred tree. The earliest shrine was a courtyard around the sacred tree below which there was a small altar. The tree was said to mark the birthplace of Artemis in the belief that Leto had leant against it to relieve the birth pangs at the onset of her labour. The story may go back to the darkest origins of the cult for a number of statues have been found around the site of a woman nursing a child. The oldest of these appear to be images of Leto and Artemis but later examples figure an infant brother. There is no doubt that this is in embryo the later Apollo. He too had by some traditional accounts an origin in Asia Minor. In that region the field mouse had once been his totem. Could this superlative god of light once have been a lowly Middle Eastern corn spirit? Even as late as the Iliad we see him on the walls of Troy, little more than a tutelary god of the neighbourhood. At Ephesus Apollo remained a child. Among the Greeks he rose, with his luminary the sun, to greater patriarchal prominence.

Elsewhere the picture was much the same as erstwhile water, wind and vegetation gods solarised the surrounding lunar landscape. In Mesopotamia the Zodiac, still known as the Belt of Ishtar to the Babylonians, became identified with the sun's ecliptic. Its old lunar mansions were transformed into the stations of the sun through the solar years, the origins of our own astrological zodiac. Across this celestial promenade the sun barque now sailed. *The Book of the Pyramids* describes for us how, after his morning bath, the sun god Ra would get into his boat and, in the company of his scribe, the loyal Weneg, inspect the twelve provinces of his new solar kingdom, spending a daylight hour in each. The moon barque still traversed the night sky but now only as a surrogate. *The Book of the Dead* tells us that the moon god Thoth was only there because Ra ordered him to take his own place in the sky whilst he proceeded on his own nocturnal path through the underworld. The old lunar calendar that had probably existed since Palaeolithic times because the luni-solar one we know of twelve lunations numerically gerrymandered to fit the solar year of 365 days.

The lunar pantheon, too, left its mark on the new solar one. As the goddess had been adored in triad in honour of the waxing, full and waning moon, the godhead split into triadic shape. We can see the outline in the rule of the three Greek brother gods, Zeus, the sky god, married Hera, formerly the Moon goddess and Queen of Heaven. His watery brother, Poseidon, married Amphitrite, once the goddess of the Deep. Hades became the husband of the crone, the goddess of the underworld, whom, as a maiden he first took by force and summarily raped. Behind the pantheon the cosmology also altered shape. The earth mound became the Egyptian solar pyramid. The moon tree was turned into the solar obelisk. The myth of the first moon-rise in the primal night was replaced by the rise of the sun on the first day. According to the priests of Heliopolis in Egypt the sun god lay under the name of Atum in the darkness of the primal sea. With his eyes shut he enclosed himself in the bud of a floating lotus flower until he rose by an effort of will from the calyx and appeared in the majesty of his own light under the name of the sun god, Ra.

In some cases the moon god would have held his own in the night sky while this invasion of the sun was going on. Thus we find Thoth, the Egyptian, and Nanna, the Sumerian, moon god, still in full possession of their powers at the end of the process. It is possible, however, that elsewhere the feminine principle reoccupied a weakened moon although now very much as the lesser principle. Some evidence of this may lie in the unstable status of the Sumerian moon goddess Inanna who later became Ishtar, Babylonian goddess associated more with the planet Venus. In Sumerian myth she was daughter of Nanna, the moon god. A persistent tradition also connected her to An, Sumerian god of heaven. In one tale she joined with her brother Iskus, god of storms, to attack her father, Nanna. Her intention was, by driving her father from the skies, to marry An and become Queen of Heaven. Nanna actually managed to come out of this with his powers intact but a late myth, the Elevation of Inanna, tells how An finally married her and conferred on her all his powers.[6]

The same paradoxical development may have led to a secondary consolidation of the powers of the goddess in the earth. Driven from the constellations by male gods and heroes, there was only one place for the goddess to go and that was in the earth, there to be reconstituted usually in a more malevolent form. An example of this fall from grace was the Greek goddess Hecate. The mythographer Hesiod made her the daughter of Perses and Asteria, both symbols of Titanic light. The parentage is what we would expect of a moon goddess, probably of magic in the waning phase. Her lunar character she retained albeit as the daughter of Zeus and Hera. It was said that she aroused her mother's anger by stealing her rouge to give to another moon goddess, Europa. To avoid her mother's wrath, she fled to earth and hid in the house of a woman recently brought to bed with child. The contact rendered her in need of purification which she received by plunging into the river Acheron beneath the earth. That was how Hecate became the fearsome goddess of the Underworld. Conceived now as a goddess of the infernal dark, she developed a taste for the black arts. Pillars to her carved with three faces could be found at the crossroads she haunted with her Underworld dogs and the spirits of the dead.

Yet, for all the centuries it spent in the shadow of the sun, the moon never wholly lost its halo of sanctity and the roots of fertility still remained deeply embedded in the earth. High up in the solar pantheon the new sun god still glanced down uneasily at the old Earth Mother and her daughter recently re-invested with the moon if, that is, she had ever truly lost her prerogatives there. Legitimacy was probably still a lunar concept. In many lands dying sun lovers not yet solarised, some fated never to enjoy such privilege, still descended to an early death to fertilise the soil of earth.

Lunar priestesses perhaps still celebrated the old mysteries. In such circumstance it is not inconceivable that marriage into the line of the old lunar priestesses would have been considered necessary to legitimise the new solar priest-king. The memory of their marriage ritual may be enshrined in the myths of Crete. Earlier we saw there how the queen Pasiphae attempted to mate with a great white bull. Now the bull is a symbol that underwent solarisation in myth. The bulls' heads we saw at Catal Hüyük may have been no more than the symbol of the primal power of Earth. It may even have been a symbol of her daughter the Moon.

Certainly those found later in Crete are without exaggerated male characteristics. The genitalia are not fore-grounded in any way.

By the time of the Ancient Greeks, however, the bull was already established throughout the Mediterranean as a powerful male solar symbol. As such it would eventually become the central symbol of the cult of Mithras, a powerful competitor to the early Christian church. The cow, in contrast, always retained its lunar linkage. Have we therefore in the grotesquerie of Pasiphae's tale a distant folk memory of the nuptials of the solar priest king and lunar priestess, a shamanistic dance, perhaps, in which each impersonated the bull or cow totem of their clan? This might well be judged just one hypothesis too far if it were the only case of its kind but there are too many bovine connections elsewhere for it not to represent a resonance of ritual in myth.[7] There is the rape of Europa by Zeus in the form of a bull. Europa had powerful links with Crete. She was a moon goddess. So too was Pasiphae. Pasiphae's daughter Ariadne, another lunar goddess, absconded with the Greek hero Theseus, who murdered the bull-headed Minotaur. His son Hyppolytus, in turn, was dragged to his death under the wheels of his chariot when his horses took fright at the bull of Poseidon rearing up out of the sea and Poseidon, of course, was the very god who had started the ball rolling by afflicting Pasiphae with a love for the bull in the first place.

So much is speculation. In time the solar son/lover would cease to descend into the detritus of Earth after marriage to her daughter. His marriage might survive but after the annual nuptial celebration held now on some high ground, a mountain top, perhaps, or a ziggurat, he would return whence he came, to the heavens. The god was still part of the old cycle that had embraced earth and the heavens but he was now at its summit in the ethereal regions once the province of the exalted lunar goddess. Seeing him there in his lofty eminence a thought must have occurred to his temple priests. Like them he could reproduce himself. The concept of fatherhood was henceforth projected on the sun. The solar son became the solar father.

The sun, however, remained just one luminary among many others. The heavens as a whole were the ultimate prize. Only by embodying the sky as a whole, not just the sun, could this omnipotent god finally free himself from the demeaning obligations of the old son/lover. Surely the seed of such a celestial being was too precious to be given gratuitously to the earth? If he were truly to fulfil the role that the priests had in mind for him then he would need to reproduce himself under an entirely new dispensation. To preserve his integrity he would have to create the world afresh. The new sky father would have to metamorphose into a creator god to liberate his seed from the polluting earth.

The primitive mind naturally thought of the beginnings of things in terms of giving birth. We have seen how in the primal matriarchal myth of creation the goddess gave birth parthogenetically to the earth. Her replacement, however, confronted male priests with a real dilemma. The creator god lacked a womb. His incapacity in this respect led the Egyptian priests of Heliopolis to ponder some alternatives. At first the analogy between semen and saliva suggested itself. Of the two, saliva had the more pristine force. Life-giving though it was, semen was sullied by its attachment to the womb. By this criterion even vomit seemed a more prestigious effluent. Hence the priests had their god Atum spit out the god Shu, of the air, and vomit up Tefnut, the goddess of moisture.[8] Ejaculation could match vomiting and expectoration as isolating acts of male creation only if somehow it could avoid the womb. This is why in another version we find the beginnings of a pantheon produced by the semen of the god's masturbation. At Memphis the priests went further. Keen to push the claim of their own god, Ptah, they made an identification, clearly they felt to the detriment of Atum, between the semen and fingers of the latter in the act of masturbation and the teeth and lips of Ptah which now, by the act of utterance alone, set the universe in motion.

In the period when these myths were being formed Egypt was comparatively free from foreign invasions. It did suffer one massive incursion from the north in the shape of the nomadic Hyksos. But by the time these arrived on the scene the long, inexorable decline of the kingdom had set in and the mythology had begun to fossilise. The consequence of her long period of uninterrupted development was that Egypt experienced a gradual evolution to patriarchal dominance. The tranquil nature of the change is encapsulated in the myth of how, on the orders of Nun, the primal sea, Nut, the cow goddess of the sky, raised Ra, the sun god, on her back and lifted him high into the vault of heaven. Once there, he joined with Horus the falcon god, to reign over the sky of Egypt as Ra-Harakhte. Ultimately, however, his regal credentials derived from association with the creator god, Atum, with the effluents of whom, as we saw, the universe began. Patriarchal Egypt paid a price for this pacific change. The sky was never completely masculinised. No matter how encompassing the power of the male god in the sky it remained the starry belly of the cow goddess of the night. It was from her every morning that the sun god, Ra was born like a sucking calf. Other peoples were far less fortunate, with dire consequences for their religious development.

The entire movement we have charted leading to the gradual ascent of the male through successive divine embodiments as a god of water, corn or vine, wind, moon and sun had been propelled forward, as it were, by the discovery of the sperm. Threatened with collapsing in upon itself through the gap opened up, an entire mythological system had been forced to fill the void by ironing out the phallic principle. Where, as in Egypt, no alien external pressure was applied to the change, the system altered shape peacefully, organically we might almost say, and from within. The change in Egypt was interminably slow and the myths that resulted represented the accumulation of a series of compromises between the demands of alternately powerful male gods and their protagonists, the priests. In other lands, too, the transformation might have taken many centuries to complete were it not for a more violent impulse from without that drove it more rapidly and more radically along the path to masculine symbolic dominance.

At the end of the Neolithic Age, in the era known as the Chalcolithic, and with increasing frequency in the succeeding Bronze and Iron Ages, the old Goddess culture was subjected to a series of hammer blows along two massive fronts. Its attackers, first in the north and then in both north and south were descendants of the old Palaeolithic hunters who had turned to herding cattle and in the course of their centuries spent in transmigration of the deserts and the steppes,spawned an élite of mounted warrior herdsmen. They came in wave after wave that brought Hittites, Mitanni, Hurrians, Kassites, Achaeons and Dorians down from the northern steppes and, to complete the gigantic pincer movement, Akkadians, Amorites, Canaanites and Hebrews up from the edge of the southern deserts.

To the Neolithic farmers the invaders brought a new Dark Age. Communities that had been peaceful and sedentary for many centuries were submerged in serfdom beneath warrior castes that were violent and unstable. Whatever the matriarchy that had endured thus far, it was unable to absorb a succession of so many alien inundations. The cataclysm came from a true clash of cultures.

To the invaders the role of the sperm in procreation was the warrant for a much more violent aggrandisement of the male. The symbolic coil of mother right was prised apart by the new radical rights of fathers to the power of life and death over their own genetic investment. The patriarchal family became the property of the father who held sway over it like the ruler over his serfs. Beneath the warrior caste was a new male priesthood who practised human and animal sacrifice and buried the living wives of their dead rulers along with their servants and other accoutrements in their graves.

The priests were part of the new social order and propagators of the myths that underpinned it. The images they worshipped were reflections of their own rulers in the skies, bellicose gods of not just the rising sun but the gathering storm, wielders of the battle axe of the skies, the thunderbolt. To the old goddess the new gods came with a sword of vengeance. Many ancient myths have been interpreted as accounts in coded form of the capture of matriarchal shrines and the mass rape of the resident priestesses.[9] Even so, the former servitors of the old deities would probably have struggled hard to hold or restore their last few lunar prerogatives. Traces of this may lie in the many stories in Greek myth of how Hera, a former moon goddess, constantly plotted against her husband Zeus. Her conspiracies always failed, however, leading only to yet more bullying and ill-treatment from this god.

The old matriarchal culture had had two principal myths symbolically inter-connected, one a ritual myth of death and resurrection, the other a primal creation myth. Once men had broken into the goddess pantheon, both represented cultural inheritances ripe for masculine appropriation. As the ritual myth was the more accessible of the two, male gods could use the momentum from its capture to achieve a trajectory of transcendence that led them to their ultimate prize, a part in the act of creation. We have seen how in Egypt the gradual elevation of the gods to the skies had led their priests to create for them their own creation myths. What happened elsewhere as a result of invasion was that this transformation was accelerated by the arrival of an alien pantheon headed by a new sky god. The Egyptian god Ra was a sun god still when he entered his inherit-ance and he retained his solar feature.

However, before the solar gods of other people could acquire their full celestial inheritance they were absorbed or simply toppled from their eminence by the new, more combative sky gods from the deserts and the steppes. With the arrival of these wielders of the thunderbolt, these gods of rolling thunder, the next act of transcendence of the male was to take a savage form. Unlike their Egyptian counterparts these gods would not be content with fashioning their own vomit, spit and semen in search of a duplicate for the womb of the goddess. They would expropriate the womb itself to equip them with a creation myth. The patriarchal cosmos they designed would be ripped out of the belly of the goddess. Her innards would be little more than spare parts in the hands of the new creator gods. And, in the course of this, matriarchy as a whole would be pulled up root and branch. The Mesopotamian story of how this all happened is preserved for us in what the Babylonians called the Enuma Elish.

The tablets recounting the *Enuma Elish*, the Mesopotamian myth of creation, were discovered among the ruins of the palace and library of the ruler Ashurbanipal at Nineveh in the course of the last century. The original form of the text is thought to date from the period when the First Babylonian Dynasty was the paramount power in Mesopotamia, between 1894 and 1595 B.C. The general belief among scholars is that the poem was used as part of a set ritual and was recited on the fourth day of the Babylonian New Year Festival. The point of the poem is only partly to tell the story of the creation. Its central theme is really the glorification of the sky god Marduk, identified with the planet Jupiter. Marduk was almost certainly a late arrival in the Mesopotamian pantheon, the god of earlier Babylonian invaders, perhaps from the mountains to the north.

The poem begins with the goddess Tiâmat of the salt waters commingling in the primal dark with Apsu, her consort of the sweet waters of the rivers and streams. Apsu was very much the lesser being for Tiâmat was the mother of everything and in her bosom in the watery deep she nursed the Tablets of Destiny, a kind of book of fate, in which the destinies of all things had been written since before the creation. From the union of this primeval pair came a succession of gods who formed the beginnings of a pantheon. The energy of these younger gods drove Apsu in time to attempt to suppress them. In the ensuing battle he and his wife came to personify the dark forces of chaos pitted against the gathering strength of the young masculine gods of light. Apsu was the first casualty of this titanic tussle, provoking Tiâmat to avenge his death by spawning a truly monstrous brood of acolytes and calling down upon her adversaries the cosmic powers. These she put under the command of her lieutenant, the powerful Kingu from the kingdom of darkness. Protected by one of her spells and with the Tablets of Destinies pinned to his chest, he evoked such fear and trepidation that the gods withdrew from the field, leaving the way clear for the rising god Marduk to enter the lists alone as their champion. In the heat of the battle with the redoubtable Kingu Marduk managed to divine his opponent's plans by staring into the 'womb' or 'belly' of his mistress Tiâmat.[10] Then, trapping her army with his net, he wrenched the tablets from Kingu's chest and affixed them to his own.

Victory over the goddess was now within Marduk's grasp. It only remained for him to create the universe afresh from her parts.

With this in mind he split her 'like a shellfish' into two crustaceous halves. From one hemispheric part of the shell of her corpse he formed the celestial sea above; from the other the sea below, the terrestrial ocean. The reconstruction of the cosmos from the corpse of Tiâmat betrays the source of this tale in our primal myth. Tiâmat was originally the goddess of the celestial sea from whom the earth emerged. The vision of the earth encircled by a watery shell was less than reassuring to men who had launched an assault on the image of the goddess that embodied it. A more mechanistic age demanded that the integrity of the celestial fabric be preserved lest the encompassing waters burst in from above or below as occasionally, of course they did in storms and floods.

Aware of such an eventuality, Marduk set up barriers with guards so as not to allow the waters to come rushing in. Marduk was very much a Babylonian god and the suggestion has been put that he inherited his role of monster slayer from an older Sumerian myth in which Ninurta, the son of the Enlil we encountered earlier, slew Kur, another deity we have had cause to note, the predecessor of Tiâmat, and erected a stone barrier on her corpse to hold back the ensuing inundation of the salt sea.[11] To this earlier role of monster slayer and stemmer of the sea Marduk evidently added the far more revolutionary one of masculine creator of the universe. If there was a fusion here of two texts then it is intriguing, for it suggests that patriarchal mythographers could only reduce the primal myth in two successive phases, extruding the goddess in the first of them and making Marduk her replacement in the second.

The legacy the new creator god left to men was the establishment of a new order in the sky. His work here completed the process that began when the first lowly water god appeared, little more perhaps than the tutelary spirit playfully reflected in a brook or stream. Now all the heavens were to be the domain of his lordly descendant. In his new kingdom, the text tells us, the great Marduk constructed stations for the gods and fixed their astral likenesses as constellations. He determined the time span of the year, it says, and for each of its twelve months appointed three defining constellations. He was acting bold in doing thus, taking virtually in hand the fate of men for this, the Babylonians believed, was written in the movements of the heavens. The moon, too, he alone now caused to shine, making it the creature of the night. At the end of all this labour man also he created. At first, he thought of doing this entirely himself by causing his own blood to solidify into bone, a trace, possibly, of an earlier folk memory of gestation from the coagulation in the womb of menstrual blood. Later, an alternative was proposed by the other gods, to use the spilt blood of his former foes, the spawn of Tiâmat.

There is no challenging the significance of this myth in the inexorable rise of patriarchy. Its influence can be seen in parallels throughout the Ancient World: in Hittite Anatolia, in the battle between the storm god and the serpent Illuyankas; in Canaan in the struggle between Baal the storm god of Mount Saphon and the serpent Lotan; in Israel in conflict between the sky god Yahweh and the monster Leviathan; in India in a similar contest between Indra, lord of the mountains and the goddess Danu and finally in Greece in three encounters of gods with serpentine foes, Zeus with the monster Typhon, Hercules with the snake Ladon in the garden of the Hesperides and Apollo with Python in the gorge of Parnassus.

What was destroyed in these combats was the divine sanction of a matriarchal order. That order, which had held sway over men for millennia, could henceforth be expelled from their conscious thoughts, an image of darkness and confusion that their own creator god had vanquished forever. The belly of Tiâmat had once enclosed a vision of the world. Life in the belly had been the living, breathing affirmation of the presence of the goddess. 'The world is full of gods', said the philosopher Thales, recalling much later a dim remembrance of a divinity once immanent in all nature. Returning eternally to the source of her powers in the earth, her moon daughters had found the sustenance to produce each new generation. Around the whirling spindles of their wombs the goddess had spewed forth from her belly the threads of life that she twisted and spun into the bodies of men. That was the meaning of the Tablets of Destiny in the very bowels of the goddess.

Fate had been feminine, which is why Marduk had had to eviscerate the body that encompassed it. Freed from her entrails, destiny could become the possession of the young male gods. As a metaphor for this we can see the way in which the legend of the Enuma Elish itself was used at the Babylonian New Year Festival. A centrepiece of the ceremonies in which it was recited was the casting of the destinies for the coming year. The casting took place in a special chamber of destiny in Marduk's temple where he and the other gods were believed to assemble during the festival to decide the fate of everything for the coming year. This power to determine fate had been the real prize, the poems make clear, for which Marduk had agreed to champion the cause of the gods.

From the gutted shell of Tiâmat's body, the last broken relic of the primal myth, men emerged blinking into the new dawn of their own creator gods. The world they saw about them presented now a boundless landscape for the play of their untrammelled will. On that landscape they would leave their mark in the centuries to come. It would be their fate to create a world more linear, hierarchical, more rational and mechanistic. Unseen by them, the snake had slid from the rotting carcass of the goddess and then vanished in the earth. The eternal return it had symbolised might still engage the imaginations of philosophers but for mankind as a whole the cyclical was doomed as a richly accommodating vision of the world.[12] The broken remnants of the old pantheon would follow the snake into the earth and the outer darkness. The crone had always inhabited these regions. The goddess had always had her darker side. Now her nether world was flooded with these refugees from the heavens. Soon the dark side of the old goddess would come to predominate. As goddess after goddess fled from the heavens and sank into the earth only those acceptable to men remained behind to grace the celestial regions of the pantheons.

Virgin goddesses, meek helpmates and nagging harridans might still hold their own in the sunlit world of public places. The rest, like women themselves, were banished to the shadows. High indeed was the price paid by goddesses once so powerful in their own right to prolong their presence in the light for the world of light was now a stage for men to posture and cavort before their own reflections in the gods. Beyond this world the dead had always found a welcome refuge in the womb of earth. The goddess had been the goddess of death in life and life in death. Yet the womb as tomb had never been a forlorn and dismal place of no return. It was through its labyrinths that souls had passed to the orchard in the Elysian fields. The memory of the scented breeze of this paradise lingered incongruously on in the minds of men for whom the underworld had become a dark and empty nightmare of a place, full of dust and flitting shades. On the threshold of such a world even the new gods of light would hesitate to tread. Only the Egyptians, who avoided the divine bloodshed we have witnessed, managed to retain the thought of the after-life as a pleasing place, a happy sensual after-taste of earth. Yet even they never quite banished the dark and sinister from that thought. Their ship of souls on its way to paradise had to fight for its life against the assault of a serpent that lurked in the watches of the night.

The underworld, it has been said, was the true subconscious of the Ancient World. The dark and chaotic forces it saw at work in it were the equivalents of the symptomatology of our modern psychiatric illnesses. Here as elsewhere we are left with a sombre inheritance from these sad events for, in being forced down deep into the earth, the old celestial goddess turned demonic in the male psyche. There in the subconscious of men she would remain ever at the ready, like a greedy succubus, to prey on them. Her power to torment them is apparent in the Erinnyes, the Furies of the Greeks. The mission of these infernal deities was to punish all those who transgressed the most primitive of the rules governing the conduct of men. Blood guilt from parricide came within their reckoning as did the sanctity of oaths.

They were daughters of Earth, all agreed. 'Daughters of the Earth and the Shadow', Sophocles called them. It was above all when a son's hands were stained with his parents' blood that these 'dogs of Hades' emerged in their most fearful aspect. It was then they would appear on the threshold of the accused with bloodshot eyes and blood-red girdles, their hair a mass of hissing serpents. Their cult spread throughout the whole of Greece.

Later, more civilised Greeks tried to tame them under the title of the Eumerides, 'the Benevolent Ones', but the old fears still remained. They would surface again after hundreds of years, a nightmare on the brain of the deranged misogynists who led the witch-hunts of the Christian West.

What the Furies had once enshrined was the ancient kinship law of Mother Right. In the cosmology of that world earth had emerged out of the primal waters of the goddess in the shape of the first mound. Creation so conceived was no more a matter of causation than birth itself had seemed before the discovery of the trigger of the sperm in the act of procreation. Even less was it seen as an act of conscious will. The world could not be 'willed' into being from the womb of the goddess anymore than the myriad animal and plant life that emerged serendipitously in the seasons of their fertility. For a male creator god to make the world, however, involved an entirely different order of creation.

What the Egyptian Atum and the Babylonian Marduk with considerably more violence made was not of the same substance as themselves. No matter how the male creators massaged the imagery of spit, semen, vomit and spilt blood they could never create a world out of themselves in a way that was so palpably the case in the old cosmology of the goddess. Without a womb they could not help but transcend their own creation. The spirit of the goddess had always been inherent in the material world. The spirit of the male creator, however, tended to float free of its material creation in an ethereal world far above. The concept of the divine as immanent was lost. The world the male god forged was no more a part of him than the shot sperm was a part of the womb. It was merely a projectile hurled off from him, once hot, but cooling to inertness. How could it be otherwise when the old womb of the goddess still lay in an earth the lordly sky god only rarely deigned to visit? His realm was the world of celestial light. In fact, his spirit was that light.

Where the shafts of light failed to penetrate was the realm of the goddess. Her last remaining kingdom was beneath the earth. Thus matter was identified with her darkness. By way of contrast, light became identified with the values of the new order in the airy world above. Thus light turned ethical. It lost its playfulness, its vivacity, for it now had to battle with the polluting shadow of the material world. With this development mankind was well on the way to a dualistic vision of the world in which the powers of light and darkness would struggle for supremacy till the end of time. The thought that what now seemed sinister and chaotic in the old goddess world might one day come back to haunt them hovered menacingly in the minds of men. It was to prove a fertile source of phantasmagoria in the centuries to come. It would never be so easy again for men to live unselfconsciously on the surface of life.

In the brave new world outside of the belly of Tiâmat the sudden insecurity of life created a dilemma to which the spirituality of the liberated man was compelled to respond. For those men who were to experience the true agony the dilemma brought, the journey of the soul would ultimately confront the choice of light or darkness. There would be those who as time passed would choose to flee the dark and escape to the light in search of an immortality that would complete the transcendence of the material world. Other men, however, would turn to face the darkness. It would be their fate to carry the torch down into the bowels of the earth to corner the crone goddess in her lair. For them life would become a sombre quest to harrow hell, an endless trek for meaning in the emptiness, a search for masculine enlightenment in dark and feminine places. In the course of their descent into the darkness mythic representations of such men would become the heroes of the last phase of the patriarchal colonisation of the old empire of the goddess: the invasion of the underworld.

The idea is already there in a primitive form in the mythology of Mesopotamia. The story in question concerns how Nergal, the Mesopotamian Mars, became ruler of the nether world. Till his arrival on the scene it had been the province of Ereshkigal, the sole ruler of this dark estate, and the one who had brought Inanna to her knees. The story begins with an invitation Ereshkigal receives from the gods to attend a banquet in the world above. She cannot leave the world of the dead but she sends as her ambassador Nantar, Fate, the demon of death. The banquet ends in disarray when Nantar is insulted by Nergal, the god of war. An outraged Ereshkigal demands his extradition to the under-world. The gods are forced to comply but are loath to consign Nergal to his fate without at least the benefit of reinforcement. Fourteen demons, an interesting lunar number, are sent to accompany the god of war. On his descent, he posts them at each of the fourteen gates, until at last, clearing the remaining gate, he storms the palace and threatens to decapitate the goddess. Relenting to her pleas, he agrees to become her husband instead and thenceforth co-ruler of the dead. His symbol as joint overlord would be a sword or a lion's head.

The coup that drove Ereshkigal from her throne paved the way for the Hades of the Greeks. An underworld with a male overlord put the final seal on the patriarchal legacy. The legitimation of the new order would be complete when the colourless Hades was satanised in the shape of the Christian Hell. The goddess would then be denied even the role of combatant in the battle for the souls of men. Yet the repercussions of Nergal's raid go wider still. They concern fate in fact, or rather the attitude to it we call fatalism. It was the conflict with Nantar, Fate, we recall, that caused the raid. What was at issue in the struggle that ensued was the conflict between the fatalism, the acceptance of fate, that grew naturally from a bounded, finite and cyclical, vision of the universe and the thrusting will to power that had to cope with the real politik of the new, and increasingly chaotic world of men.

To the incoming patriarchs only the active will of their creator could bring a resolution to this case. That was why Marduk had to meet annually with his fellow gods to cast the destinies for the coming year. Naturally any tool to hand was useful in this task which is why, by a paradox, he stole the Tablets of Destiny, paradox because their existence rendered superfluous his annual cast. The tablets had been the possession of Tiâmat. More than that, they were her, in a sense, for she was Destiny. Curiously, in her different forms as separate goddesses, she never lost this link with Fate. So when her goddesses descended into earth they carried down with them the shadows of her old prerogative to decide the fate of men. Earth thus became the last refuge of fatalism until, that is, Nergal came.

We have come a long way from our dying vegetation god. Nergal had burned a new trail for men. Soon others would follow him, going down alone, not as the suffering redeemers of the earth but as heroes on a quest. The nature of that quest always ultimately concerned the nature of men's fate in a potentially malevolent universe. Significantly, first signs of this development can be seen in the same region of the world from where the tale of Nergal came. The hero of the saga is one Gilgamesh, a renowned king of Uruk in Mesopotamia. His patriarchal credentials are there to see in his relations with the goddess Ishtar. Beloved by the goddess, he chooses to spurn her. Among the reasons for his reluctance to succumb to her he cites, intriguingly, the fate of her former lover, Tammuz, for whose early death she had decreed an annual act of mourning. Clearly this was a path the young Gilgamesh did not intend to follow.[13] This is doubly intriguing for a number of commentators have pointed to his strong association with the sun.[14] Her angry response to his scorning is to call upon her father for the destructive power of the Bull of Heaven. Gilgamesh destroys the bull with the help of his friend Enkidu.

The description of Enkidu has a number of lunar features and it is interesting that he dies as a result of the battle with the bull. In his solitary despair at the death of his friend Gilgamesh becomes aware of the general imminence of death. To avoid that fate, he journeys to the underworld in search of everlasting life. In his voyage we see the last vestigial trace of the descent of the maiden but with her redemptive death now transmuted to a quest. This time, however, the journey is in vain, providing a tragic theme with the power still to move us. As time passed, the abstract meaning of this myth slipped from the grasp of later, less civilised peoples. It became barbarised into the plundering forays of a Theseus or a Hercules. In Gilgamesh we still sense the tragic consciousness of loss, at the hollowness of the inheritance Marduk had bequeathed.

1 Fontenrose J. The Ritual Theory of Myth. University of California
        Press, Berkeley, 1966.
2 Jakobsen ibid 1976 p. 122.
3 Jakobsen ibid 1976 p. 123.

4 Jakobsen ibid 1976 p. 103.

5 Jakobsen ibid 1976 p. 104.

6 Jakobsen ibid 1976 p. 137.

7 cf Baring and Cashford, ibid 1991.

8 Brandon S. G. F. Creation Legends of the Ancient Near East. Hodder and Stoughton, London 1963 p. 22.

9 Graves R. The Greek Myths Vols 1 and 2. Penguin. Harmondsworth 1955.

10 Wallis Budge E. A. The Babylonian Legends of the Creation. Harrison. London. 1921 p. 20.

11 Brandon S. G. F. ibid 1963 p. 102.

12 cf Baring and Cashford ibid.

13 The Epic of Gilgamesh (ed. with an intro. by N. K. Sanders) Penguin Books London 1972 p. 86.

14 Hawkins G. S. Mindsteps to the Cosmos. Souvenir Press London 1984 p. 33.

Chapter 4

The Lonely God

We have charted the general downward slide of the goddesses into images of malevolence and obscurity. We have seen these driven from the moon first, then the sun, and, after returning for a while to a lesser moon, eventually from the heavens as a whole. Driven back down into their last redoubt in the earth, they were even forced in time to share their kingdom there with a new male overlord. Their relegation was reflected in the changing pecking order of the pantheons. With their former titles gone or, if surviving, often expropriated by male arrivals in the pantheon, they were gradually shunted down the hierarchy of gods.

In Sumeria the great goddess Ninhursag, the queen of the mountains, once a very powerful figure in the pantheon, was, by the beginning of the second millennium, already the last to be mentioned in the roll-call of the gods. Critical to the engineering of this massive shift in status were the editorial activities of temple priests. It would be absurd to posit on their behalf a conscious conspiracy to demote the femininely divine. It was more the case that in a world in which legitimacy was increasingly attached to the male principle in all walks of life male gods inevitably took up more interpersonal space in the divine narrative. In the whirling conflict of these gods for the spotlight centre-stage the much diminished goddesses were simply elbowed to the wings. The driving momentum behind the struggles for supremacy of the male gods was the motives of their servitors and beneficiaries, the priests. They rewrote the myths constantly to serve their own ends and give legitimacy to themselves and their kings. Religion thus became a branch of power politics in the life of the state.

We have seen how at the end of the Neolithic Age power came to lie with the distributors of the storehouse grain. The ultimate controllers of its distribution were the descendants of the patriarchal invaders, kings who patrolled their conquered lands with their retinues of warriors and priests, elevated above their subjects by the possession of slaves, herds, treasure and the very earth itself. These monarchs were effectively great landlords on horseback, lording it over the descendants of the old Neolithic farmers who were forced now to give tribute and were denied legal title to their land. Grain was the tribute they paid, delivered to the royal storehouse.

The kings returned from their estates at night to the safety of their walled cities. These were the former Neolithic urban settlements now converted into fortresses from the parapets of which the rulers eyed the dark, conquered land beyond with fear and suspicion. It was not long before these fortress monarchies began to coalesce into the archaic states and empires of Antiquity. The greater the treasure of the local king, the more silos he possessed, the more able he was to make neighbouring kings his vassals, his 'sons' to use the diplomatic language of the time. The same surplus of wealth made it easier for him to create a bureaucracy bound to him and yet functioning by remote control through the impersonality, the moral neutrality of the diplomatic missive and the royal order. The bureaucracy in turn enabled him to control and co-ordinate a more complex societal division of labour.

The division of labour controlled by these early monarchies went into over-drive at the beginning of the Bronze Age. What triggered this movement towards increasing complexity and sophistication was the installation and surveillance of large-scale riverine irrigation systems. Populations that had grown on the grain surplus pressed against the margins of fertility of arid lands and threatened to exhaust them unless their natural moisture was replenished by surpluses of water that existed elsewhere.

Constructing the necessary conduits and canals was a truly massive operation requiring careful forward planning. The riverine waters had to be drained, channelled and distributed over wide expanses of land. The work of digging and banking placed manpower resources at a premium. It demanded the routine mobilisation of subject peoples. Where these did not suffice, wars were fought to conquer fresh workers for the new canals. A compulsory labour system required the expansion of a bureaucracy to oversee it. Irrigation became the prototype of all public works operations of the Ancient World. The much greater, much more intricate subordination of subjects it entailed was probably the major stimulus to the rise of the great empires of Egypt and Mesopotamia.[1] So much of the pattern it enforced was to become typical of patriarchy on the grand scale: in particular its linearity, its rationality, its hierarchy, its subjugation, its preoccupation with mechanism and manipulation.

Compulsory labour service was thus added to the burden of the tithes of grain to the royal storehouse. In an agrarian society the way to ensure the flow of such goods and services was to attach the obligation to deliver them not to the individual peasant but to the land he worked. Working the land thus became bound to the duties and charges imposed upon it. Invading monarchs took the system of subjection with them, decreeing it as a natural law for the conquered, often uprooting and transplanting entire populations like any other material resource, the better to utilise their skills and muscle-power. Even where, as in Egypt, the system was homegrown it never lost its brutal aspects.

Under the crushing burdens of the pharaohs and their manorial lords, Egyptian peasants fell first into debt, then into debt slavery, ending up always in the same subjugated state. Here as elsewhere the peasant degenerated into little more than a farming implement. When his parcel of land was mortgaged or sold, he found himself necessarily included with the livestock. Soon all the peasants of the lower Nile would be virtual royal labourers with their crops expropriated in accordance with the pharaoh's instructions. To the state these workers were little more than fiscal units.

The new, much harsher patriarchal world was a world of clientage. Heavy though its obligations were, men feared most of all the threat of ostracism from the system, for a man without a master was unprotected. An omnipotent system based on fear and forced labour spread throughout the Middle East, creating profound feelings of alienation which Christianity would later exploit.

At each level of this pyramid of subordination through king, priest, soldier, bureaucrat and lowly peasant, the patriarch represented his family as a unit in matters dealing with the state. In fact, the whole system was built on the metaphor of the patriarchal family. The metaphor even extended to relationships with other states. The Pharaoh addressed his client kings as sons and expected to be addressed as father in his turn. The patriarchal family was now almost everywhere the residential and economic unit. It was the only acceptable channel for social and genetic reproduction. Property passed through the male line, usually to the eldest son, in a kinship network obsessively preoccupied with purity of blood. The inviolability of all property owners' sperm had at all costs to be preserved. In the case of the greatest property owners of all, the Pharaohs, the anxiety reached such an extreme that it broke the incest taboo and sanctioned marriage between royal siblings of the ruling house.

Women, their wombs now no more than a hothouse for the sperm, warm, fecund, but potentially pollutable by other men, were exchanged in marriage deals between patriarchs at every level. Like cattle they had the status of a kind of primitive currency circulating between males. Husbands had complete power to punish and repudiate their wives. In some cultures they had the powers of life and death over them. Women, indeed, were probably the first war captives and the first slaves. Like slaves they were a legal attachment to the master's household. 'I am a woman' was a formula used by men to express their own political subjection. Ill-treatment of women, of course, threatened to debase them as a currency, rather like de-facing the coinage of the realm. It was conceivably out of the anxiety to prevent this happening that the concept of legitimate marriage and with it the more civilised treatment of wives developed. We can see the change in attitude already occurring in the legal code of the Babylonian ruler Hammurabi. Henceforth women would find some defence, at least. in the sanctity of property.

110

Close to the top of the pyramid of the archaic state were the temple priests. They were the bearers of the patriarchal religion and the guarantors of the legitimacy of the king. Members of the ruling class, the chief priests, were often scions of the aristocratic clans descended from the retinue of the original conqueror of the land. For the heirs of that conqueror legitimacy remained indispensable. It could be bestowed either through the apotheosis of the ruler or some other message of divine confirmation. Rulers were convinced by their priests that their power was granted to them as a fief of their sky god. In Babylon royal ownership was expressed as a surrogate for divine possession of the land. Such convictions gave archaic empires the flavour of theocratic states. In extreme cases the monarchs adopted the apparel of their priests. The chief landlord of the realm thus became a priest-king forced often to submit to a ceremony of re-investiture under the eyes of his priests. In return for the legitimacy they conferred the temples received land and other property as gifts. As much as a half to three quarters of war booty was regularly given to the priests. Great power and wealth thus accrued to the temples.

The wealth of temples like that of Amun at Egyptian Thebes was legendary. In addition to the royal granaries a second source of power emerged: the temple treasuries. Supported by their wealth, the temples developed their own bureaucracies which in the day-to-day administration of the state were frequently inter-linked with those of the king. Both bureaucracies were staffed by scribes who were usually educated in the temple itself. Their learning therefore added to the power of the priests. The end of this process of accretion saw the priesthood developing into a separate estate, an alternative pyramidal power source to the king. Inevitably, when they tinkered with the pantheon, the priests sought legitimacy not just for their rulers but also for themselves.

Nowhere was the issue of legitimacy greater than in Egypt where four large temple cults were engaged in a constant struggle for supremacy, at Hermopolis, Heliopolis, Memphis and Thebes. We have seen how in their conflict with each other they strove to reinterpret the ancient goddess myths to suit themselves and then competed with each other for the site of the original primal mound, a concept that gave rise in time to the prototype of the pyramid. Each tried to co-ordinate the others' systems into a single cosmology that pointed to the creation of the world by their own tutelary god. The end result of this reductive syncretism was a mythological system with all the properties of a layered quilt, a complex patchwork, almost unstitchable by the modern historian of religion.

With the movement to the solar paradigm the reductionism gathered speed. Victory looked finally to have been won by the solar cult of Ra at Heliopolis. A sure sign of the dominance of Heliopolis is that so many lesser, local gods could only survive by assimilating to this sun god. Soon even the great creator gods of other cults were queuing to receive Ra's imprimatur as the priests at Heliopolis sedulously furthered the cause of their god. We have already recorded how they re-edited the tale of Atum the more closely to identify him with the solar cult as Atum-Ra. Heliopolitan priests had, in fact, always laid a claim to the creator Atum. His most powerful competitor, the god Amun, was, however, linked to Thebes. Even more popular than Atum and therefore riper still for customising as a solar god, he was not long appearing under the name of Amun-Ra. In the meantime Ra had also absorbed Horus the falcon god of sun and sky in the name of Ra-Harakhte.

There was a price to be paid for ingesting other gods. By constantly increasing his absorptive capacity, the priests at Heliopolis necessarily made a vaguer generalisation of their god Ra. Only the abstract and disembodied can assimilate so many different myths. Such is the pattern that obtains when religious militancy enters myth. Already, by the time of the eighteenth dynasty, most notably in the reigns of Thutmosis IV and Amenophis III, we detect a tendency to think of Ra as just the solar disc. The word for the disc itself was "Aten". We frequently hear of Ra as the occupant of the disc as it transited the sky. The conception had some useful spin-offs. The eighteen dynasty was a time of imperial expansion. By association with the travelling disc the pharaohs gained a moral claim on other lands. Their natural hegemony was said to extend to all the lands encircled by the sun-disc from the heavens. To reinforce this claim, the symbol of the disc was borne before the imperial army as it formed for battle. Subtly, the symbol was graduating from a mere manifestation of the god to his sole epiphany, in other words, virtually the god himself, Aten-Ra, or simply Aten.

It was in the reign of the pharaoh Amenophis III that the actual deification of the pharaoh as the sun disc really began. Previously the divinity of the pharaohs had taken a diversity of forms. Increasingly now it would be circumscribed by the disc of the sun. Amenophis III, for example, referred to himself as the 'dazzling sun disc'. Inscriptional evidence suggests that the pharaoh initially saw himself as a kind of co-ruler with Aten, perhaps his regent on earth. Later, however, the image of the pharaoh came to predominate in the various representations of the cult.

Under Amenophis III the worship of Aten had been more or less in harmony with that of other gods. The situation changed with his successor. Amenophis IV ascended the throne in 1377 BC. By a strange paradox this most effeminate of men - the medical consensus is that he suffered from an extreme form of eunuchoidism, the product of an endocrine disorder which stunts the growth of secondary sex characteristics - was fated to carry the masculinisation of the pantheon to its greatest extreme. It was he who proposed that the sun disc be made an object of universal worship to the virtual exclusion of all other gods. The pharaonic Aten was to become the sole focus of a totalitarian state cult. Part of his motive, no doubt, was hostility to the priests of the God Amun who had grown powerful enough to vie with Aten as a potential candidate for such a cult.

The priests of Amun had grown in influence with their god and formed now a kind of second estate, an alternative power source to the monarchy. Partly, therefore, to curb their growing dominance in the state, the pharaoh decided in the fourth year of his reign to make a complete break with the old religious order. In what must have seemed a breathtakingly radical act at the time, a totally new departure, he built a new capital for his god called 'the Horizon of the Sun Disc' at modern Tell-el-Amarna. He followed this by changing his name to Akhenaten, meaning 'he who is useful to Aten'. At about the same time he celebrated the jubilee of this new father god together with his own, an unprecedented act in the traditions of the time, to reveal to the people how their destinies were linked.

Akhenaten's new regime was short-lived. His successors reversed his decrees. His capital was eventually abandoned. In reaction to his own intolerance, his statues were savagely defaced. In a manner reminiscent of a modern totalitarian state he became the great non-person of Egyptian history of whom all trace had been removed while the sun disc he had hypostasised returned to a far less elevated status as a simple manifestation of the god. Yet for all its apparent failure the reign of Akhenaten was of lasting significance, nonetheless, for, if we examine it in detail, piecing together what little evidence remains, we find it foreshadows the way in which patriarchal religion was to develop in the centuries to come.

The cult, to begin with, was a curiously cathected combination of bland materialism and figurative abstraction that seems almost to convey a premonition of the life of modern patriarchal man. The materialism was rooted in the fact that Aten as the solar disc was, no matter how worshipful, still a visible part of nature. This naturalism was preserved in the pleasing fable of how the first occupant of the disc, the sun god Ra, had emerged out of an unfolding lotus flower in the primal sea. Stemming from this naturalism was another very modern feature that became a characteristic of the cult, a vague universal love for all living beings. Extended to the worshippers themselves, it created the ideal of a universal co-fraternity of believers under a common fatherhood, almost a kind of humanism, in fact. As the expression of Aten in the mundane world the reigning pharaoh was the natural ruler, the father on earth, as it were, of this religious brotherhood. Only he could truly know the heart of Aten. There is a portent here of the future worship of the Roman emperors as the 'unconquered sun' and, in a direct line from them, of the Caesarism and virtual deification of our own twentieth century totalitarian dictators.

The abstraction was absolute and patent in every aspect of the cult, raising the image of the male father god to truly ethereal levels as a universal object of worship. A universal god, however, can brook no rivals. He easily becomes a jealous god. The spirit of Aten was ruthlessly intolerant. To its claim to universal truth only one response was permitted. All were compelled to submit to this god. To do otherwise would have seemed perverse to his worshippers for once all truth is distilled in the rays of the solar disc no further revelation can be expected. The reductionism spread to every aspect of the cult. Depiction of other gods was subject to an interdict as were all cultic acts apart from a bleak and rudimentary offering to the image of Aten. Temples of other gods fell into desuetude.

The revolution did not stop there. The reductionist drive led to an outburst of iconoclasm against other cults. The names of other gods were effaced, a horrific act in the context of the times for the names were thought to embody the numinous spirit of the gods. In temples throughout the land the hieroglyphs of the chief opponent to the cult, the god Amun, were chopped and chiselled out. The acts of mutilation went on for years in a kind of puritan frenzy. Even the literature of other cults was destroyed, a foreboding of more modern 'burning of the books'. There was to be no more mythology. The sun god had no mythology any more except for the few shreds that clung from the old cult of Ra. Priests were not allowed to make an anthropomorphic representation of the god. The excision of all such symbols denied worshippers any hope of mediation in their act of submission to Aten. The human spirit found itself alone in the presence of this scorching god. There was no intermediary, nothing to channel the direct and immediate effusion of the soul.[2] Age-old aspirations were left unsatisfied. The kingdom of the dead was ignored. The funerary practices of the priests of Osiris, the underworld god, were purged.

As a god, Aten hovered over the threshold to the after-life, a stark, dazzling disc that burnt the eyes of his worshippers and blinded them to the nature of the world beyond. The compassionless character of this god is reflected in the way he was worshipped in his religious capital. The whole region of Tell el-Amarna is a veritable holocaust of the sun from March to November. Yet his servitor, co-ruler and self-proclaimed son insisted on a shrine open to the sky and almost totally devoid of shade. Here in the inferno not only the rites but also diplomatic audiences took place. A curious comment on the extremism of the cult has been uncovered in one of the tablets uncovered at the site. It records the astonishment of the king of Assyria that on a recent mission his ambassadors to the capital were kept standing for so long under the hot sun. If the pharaoh, the complaint goes on, chooses to stand and die in the heat of the sun, then all well and good, but why should foreign embassies be forced to suffer with him?[3]

Once Akhenaten was dead and the reaction had set in, the various gods returned and the temples were full again. This evident return to normality was deceptive. After his reign things were never quite the same again. The after-image of the brilliant Aten had been burned into the retina of his worshippers. Their gods henceforth would carry the outline of Aten, the shape of an overarching absolute god of whom the earth could only be a dimming aspect. With Aten a new religious consciousness had dawned, a new vision of the divinely masculine. Already apparent is what that vision could become once its last connection had been cut to the earth. So condign a failure in all that he did, Akhenaten had yet set in motion a process that would end in an abstract and omnipotent father god, a patriarch in the skies, complete in his solitude, without a goddess or familial ties.

Remote though he appeared, Aten did at least have a visible embodiment in the natural world in the light of the solar disc. This naturalism in his cult is a testimony to the more evolutionary development of the Egyptian male creator god. In contrast, in Mesopotamia, as we have seen, a violent break with the old goddess cult had taken place. Like Aten, Marduk was a single all-powerful creator god, paramount in the heavens. Unlike him, however, he had not risen to the sky from a lotus or on the back of a cow goddess. His celestial apotheosis was much more radical and, for a creator god, far less demeaning. He had simply cut the world out of the belly of the goddess and then levitated to the heavens to observe his handiwork. His exaltation thus involved his own violent deracination from the earth.

Aten lit up the material world wherever it caught his solar rays. Marduk hovered above the world of matter he had forged. His absence left the imagination of his worshippers a prey to demonic forces. Only his annual return to determine their destinies for the coming year at the New Year Festival prevented their perilous universe collapsing into hideous chaos. Sadly for Marduk, he had come to power before the reduction of the pantheon to a unitary phenomenon. He had therefore to drag a retinue of lesser gods in his trail. He lacked the august isolation of the Egyptian Aten. Eventually these two visions would merge to produce a father god with all the wilfulness of Marduk but with the added pedigree of an isolated Egyptian creator god who had lain in the primal dark before time began.

The goddess had been immanent in a world that had miraculously issued forth out of herself. The world was to that extent an aspect of her own interiority. The Mesopotamian creator god had no such tie of propinquity with his own creation. Its matter would remain forever a product of his handiwork, no more than a tool or an artifact for the expression of his conscious will, irrevocably an otherness external to him. The image of the god that would emerge from the fusion of Marduk and Aten, let us call him for the moment Aten-Marduk, could hardly be encompassed by his own creation, his artifact in other words. No visual representation, no icon could suffice for him for by the sheer fact of its manifestation in the world of matter he had created it would diminish him. His essence could only be captured transcendentally. By the same logic his intentionality, his will could never with any degree of certainty be known. Hence no act of contrition could be sure to appease him. The injunctions of such a god could at best be heard, not physically, as a voice that is, but in the unvoiced word, in the very soul of man. The scene was set for the development of conscience, of guilt, of an inner turbulence unknown in the old goddess cult.

The key factor in this development was the personalisation of the relationship with the god. The tendency to imagine a commonality of interests with one's god, a mutuality of rights and obligations expressible almost in contractual terms, has probably always been part of the primitive religious stance. From such a god a little guidance, perhaps even some justice and compassion might not be thought unreasonable demands. The source of this expectation may have lain in the notion that each individual had a tutelary god and that this divinity was responsible somehow for his potentiality for success in daily life. The lucky individual was described in Sumerian as having acquired a god.[4] In its earliest form the concept would have been quite physical. The benefactor was thought of as dwelling in the body of the man rather in the way that characters in the New Testament were believed to be possessed by incumbent spirits.

As an extension of this the idea developed that a truly personal god would probably always have been there anyway, influencing the fate of his chosen protégé at decisive moments of his life. Whole families were believed to have such gods, which were engendered at birth and bound by unwritten contractual ties to give help and guidance to each generation. The dilemma came with the abstraction and disembodiment of the god. How do you control a single, all-powerful, all-knowing creator god who is unseeable, unknowable and yet dwells within you, rendering you infinitely accessible and vulnerable to his slightest whim?

The very proximity, approachability of such awesomely unstable power inevitably creates anxiety in the worshipper. It is a contradiction, of the naked worshipper in the presence of the alarming singularity of the universal god who just happens to be afflicted with an obsessive interest in his fate, which has stricken monotheistic religions ever since. At its worst, feeding on the anxiety it generates, the singularity develops pathological and quite unappeasable ego needs. The worshipper responds by striving desperately to search for cues in his own interiority from the in-dwelling god to try to achieve a state of grace, a release from the stress of spiritual remoteness from his god's ungoverned will. The anxiety is the origin of the ethical creed.

By defining the obligations the individual must fulfil to appease his creator, some hope is offered that the appetite of the latter for endless subjugation can be sated. Translating the will of the god into the rules of ethics renders it more predictable, more manipulable even. In fact, a kind of balance sheet results in which the worshipper can stand in a manageable relationship of credit or debit with his creator. Fulfilling obligations builds up personal credit. As the vicissitudes of life can lead the weak or unwitting individual speedily into debit, the sooner credit is accumulated the better. It acts as a kind of insurance device, a call on the goodwill of the creditor to overlook the occasional lapse into the red. The strongest kind of credit naturally involves the worshipper suffering for, had the god not wanted him to suffer, the entire system would not have had to be installed in the first place. Hence the need to anticipate the god by inflicting credit-worthy suffering prematurely upon oneself. In a nutshell, the concept of the righteous sufferer.

Nowhere did this attitude reach a greater extreme than among the people of Israel. As to the origin of this people a great deal has been written although much of it is speculative. The Bible tells of a sojourn in Egypt lasting over four hundred years. Whether there as invaders, mercenaries, or slaves, they would no doubt have been familiar with the theology of the Egyptian sun god. Significantly, it was in the century or so after the death of Akhenaten that they began to appear in the highlands to the east of the Jordan river.

The Old Testament recounts a number of wars with successive coalitions of local kings. As refugees from the land of Aten, the Israelites were in the vanguard of the patriarchal revolution. Psalm 104 in the Old Testament bears an uncanny resemblance to a famous hymn to Aten. Whether the Israelites arrived at the Jordan river with a fully-fledged monotheism based on the cult of Aten is debatable. The Old Testament would have us believe that they already had a covenant with their god Jehovah but the earliest of its books date from centuries after the events they purport to describe and are almost certainly a projection into the remote past of the theology of a much later period.

The land of Canaan the Israelites invaded was a buffer zone between on the one hand the Egyptian and on the other the Assyrian and later Babylonian spheres of influence. Already fought over for generations before the Israelites arrived, it provided both warring sides with a trade route, a cultural cross-roads and a convenient military highway. This accessibility to both spheres of influence must have had an impact on the Israelites' beliefs. It certainly made their survival as a people somewhat perilous. As with all buffer states, their vulnerability increased whenever the power balance that normally guaranteed their freedom was upset. This began to happen with depressing frequency once Egypt slid into a slow but permanent decline. Their worsening situation was not helped by the division of their kingdom in 922 B.C. From that time on the northern and southern tribes, Israel and Judah, went their separate ways.

It was Israel that succumbed first, falling to Assyria in 721 B.C. Judah survived until 587 B.C. when she too fell to Assyria's successor, the Babylonian state of Nebuchadnezzar. It was the custom of these Mesopotamian powers to transplant potentially troublesome conquered peoples. The Israelites clearly fitted into this category for in the days of their autonomy their kings had constantly intrigued with one side or the other. The people paid the price for this in the form of a lengthy exile in northern lands. It has been suggested that they may have been set to work on the Mesopotamian canals. Not all the Jewish people were taken north. The poorer people remained behind to tend the land.[5] Most of the ruling class, however, would have gone, including the priestly intelligentsia. Their descendants did not return until after Babylon itself had fallen to another northern successor state but this time one ruled by a more liberal and far-sighted man, Cyrus the Great of the Medes and Persians.

In their centuries of exile the Jewish priests would no doubt have become familiar with the cults of the Mesopotamian peoples around them. Their beliefs about their own patriarchal god could scarcely have been unaffected by such a long process of familiarisation. In a sense their experience as exiles was unique. A southernmost people, refugees from the land of Aten, they spent many years as reluctant guests of the worshippers of Marduk. If any cultural borrowing between these two visions of god took place then surely the Jewish people were the prime candidate for the role of carriers and transmitters. The experience would have given a powerful creative boost to their already developing monotheism. It would have placed them in the forefront of the patriarchal revolution, at its cutting edge. That revolution was close to the heart of the prophets who claimed to speak on their behalf. Indeed, as we shall now see, in their centuries-long defence of it they had already more than proved their worth.

When the Israelites first arrived in Canaan after their long trek from the Sinai peninsula they found a land inhabited by many peoples. The main population was the Canaanites themselves but the Bible mentions also Amorites, Jebusites and Hivites1 and the powerful cities of the Philistines in the south-west. Materially, these peoples were superior to the Israelites. The Canaanites were wealthy traders with an art and architecture of a sophistication beyond the grasp of the invaders. The Philistines were skilled metallurgists who ran a flourishing agri-business in forging metals for agricultural purposes.[8] In religion, however, these peoples were more primitive and backward than the Israelites, primitive and backward, that is, in terms of our schema, for they were at an earlier stage of patriarchal development. Their belief system had begun to change under the influences from Egypt and Mesopotamia yet still retained many significant goddess features.

From the evidence of the Bible we can see that these goddess features appeared quite menacing to the patriarchate of the invaders. In fact, the diatribes of the prophets against these very features give us an idea of what Canaanite religious practices were like. Since 1929 this evidence has been supplemented and confirmed by the religious texts uncovered by the excavations at the ancient city of Ugarit, modern Ras Shamra, in the north. These texts give us a clear picture of the pantheon, the rites, the prayers and the myths of the Canaanites.

To begin with, we can see that the religion of these peoples was anything but monothcistic. There seems to have been a large number of gods and goddesses in the religion often from different pantheons but enjoying a fairly happy relationship of co-existence. There was Astarte, the Syro-phoenician goddess, in the north. There was Rahab, the goddess of Jericho, sadly written into the Old Testament as a prostitute with a brothel in the town. Milcom was worshipped by the Ammonites as also was Molech, his altars stained with the blood of human sacrifice. The greedy Chemosh was the god of Moab. Baal, Aleyin, Anath, Asherah and El were the chief gods and goddesses of the pantheon uncovered at Ugarit. From the evidence at this site we get some idea of how far the divinely feminine had retreated before the slowly advancing male principle. The Canaanite moon, for example, was already masculine, the god Yarih.[6] The sun, however, was still obstinately feminine in the shape of the goddess Shapsh. Memories of the original mother/daughter duo still survived, but rather opaquely in the image of the Canaanite Elysian Fields, called the field of the goddess Asherah and the girl, her daughter Anath.[7] The goddess principle remained powerful in the after-life. A carved panel on a royal bedstead from Ugarit depicts two kings sucking the breast of a goddess figure, drinking the milk of eternal life.[11]

Despite all the patriarchal changes going on around them, the goddesses, it seemed, still retained a powerful hold on the imagination of the people of Canaan. They were worshipped in a tree and pillar cult and the countryside was dotted with the sacred groves of Asherah. Worship there was linked to a cult of prophecy under the auspices of the priestesses. The use of the sacred tree as a source of prophecy was taken over by the early Israelites. On the eve of a battle against the Philistines, for instance, King David felt compelled to wait for a message from the wind among the leaves of some mulberry trees before giving the order to attack. Other aspects of the goddess cult were not so readily accommodated. Their shrines were the setting for orgiastic fertility rites. In these the sacred prostitutes used sexual commerce as a form of sympathetic magic for the crops. Some of these prostitutes were women but those who drew the particular wrath of the Jewish prophets were men. They were the 'qedeshim', the dog priests, male transvestites sodomised in the rites.[9] The religious significance of such practices we have already described. Naturally this would be lost on the Jewish prophets.

In Canaanite mythology the old mother/daughter partnership had begun to fall asunder under the pressure of the male principle.

Both Asherah and her daughter Anath had been married off to El, the now ageing head of the pantheon. By him they had given birth to the dusk and the dawn. El was a bull god of the mountains. Originally his sacred marriage may have been imposed on the goddesses by an invading cult of sky god worshippers. Alternatively, he may once have been an indigenous dying son/lover who had either merged with the invading sky god or risen to the mountain tops of his own accord. By the time the Israelites came he had been upstaged by younger gods. In the texts from Ugarit he seems something of a recluse on his mountain peak. His status there was lofty enough for the Israelites to identify him with their own Jehovah.[13] A trace of the eminence of the old mother goddess he had married still remained, however. Asherah is referred to as the consort of El and the mother of the seventy gods. Evidently she had once borne the entire pantheon without much assistance from El.

If Asherah recalled the ancient eminence of the goddess, her daughter Anath was a reminder still of the terror she had once inspired. This forceful, thrusting goddess was huntress, warrior and guardian of the crops. The power and influence she preserved can be gauged from the fact that when Baal, the most powerful of the younger male gods, wanted permission to have his own palace built he had to suffer the indignity of begging Anath to intercede on his behalf by asking Asherah to get El to give him authorisation to go ahead. Indeed, El himself was so afraid of a direct appeal from this goddess that at the very thought of meeting her face-to-face he hid in the innermost chamber of his palace and in this cowed and fearful state granted her request.

If El had ever been a vegetation god then by the time the Israelites entered the land his role in that respect had already been usurped by the god Baal. Baal too was by then a mountain god, a storm god and a bull god but one who had not yet managed to relinquish his old role of a dying and resurrecting fertility god. In other words, he was a rising male god caught in mid-elevation along the ascending path that would ultimately lead to the lordly heights inhabited by El. That this would have been his destiny had he survived the sojourn of the Israelites in his lands is apparent form the fact that his role in the Canaanite fertility myth had already passed in large part to his son, Aleyin.

If Baal was the 'Rider of the Clouds', as the Ugarit tablets call him, then his son was the earthier aspect of him that still remained. Aleyin was, in fact, known as 'the Baal of the Earth'. His claim to this title lay in his rulership of the sweet waters of the earth as the god of rivers and springs. In the myth Baal, or rather the part of him that was Aleyin, engaged in an annual battle with Mot, the god symbolising death. In the course of it he was killed. His death sent the goddess Anath wandering off grief-stricken in search of his remains. Her grief unrequited turning to a thirst for revenge, Anath murdered Mot, winnowed him like corn and chaff and then planted him like the seed. The planting of this harvest spirit was the prelude to the resurrection of Baal. Had Canaanite religion survived, in time Baal would probably have displaced El on his mountain-top, leaving his role as a vegetation god to be played entirely by Aleyin as a separate god. The need for a successor in that role says much for the retentiveness of the vegetation god in Canaanite myth. It is as if Canaanite religiosity was simply too sensual, too earthy, too full of feeling for the fertility aspect of the goddess, to completely abandon the concept of a dying and resurrecting vegetation god.

At this distance in time and in the aftermath of the ultimate triumph of patriarchal religion in the West, it is hard to imagine just how threatening the surrounding Canaanite religion must have seemed to the Jewish religious establishment. The early material superiority of the people of Canaan, their greater sophistication in the arts of urban civilisation, must have made their religion doubly attractive by sheer association in the minds of the materially more backward people that had conquered them. Uncouth though they were in the civilised arts, the conquerors, however, were in the vanguard of a revolutionary movement in religious thought that would one day carry all before it. At the time all this was in the future, though, and the priestly guardians of that patriarchal movement must have sensed constantly around them the ever-present threat of counter-revolution from cults still pulsating with the rhythms of the old religion.

The history of the Old Testament can be read as the story of the struggle of the priests of Jehovah to contain and, if possible, eradicate this cultic pollution. It is by no means a story of unalloyed success. Periods of apostasy among the people when the battle seemed lost alternated with violent, often bloody spasms of repression. From the strictures of the writers who recorded these events and the angry tirades they voiced through the mouths of the heroic defenders of their faith we gain some idea of just how real the threat seemed, how quick the Israelite people were to desert their own religion and go whoring after the foreign gods. The fiercer the fulmination against a practice, we can presume, the more likely it is to have been deeply prevalent.

The Jewish prophets were less interested in the details of the cults than in the general threat they represented but, if we examine their denunciations, we can see there were two major objects of their rage. These were the worship of Baal and the worship of Asherah. Baal was a mountain god and it is he no doubt who figured in the rites the prophets condemned that took place on hills and mountain-tops, and, generally in 'high places'. There were also 'houses of Baal', presumably temples to this god, in some of the towns, notably in Samaria.[10] Asherah was a more confusing threat. In the minds of the writers of the Old Testament she is often identified with Syrian Astarte under the name of Ashtaroth.[18] She had a tree and pillar cult and was worshipped in rural areas in sacred groves. It was probably in her honour that the orgiastic rites were held that so outraged the prophets. The Jewish people must have taken part in these in large numbers for they are specifically enjoined not to dedicate to Jehovah gifts earned from the 'hire of a whore or the price of a dog'.[14] The 'dog' in question refers to the sodomitic practices of the 'dog priests' of the temples. So strong was the affection of the people for these two deities, Baal and Asherah that Gideon, a patriarchal reformer, had to destroy their shrines at night for fear of the popular reaction.[15] When the apostasy of the people was at its most extreme the shrines seemed to be everywhere, 'groves on every high hill and under every green tree'.[16]

It did not help the cause of the prophets that the kings of Israel proved even greater reprobates than the common people. The list of prophets declaiming against the cults from Elijah to Jeremiah is matched by an even longer list of kings guilty of the worst kinds of apostasy. Desertions to the goddess were particularly notable under the regency of queen mothers - Athaliah1 and Maachah2 are cases in point - and whenever there was a powerful foreign queen in the land. At such times priests of Baal and Asherah had the ear of the king and access to the royal court. The much reviled Jezebel had, it was claimed, as many as 850 of them that did 'eat at her table', in other words, a charge to her household and we assume therefore part of her retinue.

A great collector of foreign queens was probably the biggest royal backslider of them all. Solomon kept virtual open house for the gods of the wives, seven hundred of them, who had 'turned away his heart'.[19] He was not just a passively accommodating husband, however, and was frequently observed burning incense and sacrifices 'in the high places'.[20] The heretical tradition to which he had given the royal seal of approval continued long after his kingdom had split into the two states of Israel and Judah. Both states were prey to a constant oscillation between apostasy encouraged from above and similarly engineered periods of repression.

In Judah the worst recreants were Rehoboam, Ahaz and Manasseh. Purification from their polluting influence came in the reigns of Asa, Jehoshaphat, Hezekiah and Josiah. In Israel the two Jeroboams and the notorious Ahab were the worst offenders. Of the purifiers Jehu was most notable. From the description of what the purifiers had to do to restore the faith we can see just how far the excesses had gone among their predecessors. In the general upshot of Josiah's reforming zeal we find that among the many aspects of the cults destroyed were the special quarters in the temple assigned for the use of the sodomite priesthood. Next door to these was the house, a veritable cottage industry it seems, where women wove hangings for the sacred groves.[12]

The struggle with the Canaanite gods lasted for the best part of a thousand years. It was till continuing when in the sixth century the battering rams of Nebuchadnezzar were breaking down the gates of the last few independent Jewish towns and cities. It endured throughout the years of exile. Indeed the exile itself was interpreted as a divine punishment for the disloyalty of the people to their god. Nowhere in the Ancient World were the battle lines so clearly drawn between the developing patriarchal religiosity and the remnants of the old goddess cults. The effect of the war of attrition along this front was to give Judaism its purifying vision. Its preoccupation with ritual purity was sharpened to obsession by its endless struggle to free itself from the polluting influence of the cults.

As in any strategy of permanent revolution, the embattled people were constantly enjoined to be ever at the ready to defend themselves against the perpetual threat of the counter-revolution from within. The point of entry for the contagion was always the women of the land. As late as the sixth century they were the subject of a bitter sermon by the prophet Jeremiah. Their outrage had been to burn incense to the 'queen of heaven' and 'pour out drink offerings unto her'. The resentment felt by the prophets for these errant goddess worshippers fed the misogynism that fills the pages of the Old Testament. The campaign to subdue them was never-ending. Purification from their influence was the price men paid for the defence of their patriarchal inheritance. In the cause of that purity the universe turned ethical and dualistic.

The tendency inherent in patriarchy to seek the light transcendent was transformed by Judaism into a militant crusade against the forces of darkness. For the Jewish people the crusade gained added force by the extension of the search for a state of grace to the entire nation. The fate of the people as a whole was thought to depend on how they responded to their obligation of moral responsibility to their god. Without that ethical imperative the psychotic power drive of that god might well have led the people into darker paths than any they had seen in the surrounding cults. It was the voice of the prophets that disciplined it and, in disciplining it, disciplined the people.

This discipline also had its price. There was a continual search for clues in the past and the present that would somehow reveal the mood, the attitude, the intentionality to the people of this demanding god. As the end of the whole enterprise was believed to lie in some happy state of grace in which the righteous would at last be at peace with their maker, the effect of the preoccupation was to set the history of the nation as a whole on a trajectory in time towards that hoped-for state. Time, as a result, turned linear in the minds of the Jewish people. Their history became for them the linear unfolding in time of the motive force of their god. A chosen people heading for a state of transcendence cannot have other than a teleological vision of the universe. The cult of Aten from which they may have derived their monotheism had retained the cyclicality of the old goddess myth but, once a culture develops a linear conception of time, it inevitably corrodes away any cyclical motifs that remain in its myths. In the case of the Jews the myths they had inherited became simply a source of further clues as to the intentionality of their god. The anxiety to know the will of that god, his plans for his chosen people became thus a search for a truth not poetic or mystical but empirical. Soon there would come a time when any cult to survive would require some claim to historical truth, if not a manifestation of its god then a truthful biography of its founder. Already we are at the dawn of the Christian era.

1 Weber M. The Agrarian Sociology of Ancient Civilisations (trans. by R. Frank). N.L.B. London, 1976 p. 84.
2 Redford D. B. Akhennten: The Heretic King. Princeton University Press. Princeton. New Jersey 1984 p. 58.
3 Bille-De Mot, E. The Age of Akhenaten. Evelyn, Adams and Mackay. London. 1966 p. 83-4.
4 Redford, D. B. ibid. 1984 p. 233.
5 Jakobsen, T. ibid. 1976 p 133.
6 2 Kings ch. 23 v. 12.
7 Judges ch. 3 v. 5.
8 1 Samuel ch. 13 v. 19, 20.
9 Kramer, S. N. (ed) Mythologies of the Ancient World. Anchor Books. New York. 1961 p. 209.
10 Deutronomy ch. 23 v. 18; Judges ch. 19 v. 22.
11 Genesis ch. 28 v. 18-19.
12 1 Kings ch. 16 v. 32.
13 Judges ch. 2 v. 13; ch. 10 v. 6.
14 Deuteronomy ch. 23 v. 18,
15 Judges ch. 6 v. 25-29.
16 Kings ch. 14 v. 23.
17 Kings ch. 8 v. 26.
18 Kings ch. 15 v. 13.

19 Kings ch. 11 v. 3
20 Kings ch. 3 v. 3.
21 Kings ch. 23 v. 7.

Chapter 5

From the Primal Myth to the Life of Christ

It was by looking into their mythical past that the Jewish people hoped to see what plans their patriarchal god had in mind for the future of his chosen people. As late arrivals on the patriarchal scene the myths they had historicised had largely been borrowed from others. The Old Testament that contained them had been built up cumulatively at different times in the course of the first millennium. Already the old matriarchal mythology had been much worked upon by the time Jewish scribes added their own interpretations. In fact, as we have seen, the mythology had already begun to separate into fragments perhaps even before the rudiments of a written script had been invented.

When the first myths were transcribed to the Sumerian cuneiform script, they already expressed the world view of a patriarchal culture. Occasionally, as in the case of the descent of Inanna, whole sections of the earlier oral tradition survived intact. Even there, though, as we noted, the tradition had been tampered with. Elsewhere the re-editing was far more radical. The fragments that survived simply provided the building blocks for the masonry of patriarchal myth. We have seen how these blocks were re-shaped and then fitted into place. At first mythic themes were retained but with male actors inserted into roles hitherto occupied by women. Later the themes themselves altered shape when viewed from an increasingly patriarchal perspective. New masculine aspirations sought expression in the tales. New values re-interpreted the old. What had once been sacred became absurd or, worse, tabooed and polluting.

The radical turning point in this process had come when Marduk tore Destiny from the chest of the titan Kingu and then assembled the new world order out of the eviscerated belly of his mistress Ti'âmat. The impact on the psyche of this primal act of mythic violence can be seen in the replication of the story in famous battles of gods with serpents throughout the Near and Middle East. From the destruction plundered fragments floated free like debris in the world of myth. Only Egypt retained an unbroken line of tradition, tenuous though it was, with its matriarchal past. There the creator god still lay like his motherly forbear in the murky blackness of his own sea waiting patiently to make time begin. The same sea in which Tiâmat, too, had coiled washes through early patriarchal mythology in successive flood motifs. We find one of these, perhaps closest in outline to the original, in the Gilgamesh epic in the story of Utnapishtim.[1]

In this short fable, replete with lunar symbolism, the flood is sent by the gods to quell the babble of noise on earth that has been preventing them from sleeping. Warned by one of the gods of the immanence of the flood, Utnapishtim builds an ark of seven decks in, coincidentally, seven days, in which he with his family survive the storm that lasts, coincidence again, for seven days. Peering out on the expanse of water on the dawn of the seventh day he spots a mountain fourteen leagues away and there the boat grounds. On the seventh day again, he releases a dove in search of land, followed by a swallow and a raven. Finally in desperation he sets up a sacrifice in 'seven and again seven cauldrons', an act which ends in the remorse of the gods. A great deal has been written on the historical basis of this story in a memory of widespread flooding that may actually have occurred in the Mesopotamian basin in the third or fourth millennium. The idea is not implausible but, with the lunar numbers as our key, we can decode it in a different way. The whole tale, in fact, reads like a residuum of the primal myth. The boat of seven decks built in seven days is the moonboat of the goddess. Its passengers are the souls of the dead. The flood waters are the celestial seas across which it voyages each night. The mountain fourteen leagues away is the first mound, earth emerging from the sea. The three birds are the goddess herself in tri-form epiphany.

When Marduk cut the umbilical cord that attached mankind to the belly of Ti'âmat he created a dichotomy not only between the earthly and the divine but also between the earthly and the after-life. Previously the after-life had been as much within the fleshly compass of the goddess as terrestrial life. One was but a natural extension of the other. Life in the beyond was lived within a different modality perhaps but it was nonetheless recognisably like life on earth, an image of it repeated through successive mirrors. The womb as tomb in the all-embracing body of the goddess was anything but an unwelcoming place.

Post-Marduk, the modality changed. As the gods drifted ever skywards earth turned demonic as it filled with goddesses driven from the heavens and its underworld, its after-life became a sinister and chaotic place. Again, only in Egypt, which avoided these excesses, did something of the old conception of the after-life remain. There, once the souls of the deceased had been weighed and not found wanting by the judges of the dead, they led a life of leisurely labour in the fields of Osiris, cultivating the god's estates and keeping his canals and dykes in good repair. They even had little statuettes buried with them in their tombs to whom they might choose to sub-contract this work.

A similar vision may have survived among the Canaanites in the fields of the goddess Asherah and her daughter. If so, the Greeks were less fortunate. They inherited the Mesopotamian perception of the after-life. To them the Infernal Regions were a dismal place where gloomy souls took refuge. Little could grow in this world of shadows that the sun's rays never reached. The dark rivers that flowed there warned the questing hero or the travelling soul of the fate awaiting them in this world. Acheron was the river of sadness and Cocytus of lamentation. The image of the after-life as a fine and happy place warmed by the goddess's embrace endured in the idea of Elysium but only as a privilege for the few. Once it may have been the abode of all and in Homer the folk memory is still vivid enough for him to recall a beautiful meadow far to the west on the banks of the river that encircled the earth.

The clearest memory, however, survived in myth in the form of what to later Greeks was but a pleasing fairy tale, the eleventh labour of Heracles in the Garden of the Hesperides. The labour was to fetch apples from the golden apple tree that grew in the garden. The apple tree, it was said, had been the wedding gift of Mother Earth to Hera, wife of Zeus.

The garden itself was thought to lie on the slopes of Mount Atlas. This mountain was named after the Titan Atlas who was eventually punished for conspiring against Zeus by having to stand motionless with the world on his shoulders. His daughters were the Hesperides to whom was entrusted care of the tree which also had an extra guardian in the snake Ladon that coiled in its branches. Heracles was to secure the apples by a trick but more interesting than the outcome to us are the mythic symbols concealed in this tale. The garden is the 'apple land', the Avalon, the Elysium of matriarchal myth. As Hera was once the great moon goddess of the early Greeks, the tree of this garden was most appropriately her gift from Mother Earth for it was to this same tree that she had descended on her journey to the underworld.

The tree in other words was originally the axis mundi, the world tree, the umbilicus of earth. Atlas himself was but a secondary image that somehow got separated out in myth. Once he had actually been the tree his daughters guarded. The disc he then had held so patiently was not the world but the moon nestling in his underworld branches awaiting its ascent after the three moonless nights beneath the earth. In his branches also curled the snake, not a guardian at first but a symbol of wisdom, the wisdom that knows of the eternal return of all things in due course to the earth.

Earlier the suggestion was made that this vision of an after-life as a gift of Mother Earth was what once entranced the Eleusinian initiates in Crete. Ritually, the vision had been confirmed by the rites of the hanged maiden. The rites had been a celebration of the death and rise again of Kore. Her death and resurrection had been redemptive in the sense that it rescued and reaffirmed the reality of Elysium in the dream-world of the goddess worshippers.

Shadowy images of her myth lingered on in the tales of Artemis, Ariadne and Helen, the hanged goddesses and heroines we noted throughout the Aegean.

All these figures were linked to the moon and it was, as embodiments of what seemed divine and numinous in this luminary, its endless capacity for self- renewal on the moonless nights in Earth's womb, that they descended and then rose again in spirit from the earth. The ritual text that described this underworld journey through the labyrinth we saw preserved in the story of Inanna's descent. Elsewhere and much later, as we shall shortly see, this descent survived in a more abstracted form. Generally, though, the patriarchal transformation of this myth took the form we earlier observed. A dying god, son, lover sometimes brother of the goddess replaced the maidenly descent to earth. His death was mourned on her behalf by choruses of women as a symbol of the loss that seemed to threaten in the dead season of the year when the dormant fertility of his lover might yet fail to yield her annual efflorescence in the coming year. His rise too was redemptive but in a more material sense. He was almost an embodiment in himself of the corn and the grape.

This god survived in many forms and many places but where he did so he remained still the reliquary of the old women's cult. In fact he was to become something of an anachronism in a world that sought ever more transcendent images of the male god. Not all of these took a celestial form. In many later myths the redemptive death became a quest, the labours of a Theseus or a Heracles, thwarted at first, later a success, a victory over death. What began with Gilgamesh ended in a more hopeful message for men. A male hero goes down to harrow hell and finally ascends unvanquished.

If we imagine the belly of Ti'âmat as symbolising in a sense the inclusive totality of matriarchal myth then these fragments, the flood motif, Elysium, the corn gods and the hanged heroines and goddesses were the slivers that floated free when the shell of her body was smashed. Radically changed though they had already been, they now underwent further re-shaping in the hands of the Old Testament scribes. The effect of their work, which was to have such a profound influence on Western civilisation, went far beyond the embroidering of a few extra strands in the myths.

We have only to open the Old Testament and see what has been done to these myths in the book of Genesis to realise that a remarkable transformation has taken place. A new and intense moralism has changed the nature of the story-telling. Earlier patriarchal myth-making had been inspired by certain implicit values which it was no doubt assumed the audience would share, most notably, the inherent superiority of maleness as a conduit for the divine. In the Old Testament, however, we find these values distilled into the relentless injunctions of a moral creed. The motives behind this we have earlier explored. Having conjured up the volatile image of an all- powerful yet ultimately unknowable creator god with a neurotic preoccupation with their collective fate, the people of Israel had been forced to build a regime of ceremonial and dietary laws subservience to which, they sensed, would enable them to predict, monitor and manipulate the element of the diabolical in his untrammelled will. Only strenuous obedience to these laws could save the people from the righteous indignation of this god and encourage him to implement the more benevolent plans they hoped he had in store for them.

What in their imagination they had thus created was a religion of salvation based on purification through suffering. Suffering, as we earlier observed, was the contractual basis of their relationship with this god and the more painful the better. The presupposition of divine interest inherent in this collective neurosis led in turn to the image of a jealous god for surely only such a god would be obsessively concerned with the suffering of a single, chosen people. An inevitable corollary of this produced in the people of Israel what one writer has called their least amiable characteristic.[2] This was their conviction that not only was their patriarchal god the only true god but that all other gods were false, and not only false but antithetical, sinister and polluting.

Their greatest condemnation the Israelite prophets reserved for what they saw around them of the remains of the goddess cult in its dying god phase. The threat to their transcendent god seemed most ominous in a goddess whose implicit claim was that she was

135

immanent in the very earth he had created as a manifestation of his will. The very claim struck them as a devilish attempt to pervert the very meaning of that creation. We have noted the reluctance of the people, particularly the women, to follow this party line especially in periods of great stress when the male creator appeared to have abandoned Israel. To halt the slide it was not enough for the prophets to re-iterate the injunctions of their creed. They had somehow to de-idolise, to demythologise a nature saturated with the images of the goddess. Cults that celebrated her divinity in nature could then be presented to the people in their true light, as absurd or, worse, treacherous and chaotic. A religion so malevolent and miscon-ceived could only bring misery in its train as Isaiah points out in his sour strictures on those women foolish enough to plant and tend their fertility pots in honour of Adonis:

'In the day shalt thou make thy plant to grow, and in the morning shalt thou make thy seed to flourish: but the harvest shall be a heap in the day of grief and of desperate sorrow.'[3]

Naturally, the old myths were useful grist to the mill of this patriarchal propaganda machine. Where the prophets heaped scorn on the rites the scribes re-wrote the relics of the old goddess myths. Unlike the prophets, however, the scribes suffered from one significant handicap. Ever since Moses had destroyed the people's idolatrous golden calf the fertility cults around them could be presented as, at source, a foreign threat. It was not so easy to extend this censure to the myths which had actually been written into the remote history of the Israelite people. Where matriarchal excrescences still survived in myth they could not thus be ridiculed or excoriated like the rites. They had instead to be adapted. Adaptation meant they had to be re-written to carry the new message of revolutionary monotheism. This represented a considerable departure from the mind-set of previous editorial routines.

Myths that had been tampered and tinkered with from generation to generation in conformity with the patriarchal line were now restructured root and branch. In the process they were not just transformed but turned upside down, morally inverted, in other words, to express values antithetical to those that had once inspired them. Old tales were twisted into a savagely incongruous shape. What had once been symbols of immanence and exaltation in the old goddess cult were turned by the stroke of a pen into marks of pollution and symptoms of a threatening moral chaos.

We can see how the old myths were used to build the new and in some ways revolutionary world-view of Judaism in the story of the Creation and the Fall in the first chapters of Genesis. We can also observe how from the materials they had inherited the authors of the Old Testament combined both Egyptian and Mesopotamian versions of the myths to create a composite tale. Not surprisingly perhaps, their own story begins with their particular creator god on the face of the primal sea:

'And the earth was without form, and void; and darkness was upon the face of the deep. And the Spirit of God moved upon the face of the waters.[4]

The image they no doubt derived from Egyptian tradition in which Atum had lain in the deep, a spirit waiting to set the universe in motion. The word for deep 'tehum' was etymologically linked to Ti'ümat. That this was the encircling watery shell, the celestial sea in which she once swam is apparent in the course of the creation for when God made the firmament he,

'divided the waters which were under the firmament from the waters which were above the firmament.[5]

From out of this sea had risen the primordial mound of matriarchal myth and the folk memory of this continued to exercise the minds of the authors of the Old Testament,

'And God said, let the waters under the heaven be gathered together unto one place, and let the dry land appear: and it was so. And God called the dry land Earth...

From the original mound had risen the world tree, the umbilicus of Mother Earth. The tree has vanished from this Genesis creation myth but it does surface elsewhere in what has been called an alternative creation myth, the story of Noah and the Flood. This tale is in fact a straight lift from the Mesopotamian flood story described already in the epic of Gilgamesh. In the Genesis version even details like the recurrence of the number seven are preserved. As in the Gilgamesh account the voyage of the ark ends with the sight of a mountaintop. From the ark at its moorings birds are again released, only two this time, a raven and a dove, with the swallow missing.

In Genesis, however, the dove returns with in her beak a plucked olive leaf.[7] The olive was a tree sacred to the goddess. Somehow, it seems, the scribes had managed to work the tree motif back into the text. Yet, unoriginal though this story is, in one important respect it represents a radical departure from its Mesopotamian source. What has changed is the tone of it, which in Genesis is intensely moralistic. In the Gilgamesh version the gods send the flood because they are crazed by the din mankind is making. In Genesis the fault in men is a moral one and the overtones are far more sinister:

'The earth also was corrupt before God, and the earth was filled with violence. And God looked upon the earth and, behold, it was corrupt; for all flesh had corrupted his way upon the earth.[5]

It is thus the apostasy of mankind that brings the flood, and the disaster ends only when God feels the punishment is enough. The image of man implied is anything but optimistic for 'the imagination of man's heart is evil from his youth'.[9] A creature with so few morally redeeming features is clearly in need of guidelines to keep him on the straight and narrow. Hence the episode ends with God establishing a covenant with man which, interestingly enough, allows man virtually a free hand to do what he likes with the rest of his own creation. Of all other creatures not so covenanted 'into your hands', he says 'are they delivered'[12] The pattern set by the story of Noah recurs as a motif throughout the Old Testament. It is one of apostasy followed by a punishing disaster which in turn necessitates some kind of trial of suffering that has its due effect when the victim finally repents and returns to the covenant in the hope of deliverance.

From what has been said so far of the Book of Genesis it is clear that a dualistic vision of the universe in which the powers of darkness were ever at the ready to wrest the people of Israel from the light was close to the hearts of the authors of the Old Testament. Yet concealed within this disposition was a massive paradox. For a start, the Israelites were not, politically or militarily, a successful people. Around them were many peoples, first Canaanites and Philistines, then Phoenicians and Syrians, many of them still to some degree goddess worshippers, who were at different times self-evidently more materially successful than themselves. This contradiction could partly be explained, of course, by the apostasy of the people. Had they behaved themselves they too would have had the success for which they so obviously yearned. And anyway, all was not lost. As long as they returned to the true path and kept to it they would have the necks of their enemies under their heel on the final day of reckoning.

More difficult to explain was how all the tempting evil around them got into the Lord's creation in the first place. For evil we can read goddess worship for this to the scribes and prophets was undoubtedly the greatest threat. Surely an all-powerful god would have so designed the universe as to remove this menace? This is, indeed, the implication to be read between the lines in Genesis where God is so pleased with his work that he rests on the seventh day to contemplate his creation. As God could not possibly have willingly created anything so evil as the fertility cults they saw around them, a 'deus ex machina' was urgently required to explain the paradox. The answer to their problem the authors found in the story of the fall of man.

In devising the fall of man as a moral theme the Old Testament authors truly excelled themselves in inverting the meaning of the old myths for they took the symbols of the after-life of the goddess cult, the World Tree, the umbilicus of all life and the source of knowledge, its guardian snake, the symbol of immortality and eternal recurrence, the crone goddess of wisdom in its shade and the fruit from its branches which she proffered as her passport to eternity and then they distorted these images of joy and exaltation into a message of utter hopelessness and despair.

Their story begins with Adam, the first man, born out of the feminine 'adamah', the dust of the ground and therefore, etymologically at least, identified with Mother Earth.[11] His birth is followed by the creation of all living creatures, the beasts of the field, the fowl of the air and then, sadly for her status, after these, by that of his 'helpmate' Eve.

As the goddess in her wisdom phase Eve was once considerably more exalted than this would suggest. To emphasise her now much lesser role she is born from Adam's rib. Yet, etymologically again, the scribes betray their sources. Born of the feminine 'Adamah', she still retains her link to Mother Earth. Adam is given a dwelling place in the orchard of the after-life conveniently transposed to earth 'a garden eastward in Eden[12] in which grew 'every tree that is pleasant to the sight'.[13]

In the midst of the orchard the authors placed the 'axis mundi', the world tree. Adam's later connection with this tree reveals his origin in the sons/lovers of the surrounding fertility cults. The tree was for them, as we noted, a significant motif. They were either born in it like Adonis, lived in its shade like Dumuzi or were interred like Osiris in its trunk. Its original significance lay in the earlier primal goddess myth. There it was the tree of life whose branches spread among the clouds. In it the moon goddess was born and to it she returned each night and for three whole nights at a time carrying the souls of the dead to its branches in the counterheaven beneath the earth. As the key to eternal life and a metaphor of its cyclicality in the goddess cult it was thus also the tree of fate and of the wisdom which knows it. This is why the Viking god Odin hung from Yggdrasil, its Scandinavian exemplar, for nine days and nights. What he sought was an understanding of fate. That fate was for goddess worshippers one of eternal recurrence, an image epitomised in the snake which slips from its skin as the moon escapes from her shadow in her waxing phase. The fruit the snake guarded among the branches was thus both the fruit of knowledge and the passport to eternal life for the souls of the dead.

This mythic tree has in Genesis been separated into two, the Tree of Life, that is, the tree of immortality, and the Tree of Knowledge of Good and Evil.1 Now the old knowledge associated with the sacred tree was of what must have seemed to worshippers a natural law for the cyclicality it symbolised was of the eternal return of the life force to an earth from which it was reborn. In Genesis knowledge has been detached from nature and translated into an understanding of the predicaments of moral choice. Given an identity of its own in a tree apart from the tree symbol of life, this new kind of moral knowledge stands in virtual opposition to this symbol on its own ground. That ground is the duality of the authors' own moral system in which the forces of light fight a perpetual war with a darkness identified with the world of nature symbolised by the tree of life. A dichotomy was thus created between a system of ethics and the innocent sensuality of the natural world, a dissociation of morality from the sphere of the senses the effects of which are with us still. It is the fruit of this tree of knowledge of good and evil which Adam is forbidden by the Lord to eat.

The story of what followed and how it led to Adam's downfall is part of our biblical folklore. Tempted by Eve, who has been beguiled by the snake, he eats the fruit of the tree and as a result discovers like her the shameful fact of his nakedness. Covering their genitals with the leaves of a fig, the couple hide in terror of their creator, who calls to them as he walks in the garden in the cool of the day. Coming out of hiding, Adam exculpates himself to his maker by blaming Eve who in turns points her finger at the snake. As a punishment she and it and all their kind are cursed by the Lord, and Adam too for succumbing to their ploys. All three suffer banishment 'in perpetuo' for their sins: the snake to slither on its belly for eternity, the woman to multiply her sorrows in the misery of conception and Adam himself 'to till the ground from whence he was taken.'

What the Old Testament authors achieved in this strange tale was an inversion of a goddess myth whereby its symbols were turned upside down to convey the antithesis of what they once had signified. To begin with, the woman called Eve was once the goddess herself and it was she who enjoyed the shade of the orchard in the cool of the day. The snake was both her alter ego and the archetypal symbol of what she represented. The snake was not then so much the guardian as the metaphorical extension of the meaning of the tree. The fruit of the tree had always been her gift not a curse in fact but a prize, a passport to the orchard of paradise. In Genesis all these symbols were subverted. The snake was crushed underfoot for there was no room for the fatalism of the cyclical it signified in the guilt psychology of the new cult. Woman who had embodied most the cyclical on earth was set at odds with the serpentine symbol of this quality in herself. Worse than this, the fruit she offered as a token of entry to the after-life was perverted into the harbinger of the death and decay awaiting an Adam and Eve expelled from paradise. That expulsion was irrevocable in the sense that the only paradise left for man now was an extension of the path of righteousness defined by the moral psychology of his patriarchal god.

Worse still, the natural reproductive cycles of the world into which Adam has 'fallen' have been linked thereafter to sorrow, shame and guilt. At the centre of this pathological model of the natural world is the act of sex and the personification of the threat it poses to the soul of man in the sinister shape of Eve the temptress. Into the figure of Eve the scribes injected all the venom they felt for the sexual freedom of the goddess cults. Henceforth sexuality would be filled with shame. What in the fruit of Elysium had once been a symbol of extraordinary scope was trivialised into prurience and made the pitiful arbiter of mankind's fate. Not only sexuality but birth itself was to be a source of misery. As the source of both in the view of the scribes, women were twice cursed as doubly responsible for the fall of man.

Sexuality, as we have seen, was once a source of ecstatic union with the goddess and birth a confirmation of the numinous in woman. The equation of both with sin was the most perversely alienating legacy of the Genesis inversion of the goddess myth. Its consequences we see in early Christianity. They were already apparent in Saint Paul, a wilful misogynist, who could barely countenance the thought of sexual intercourse even in the marriage bed. The logical extension of this prejudice lay in the development of the concept of original sin. With this, there was to be no further innocent enjoyment of nature's gifts. The body would be mortified to free it from desire. Saint Paul himself exulted in the number of times he had been scourged and whipped. The righteous sufferer could thus take out all his anguish on his own body. Where that did not suffice, woman herself, the stimulating source of all this angst, was there ready, waiting to be punished. After all, had she not, through Eve, exposed all mankind to original sin? For the Christians, of course, there was an altogether more exalted answer in the wings. Christ, as the second Adam, could remove by his own redemptive death, the curse Eve had laid on the first.[5] 'For', as Paul so succinctly put it, 'as in Adam all die, even so in Christ shall all be made alive'.[16]

It was the thought of deliverance from all this agony that motivated those who created the Old Testament text. The thought of deliverance is the key to the Bible, its central motif, but it is deliverance in conformity with the Jewish law when after much trial and suffering the people have finally repented and come to their senses. The exact nature of this final state of grace, its coordinates in time and space, was not very clear. All that mattered was that the people or at least the righteous among them, living and dead, would find themselves in a proximity to their creator of a kind only previously experienced before Adam's fall from grace. Nevertheless, the concept of deliverance was fuzzy-edged. A far more distinctive edge attached to the suffering the people were constantly having to experience to reach the promised state. This, all could agree, was very much a phenomenon in time and space.

We have previously remarked on the significance of the failure of the people of Israel to achieve any great military or political success. We have also noted the cause of this. Caught between two great power blocs, the people could only enjoy a thriving independence when a general equilibrium held sway. The golden age to which the people looked back, the period of Kings David and Solomon, was one such time between the decline of Egypt and the rise of Assyria . For a nation waiting for deliverance through repentance from the other kingdoms of the earth there was something psychologically frustrating about this whole situation.

There was naturally a very human tendency at times to try to speed the deliverance up a bit by injecting a little activism into this endless scenario. The attitude took hold in the idea of the Messiah. Originally the word Messiah meant only a ruler whose right to rule had been symbolised by an anointing. By the beginning of the Christian era, however, and after a number of rebellions against foreign rule, the concept had been projected into the future in the shape of an eschatological warrior king who would bring history to an end by bringing down the powers of the earth and ushering in the kingdom of the elect. A whole theory grew up about the various omens and signs that would precede the coming of such a one in what were called somewhat darkly 'The Last Days'.

There were many candidates for the role of Messiah. Groups like the Essenes with their Teacher of Righteousness separated off from the mainstream of Jewish society to await the signs of the cataclysm to come. Yet the concept had its contradictions. One of these concerned the issue of legitimacy. Clearly it would have been helpful, for the purposes of general recognition, if the Messiah, when he came, had had royal blood running through his veins. As King David was about the most successful royal prototype anyone could think of, a genealogy would be required connecting the Messiah to the line of David.[17] On the other hand, no matter how royal the scion, it would have been helpful also if the deliverer from suffering had been a sufferer himself as well and not from too privileged a position. Here the concept of Messiah began to merge with that of the righteous sufferer who surfaces in the Old Testament in the dismal shape of the 'suffering servant', a sacrificial victim from a humble background who draws upon his own head and thus symbolises the suffering of the people:

'He is despised and rejected of men; a man of sorrows, and acquainted with grief: and we hid as it were our faces from him; he was despised, and we esteemed him not.'[18]

The idea that royalty could be mandated to experience the suffering of their people did not seem as fanciful then as it does today. Even less so if the royal in question were of humble origin, either ignorant of his own lineage or tactically concealing it until the time was ripe in 'the last days'. It is not difficult to see a link between this notion and that of the scapegoat. The figure of a mock king, the bearer for a day of all the afflictions of the body politic, being scourged or whipped or hurled from a cliff was a common purgative symbol in the Ancient World. We find it in a more civilised form in the ritual of the Day of Atonement in the Book of Leviticus in which a goat representing the sins accumulated by the people of Israel is driven into the desert.

All these strands wove together to create the composite symbol of a righteous sufferer, of royal pedigree but humble origin, unknown, perhaps, or despised for much of his life, who was yet the Messiah who by his own suffering and sacrifice would atone for the sins of the community and, once recognised, restore it to its true path. Make the suffering Messiah the last of the biblical prophets and generalise his message of atonement to the whole of humankind and the scene is set for the coming of Christ.

Presented in this light, Jesus Christ appears to emerge organically out of the chrysalis of Judaism and take to flight. This was undoubtedly the image of him which the Gospels strove to cultivate. With this in mind their authors took the Old Testament as their own book of prophecy and plundered it at will for evidence that predicted the events of his life. In acting thus, they saw themselves as simply rounding off motifs that went back to Genesis. Yet their work was far more revolutionary than they realised. Part of the reason for this was that the particular aspects of Judaism they exploited had already been radicalised.

We have seen how deliverance for the people of Israel could only come from repentance of apostasy and return to the law. The power in the images of the suffering servant and the Messiah lay in the fact that both offered some relief from this dreary cycle, one by atonement the other by inducing the birth-pangs of the kingdom that would end it in 'the last days'. Together they represented a short cut to divine favour and, when combined, they formed a radical departure from Old Testament tradition.

More radical still was Christianity's special contribution to all of this, the notion that the wilful creator god had undergone a change of heart and come down to earth himself to help deliverance along in the incarnate figure of Jesus Christ. What the god of the Christians was offering by this gesture was a quick fix transcendence of the Jewish laws and this escape clause effectively cancelled out the credit built up by a thousand years of righteously suffering obedience to those very laws, which is why so much of the Gospel account is taken up with conflict between Jesus and the Pharisees and scribes on the vexed issue of observance of these laws. Against pharisaical observance Jesus placed what none of his detractors could accommodate, the instantaneous embrace of the father god at the command of a loving faith:

'He that hath my commandments', says the Gospel Jesus, 'and keepeth them, he it is that loveth me: and he that loveth me shall be loved of my Father, and I will love him, and will manifest myself to him.'[1]

The effect of this justification by faith was to create what for Jewish observers must have seemed a bewildering, at times even shocking familiarity between the early Christians and their god. For this familiarity there was a price to pay. Freed from the laws designed to control his volatile psycho- pathology, the patriarchal god could roam at will in the deepest recesses of the human psyche. To restore the balance upset by the loss of these controls, the Christian Church would eventually interpose the interpretations of its priests. When these too were torn aside at the time of the Reformation, mankind was left to struggle once more with its Old Testament creator but now deeper, much deeper in its soul. Earlier we observed how, in their anxiety to know the will of their creator god, the people of Israel explored their own myths in search of evidence of his intentions. In the process they converted their own heritage of myth into a kind of history in the sense of a linear sequence of events. This activity represented a primitive form of empiricism and, in engaging in it, they were in fact sharing in a cultural development which was taking place throughout the Ancient World at the onset of the Christian era.

The essence of this development was the rationalisation of myth. Folk tales that had existed in their own mythic space and time were translated into real space and time and re-located in the misty antiquity of peoples. What the mythographers of the time were doing was creating history out of myth. The dividing line between the two had never been very clear, which anyone reading the Greek historian Herodotus soon spots, but as the development gathered pace history began to spread back in time beyond living memory and gradually envelope myth. We can see this movement of thought at work in the Greek writer Euhemerus. In his Sacred History he reduced all mythology to the apotheosis of mortal men. Individuals conspicuous for some quality of bravery or cleverness left behind a memory of them, he suggested, which was then mythologised by their descendants.

In this more rationalistic world, location in real space and time became an important criterion of truth, a claim to legitimacy that replaced that of myth. It was now a distinct advantage for any religious group looking back to a distant founder to have a biography for him that proved he did once actually exist in real space and time. On this score, however, a dilemma confronted the early Christians. They claimed spiritual allegiance to a suffering Messiah who had died to redeem mankind of its sins and was then resurrected to rejoin his father in the skies, a character, in other words, in real space and time, who by the very nature of his redeeming death and resurrection had transcended space and time and brought all previous history to an end. It was a potent symbol but one the scattered and oppressed community of worshippers had, in the conditions of the time, to turn into a biographical creation. This was no doubt why, in the middle of the first century, the word went round the early churches to gather material for the story of Christ's life. And so the construction of the Gospels began.

All the gospel writers were agreed that Jesus was a Jew who lived out his life in an orthodox Jewish environment. There was also general agreement on another point. Their founder was the last of the great line of prophets of his land and by virtue of this fact the Old Testament could be mined for predictive evidence of his life. The problem was that the purported events of that life were lived out at least two generations before most of their source material was compiled.

What the gospel writers lacked was the kind of circumstantial evidence that enriches the texture of a narrative and gives it the fictive credibility of reported 'fact'. Not only that but in two crucial areas of gap they could not draw upon the Old Testament as a source. The first of these concerned the issue of vicarious sacrifice. Now Jewish tradition was familiar with the concept of atonement but atonement by death was another matter. Agreed, the suffering servant of Isaiah was prepared to be a martyr but martyrdom is not sacrifice. It is more individually controlled, less a matter of coercion.

Christ, on the other, it could be said, although a martyr in one sense, allowed himself to be sacrificed. That surely is the significance of the story of his arrest and trial. After his death he was resurrected and here lay the second evidential gap. Jewish tradition did have a concept of the resurrection of the dead but only as part of the general resurrection of all the righteous at the end of time. The resurrection of an individual as a dramatic motif was never part of that tradition. Where, then, could the gospel writers find evidence to fill these gaps? The answer lay around them in the still surviving goddess cults.

We have witnessed the near paranoid hostility of the Old Testament scribes to the goddess religion in its dying god phase. Indeed much of the Old Testament could be read as a propaganda tract against it. Yet so ubiquitous were the fertility cults among the surrounding peoples it would be surprising not to find an echo of them in the biblical text. We have seen how the authors of that text were willing to look for source material in the ancient goddess myths and, sure enough, we do find one or two echoes of the rites themselves in the Old Testament. There is Joseph with his coat of many colours lowered into a pit whose subsequent career in Egypt is dramatically connected to the storehouse grain.1 There is Absalom, left hanging in an oak tree by his golden hair 'taken up between the heaven and the earth'2 and then slain among its branches before being lowered too into a great pit. Such stories no doubt owe much to folk memories of cults the people of Israel themselves may once have celebrated but the traces of these memories are few and far between. Hostility to the cults was enough to have any borrowings more obvious than these expurgated from the text.

In creating their own sacred writings, Christian writers were, at least at first, far less reluctant to fill out their texts with themes taken from local goddess cults. Not only were many of the early members of their congregations only marginalized Jews, who would eventually anyway be banned from the synagogue, but, as Christianity spread, it soon became less judaised in general and in fact began to gather adherents from the very heartlands of the fertility cults the Old Testament prophets had so despised. In the myths and rites of these cults the authors of the gospels encountered images of dying gods that fitted well with what they could recall of the life of Christ.

We do not need to read very far into the Gospels before we realise that their authors were very familiar with these images and ready to exploit them to make dramatic points. Their own source material from the early Christian churches would probably have consisted of sheaves of miracle stories and preaching material interspersed with lists of names of persons and places that had come down from the first Christian settlements. There were also primitive Gospel texts already in circulation by the time they began their work. The task facing the Gospel writers was how to translate this diversity of material into a powerful narrative sequence. It was here that imagery from the fertility cults came in useful. For writers searching for a tale of epic proportions it provided both the overarching theme and the adhesive to hold the story together at critical points.

We can spot the parallels easily at the most abstract level. Like Adonis and the other vegetation gods, Jesus descends from a higher level and then ascends back to it again. In his case, however, the spiral of descent and return is repeated at a lower level. The operation of the theme at two levels mirrors the dichotomy already by this time brought about by the increasing transcendence of the male god. At one level Jesus is the sky god who has cut the links with Mother Earth. In this guise he

149

descends from the heavens, is born on earth and then returns to the sky at his ascension. At a lower level within this theme he follows a second spiral of descent and return but this time as the old fertility god, the son and lover of the goddess that was. In this second, earthier spiral he dies on the cross, is placed in a tomb, descends into the earth and finally returns to the terrestrial world above at the Resurrection.

Naturally it is when we explore the lower of the two spirals of descent and return that we find the closest parallels between the life of Jesus and what we know of the myths and rites of the dying god cults. To begin with, he was born of a virgin, a not uncommon theme in the mystery religions of the Ancient World. It is worth noting here that adoration of his mother was often associated with sites linked to the cult of the virgin goddess Artemis. Like so many other dying gods he was a god of the corn and vine. 'I am the bread of life', he said. 'I am the true vine'.[23] The images of the grain and the grape run through many of his parables as well as miracle stories like the feeding of the five thousand and the turning of the water into wine. Only fitting, therefore, that his birthplace should be at Bethlehem 'The House of Bread', a village where, interesting to relate, Adonis himself was also worshipped and where, long after the purported events of Jesus' life, St Jerome was horrified to find 'in the grotto where formerly the infant Christ had cried, Adonis was being mourned.'[24] The implications of such symbolism could be interpreted quite literally in ancient mystery religions. 'For my flesh is meat indeed.' says Jesus, 'and my blood is drink indeed,'[25] a statement stark enough to shock even his disciples[26] but in the form of the bread and wine of the Eucharist it was to become the basis of an important Christian sacrament and rite.

The bread and wine symbolised the body and blood of Christ and, as in the other dying god cults, it was the mortification of his flesh which forms the theme of his passion. Anointed like a sacred king on the eve of his death,[27] he was betrayed into the hands of his captors. After his trial he was subjected to a mock coronation and scourged in royal regalia.[28] Condemned to death, he was accompanied to the place of execution by a chorus of mourning women.[29] Death comes for the redeemer as he hung from a tree on a hill.[30] We are reminded of Attis bleeding to death beneath the sacred pine and of the famous festivals of this other god for the tree itself carried processionally by the victim in the form of the cross to the spot where he was crucified.

In the sequel his spirit descended to the underworld where he spent three days and nights beneath the earth.[31] When finally his tomb opened of its own accord and he reappeared as the resurrected Lord, women fled in a state of exaltation to spread the news abroad. Thematically, the pattern is extended to the later Christian calendar of the events of Jesus's life. Born on December 25th when the sun rises from its winter solstice, the commemoration of his death has been regulated ever since in relation to the paschal full moon. In only one important respect did the pattern deviate from that of the other dying gods. Their resurrection was traditionally envisioned in the return of fertility to the earth. That of Jesus was corporeal. He actually walked the earth in an incarnate form. This had to be, for otherwise he could not have completed his other higher spiral of a sky god returning to the heavens.

Viewed from the vantage point of these events, the biography of Jesus could be seen to be interchangeable in many respects with that of the son/lovers of the goddess cults. Where these cults still survived, they remained, as we observed, very much the cults of women, for in them women still played a dominant role. In this respect, too, we can detect a resonance in the life of Christ. Throughout the gospels we find women located at key points in the text. The tradition of their prominence must once have been very strong for it survived the attempts of particularly the later gospel writers to edit it out of the narrative.

Even so, despite their attempts, the evidence is clear and points to yet another parallel with the goddess cults. Not only were women among the followers of the movement1 and conspicuous in the early cult centres,[32] they were also noted members of its inner circle of confidantes.[33] This explains how Jesus came to be anointed by a woman, significantly, one of the few facts that all four gospels are agreed upon, and also followed by a crowd of wailing women to the crucifixion spot. There, again, their presence as observers of what took place is attested by all four gospels. It is they in various guises - the names change but the principle is maintained and they were usually numbered in clusters of three - who are witnesses of the entombment,[35] intending anointees of the corpse,[36] and hence the first to grasp the significance of its absence from the tomb. They are, in fact, the first witnesses of the Resurrection in the earliest gospel6 and it is they who carry the news to the male disciples, although they are at first disbelieved.[18]

In most of these occurrences one woman is usually a Mary and of all the Maries one is pre-eminent. Outlasting all attempts by later gospel writers to diminish her role in the text, Mary Magdalene retains to the end her status not only as the leading follower of Christ but also, and on this, once more, all gospels are agreed, the key witness to the events surrounding his resurrection. Of the character of this woman the gospels leave little doubt. A woman of loose morals out of whom Christ himself had cast 'seven devils',1 she brings the shadow of the temple hierodule into the Gospel text. Behind her, indeed, the outline of the great love goddess of Antiquity can still be seen.

The resemblances between Jesus Christ on the one hand and gods like Attis and Adonis on the other seem at times quite transparent. They could almost be seen as the objects of similar cults with comparable myths and rites but for one important difference. Jesus is presented in the Gospels as the last in a long line of Jewish prophets, in fact the one who brings the entire Old Testament prophetic tradition to an end. This tradition was, it is worth repeating, a tradition of myth that had been historicised to create a mission for the Jewish people.

At the end of this tradition, Jesus Christ thus ends up, not like Attis and Adonis, with an existence circumscribed by the world of myth, but as a figure himself historicised, a prophet in real space and time or purportedly so. He therefore presents the curious picture of a fertility god for whose coming the Old Testament was ransacked to supply predictive evidence. It was a strange quirk of fate that converted the Old Testament into a source of prophecy for just the kind of cult symbol its authors so despised.

Nevertheless these Old Testament prophecies furnished the only other legitimate evidence for the events of Jesus's life.

Remove the Old Testament traditions together with the symbolism of the goddess cults and we are left with whatever remained in the sources of the Gospel writers, miracle stories, preaching texts, lists of names. When even these are found to be shot through with the symbolism of other cults, we are entitled to ask whether there was anything left that was unique to Christianity in the data of the Gospel writers. Were these writers merely propagandists who historicised and judaised the myths they found to create a workable biography for their founder? There is no suggestion of conscious plagiarism at this point although that may well indeed have happened. More likely it is that the themes they took were simply part of the folkways of the Ancient World, an aspect of its religious climate so pervasive it could not help but enter into the creation of the text. By the time the Gospels were written, we must remember, Christianity had already entered Syria and Asia Minor, where it really began to spread. These were the heartlands of the old goddess cults. The Christianised Jews and Gentile Christians who contributed most to the New Testament could hardly have been free from the influence of these cults. After all, they were still very much a part of their world.

1 The Epic of Gilgamesh ibid pp. 108-113.
2 Frye, N. The Great Code: The Bible and Literature. Routledge and Kegan Paul. London 1982 p. 114.
3 Isaiah ch. 17 v. 11.
4 Genesis ch. 1 v. 2.
5 Genesis ch. 1 v. 7.
6 Genesis ch. 1 v. 9-10.
7 Genesis ch. 8 v. 11.
8 Genesis ch. 6 v. 11-12.
9 Genesis ch. 8 v. 21.
10 Genesis ch. 9 v. 2.
11 Genesis ch. 2 v. 7
12 Genesis ch. 2 v. 8
13 Genesis ch. 2 v. 9.
14 Genesis ch. 2 v. 9.

15 cf Baring and Cashford ibid.
16 1 Corinthians ch. 15 v. 22.
17 Isaiah ch. 11 v. 1.
18 Isaiah ch. 53 v. 3.
19 John ch. 14 v. 21
20 Genesis ch. 41. 2
21 Samuel ch. 18 v. 14.
22 John ch. 6 v. 48.
23 John ch. 15 v. 1.
24 In Donne T. W. 'Bible Myths and their Parallels in Other Religions' The Truth Seeker Co. New York 1982 p. 220.
25 John ch. 6 v. 55.
26 John ch. 6 v. 66.
27 Mark ch. 14 v. 3.
28 Mark ch. 15 v. 20.
29 Luke ch. 23 v. 28.
30 Mark ch. 15 v. 37.
31 Matthew ch. 13 v. 40.
32 Luke ch. 8 v. 2-3.
33 John ch. 11 v. 19-20.
34 Luke ch. 10 v. 38-42.
35 Mark ch. 15 v. 47.
36 Mark ch. 16 v. 1.
37 Mark ch. 16 v. 9.
38 Mark ch. 16 v. 11.
39 Luke ch. 8 v. 2.

Chapter 6

Wisdom

The images of the dying god which the gospel writers exploited had been super-imposed in the remote past on the much more ancient dying goddess myth. As the symbolic descendant of the gods that had been derived from her, Christ was thus also a distant descendant of the lunar goddess. As a facsimile of her facsimile, he could be seen as simply a paler imitation of this goddess although the resemblances are clear nonetheless. Like her he was hanged on a tree, spent three days and nights with Mother Earth and had his death commemorated in the lunar calendar. Even her underworld orchard could be said to figure in his myth for he was captured in his favourite haunt, the garden of Gethsemane, 'the place of the olive press'.

The olive, we recall, was sacred to the goddess. From Gethsemane to the cross his passion like hers began and ended on a tree motif. Resemblances like these merely confirm the debt to the goddess which he shared with his fellow dying gods. As a later arrival on the mythic scene, his link with her is inevitably more indirect than theirs. Yet there is another sense in which he was also her heir and in a more direct sense. The connection is a convoluted one but it runs as a theme through later Old Testament tradition. Within that theme the goddess did in fact survive, albeit in a somewhat opaque form, to influence Christianity at its biblical source. Indeed, along with the fertility images and the Old Testament prophetic tradition, it could be said to have formed the third stream of influence on the gospel writers. It almost certainly figured among their source material. To find it, we must search once more for images of descent and return but this time not as edited masculine derivatives but as genuine if modified features of the myth of a goddess.

We noted earlier that, when the Israelites first arrived as invaders in the land of Canaan the old dying goddess cults had already largely given way to cults which celebrated the return of the son/lover of the goddess to earth. Goddesses like Anath and Asherah still figured prominently in myths and rites but they no longer enjoyed the central role they had had centuries before. This had passed to male gods like El and Baal who had largely upstaged them in the Canaanite pantheon. No doubt in some remote regions the earlier cult of the dying and resurrecting lunar goddess still prevailed but the survival would have been residual and ultimately doomed in the long term. It is no surprise therefore that we come across few vestigial traces of the old lunar rites in the early books of the Old Testament. They certainly do not figure in the diatribes of the prophets of Israel who naturally concentrated their polemical fire on the by then much more vigorous and threatening vegetation god cults. Yet one or two traces of the earlier cults can be found in the early part of the Old Testament. One of these in particular is dramatic enough to arouse our interest. It concerns the fate of Jephthah's daughter.

Jephthah was the kind of warrior leader who crops up frequently in the pages of the Old Testament. 'A mighty man of valour'[1] he had the distinct disadvantage in these patriarchal times of having a prostitute for a mother. 'Harlot' is the term used although this is often a codeword for a temple hierodule or a priestess of the goddess. Whatever the truth of this, his origins definitely put him on the matriarchal side. When his brothers grew up, he soon found himself, as a result, driven form his house. 'Thou shalt not', he was told, 'inherit in our father's house; for thou art the son of a strange woman.'[2] Like many an outcast before him he retreated to the wild where he soon gathered around him a band of warriors like himself. Such is the reputation he acquired it was not long before the Israelites come knocking at his door to help them deal with the threat of invasion from the neighbouring Ammonites. Jephthah naturally demurred at first but eventually agreed to lead their campaign to drive back the invaders. Up to this point the tale looks no different from many another Old Testament story of righteous resistance to invasion until, that is, the eve of his final assault on the Ammonites.

At this critical juncture Jephthah made a vow to the Lord that eventually rebounded back on himself. If the good Lord agreed, he said, to deliver his enemies into his hands, he would, when he returned home, sacrifice whoever came out from his house to great him. The victory he craved was not long in coming but, sadly for Jephthah, his first welcome on coming home was from his daughter and only child who came out to meet him 'with timbrels and with dances.'[3] Hearing the news of the vow from her father's mouth, she accepted the consequences of her plight with one proviso. Her request was that her sacrifice be postponed for at least two months. What she planned to do with that time is perhaps best left for the Old Testament itself to describe:

'Let this thing be done for me,' she said, 'let me alone two months, that I may go up and down upon the mountains, and bewail my virginity, I and my fellows.

'And he said, Go. And he sent her away for two months: and she went with her companions, and bewailed her virginity upon the mountains.'[4]

On returning with her companions from the mountains, we are told, the vow was duly carried out and she was sacrificed.

Now vows like this one that rebound on the self are, like divine curses and other inexplicable acts of 'deus ex machina', the devices used by authors in the Ancient World to bed into the text material that they found incomprehensible in their sources but which they nevertheless felt had to be incorporated in the narrative. If we strip away the story line from this odd tale what we are left with is some folk memory of maidenly sacrifice at the climax of rites of mourning and lamentation held by bands of young women in the surrounding mountains. Could these have been the rites of our dying and resurrecting lunar maiden? That rites they were and not just a fairy tale is confirmed by the last few lines of the story, in which we are told,

'And it was a custom in Israel that the daughter of Israel went yearly to lament the daughter of Jephthah the Gileadite four days in a year.'[5]

157

There is what seems like a chilling sequel to this tale a few chapters later in the story of the Levite's concubine. The Levites were part of the priesthood of Israel. This particular Levite had a rather wayward concubine who left him in some disarray and returned to her father's house. Obviously genuinely fond of the woman, the deserted husband duly set off to fetch her back. Well received by her father, he stayed rather longer than intended but eventually headed home with his concubine, presumably now reconciled to her fate, riding alongside. On the way back they stopped for the night in the town of Gilbeah. It was not easy to find lodgings in the town although in the end they did find someone hospitable enough to put them up for the night.

No sooner were they settled in when danger came knocking at the door in the shape of local sodomites keen to have carnal knowledge of this new male visitor to the town. The master of the house did his best to protect his guest by offering in place of him his own daughter and the concubine. Evidently catholic in their tastes, the predators took the concubine who was then abused 'all the night until the morning.'[6] So violent was her treatment at their hands that the next morning her husband found her lying in her death throes in the street outside. His response was to carry her corpse homewards on the back of his ass. Arriving home, he took a knife and butchered the body into twelve sections each rotting part of which he sent as a message to the tribes of Israel. Shocked by the barbarity of the murderous rape of the concubine and alerted by the message, the tribes gathered together at Mizpeh in Gilead to punish the perpetrators of the act.

There are one or two suggestive pointers in this primitive tale. Mizpeh, where the action ends, was also, we recall, the town where Jephthah lived. It was actually where we are led to believe his daughter's sacrifice took place. The connection is suspicious. Could these two stories, not so very far apart in the Old Testament text, refer to different aspects of the same rite? It is interesting that the host in the second tale tried to protect his lodger by offering his own daughter in addition to the concubine. She was a maiden, we are told, but she appears only to vanish immediately from the text. Could maiden and concubine be one, in fact, or at least could the image of this maiden have been associated once with what happened to the concubine. Could the story of multiple rape be a distorted account of sexual congress linked to the dying maiden rites? To carry the argument further, was it Jephthah's daughter whose body was divided into twelve parts? Did her blood cement together the early confederation of the Israelite tribes? The concubine, we are told, came from Bethlehem. This town is not far from Mizpeh. Both lie close to Jerusalem but on opposite sides. Bethlehem, we remember, had a cult of Adonis before it had a cult of Christ. Could Adonis, the dying god, have replaced a dying goddess before giving way in his turn to the Christian saviour? So much is speculation. The issues remain unresolved.

With the sacrifice of Jephthah's daughter what little we have grasped of the dying goddess returns to the shadows again. It is not till much later in the Old Testament that she emerges again and, when she does so, it is in a more civilised context and in a far more abstract and sophisticated guise. It is perhaps not surprising that she should have changed since her last appearance for in the intervening period centuries of patriarchal theological development have altered the whole tenor of the text. We find her, in point of fact, reduced to the personification of an abstract concept. Wisdom is what she personifies and we find her crying in the streets,

'Wisdom crieth without; she uttereth her voice in the streets: She crieth in the chief place of concourse, in the openings of the gates: in the city she uttereth her words...'[7]

Lamentation was an old goddess theme but in her new translucent form the goddess no longer mourns for her daughter or herself. Now the object of her sorrowing is the folly of men who have wandered from the path of righteousness. The goddess, in other words, has finally been absorbed by Jewish monotheism. It is cruelly ironic that the former object of the anger and resentment of the patriarchs should have been co-opted in the role of Jehovah's commissar. But the full extent of the power and prestige she once enjoyed is revealed in Proverbs chapter 8 where she describes how, although possessed by the Lord, she was actually brought forth before the creation:

'I was set up from everlasting, from the beginning, or ever the earth was. When there were no depths, I was brought forth; when there were no fountains abounding with water. Before the mountains were settled before the hills was I brought forth: While as yet he had not made the earth, nor the fields, nor the highest part of the dust of the world. When he prepared the heavens, I was there: when he set a compass upon the face of the depth: When he established the clouds above: When he strengthened the fountains of the deep: When he gave to the sea his decree, that the waters should not pass his commandment: When he appointed the foundations of the earth: Then I was by him, as one brought up with him: and I was daily his delight, rejoicing always before him; Rejoicing in the habitable part of his earth; and my delight was with the sons of men. Now therefore hearken unto me, O ye children: for blessed are they that keep my ways.'[8]

This is an image of such potency that the Old Testament writer who created it must surely have been, whether he realised it or not, a 'de facto' goddess worshipper. What is more, so pervasive is this last enigmatic trace in Judaism of the divinely feminine, so powerful its influence on the early Christian church that it is worth analysing it in detail to see just how it had come down from the cult of the goddess.

There is an entire literature on the subject of Wisdom in the Old Testament. The earliest examples of it are in the Book of Proverbs. This was compiled in the course of the fourth century B.C. Much of its material is older than this, however, and a lot of it can be traced back to the wellsprings of so much ancient religious thought in the heartlands of Mesopotamia. The people of Israel were familiar with the traditions of these lands ever since they had been exiled there by successive Mesopotamian powers. Their exile ended officially in 538 B.C. All were free then to return. Most, it seems, chose to stay and it was in the unbroken schools of thought they established there that the Wisdom tradition was formed. Mesopotamia, we recall, is the region where the tablets recording the myths of Inanna and Ishtar have been unearthed and it is the image of these goddesses we see partially restored in the Old Testament figure of Wisdom.

Like them she is a blend of boundless, unconditionable love and occult knowledge. Like them, too, she has her dark side.

'I also will laugh at your calamity', she warns, 'I will mock when your fear cometh'.[9]

She shares with them the symbol of the tree of life.[10] She copies their descent although such now is the state of divine transcendence that hers is not like theirs from the earth to the underworld but to earth from the heavens above. Her descent is a cause of lamentation[11] not only hers but her maidens as well.[12] For her as well there is the hope of return. She retains their lunar number symbolism. Seven pillars of wisdom support her house. Mother, bride or handmaiden of the patriarchal god, she remains the goddess in all but name.

Such a pre-eminently feminine symbol could not remain forever so close to the spreading power of the patriarchal god. At the time the proximity of the two divine principles must have seemed confusing. There is a mercurial aspect to Wisdom personified, a lack of definition in her role and status. Was she there with the Lord by his side helping him in the Creation or was she too his creation, a figure he had forged himself as a useful apprentice? Such doubts must have induced some tension and it is not surprising, therefore, that, as time passed, Wisdom began to suffer some diminishing in her status. How this occurred is worth exploring for it was to have notable effects on the Gospels' conception of the career of Christ.

The Gospels were compiled in the first century A.D. The general consensus among scholars is that the first gospel Mark was written at the earliest around A.D. 55 and much more likely in the early seventies, with Matthew and Luke following some time in the 80's and the last one, John, after the turn of the century. Who their authors were is still disputed. Less a matter of debate is the nature of the audience they wrote for. This consisted of largely Greek-speaking gentile and Jewish Christians scattered around the great urban communities of the Eastern Mediterranean. In this cultural world the old idea of Wisdom began to metamorphose around the beginning of the Christian era. As a divine principle she began to be first symbolised then masculinised in the image of the Holy Ghost or Spirit. As Christian doctrine developed, she was then defined as the third member of a masculine Trinity: god the father, god the son and god the holy ghost. The division of the Trinity is an interesting notion in itself for it suggests a last faint echo of the old Trinitarian goddess figure that had otherwise long since disappeared. This attempt to incorporate the vestiges of the goddess into the developing mythology of Jesus Christ was not at first entirely successful. The last category to be defined in the Christian pantheon, the Holy Spirit never achieved the definitional clarity of the more tangible father and son. To add confusion, the symbol retained a number of its old feminine accoutrements, most notably the myth of its descent. A glance at the Gospels reveals how their authors tried to cope with this confusion.

Wisdom can still be found occasionally in the Gospels lingering under her own name. We find her explicitly in the text of Matthew, the most Jewish of the Gospels, in chapter 11 verse 19 and chapter 13 verse 54 where Jesus's detractors in his own land around Nazareth use her to question his credentials, 'Whence,' they ask, 'hath this man this wisdom, and these mighty works?'

These are fleeting references, however, and do not alter the drift which is towards the absorption of Wisdom into the image of the Holy Spirit. The incorporation was not easy for the Gospel authors. Old symbols and associations still clung to Wisdom and forced contradictions in the text. Most intractable of all was her ancient prerogative of descent. This we first see in action at the beginning of the earliest Gospel, Mark, where it is used to make Jesus look like the inheritor of the earlier and well attested mission of John the Baptist. As a young movement it was important for the early Church to establish such credentials. In the course of Jesus' baptism by John the author of Mark has 'the Spirit like a dove descending upon him.'[13] The dove, of course, was an old goddess symbol. Later Gospel writers tended to de-emphasise the role of John in this encounter but the fact that all four refer to it establishes its importance in the propaganda of the early Church.

Now the fact that the author of Mark has this ancient goddess force exercise her old prerogative and descend from on high into the figure of the baptised Christ suggests logically that she could not have been within him in the first place. In Mark this is evidently the inference we are left to draw, for there is no earlier mention of her presence in him in the text. Mark's Christ like that of the other Gospels has his own myth of descent. In fact, as we have seen, he has two descents, from heaven to earth and then to the tomb and back again. The issue which the author of Mark failed to face was that if the descending god requires a third descent from an external source and in adulthood at that, to get his mission rolling, then surely the significance of his own descent into incarnate form in the first place is so much the less. There is evidence that later writers saw this weakness in the story. No doubt this is why Luke in particular has Jesus's own earthly mother Mary actually impregnated with the Holy Spirit. That way, the two descents, of Jesus to earth and of the Spirit into Jesus were effectively collapsed into one.

The earlier contradiction was not entirely ironed out of the text for Luke still has the Spirit descending upon Jesus, as if for the first time, in his baptism by John. There was also a price to pay for including this device in patriarchal doctrine. By seeding the womb of Mary with the Spirit the author of Luke was laying the ground for her later elevation in the Christian pantheon. More significant for Christian dogma, however, was what happened in the Gospel of John. Here, in the last of the Gospels, the development we see beginning in Luke is taken to its logical conclusion. As the incarnation of the Spirit, the Spirit of divine truth, the saviour becomes the incarnation, in effect, of the Word of God, the Word 'made flesh'.[14] This transformation of Wisdom went hand in hand with her masculinisation. This was almost certainly facilitated by the translation of Gospel material from Hebrew into Greek. We can trace the process in the changes of gender that occurred in the text. The feminine Hokhmah, Hebrew 'Wisdom', the Greek 'Sophia', was transformed into Greek 'Hagion Pneuma', Holy Spirit, neither masculine nor feminine, which increasingly in John gave way to 'Logos', the Greek masculine 'Word' of God.

Mary's impregnation by the Holy Spirit ensured her eventual near-deification by the later Christian Church. 'Near' remains the operative word for Mary as the mother of Jesus was never more than a conduit for the divine. This does not mean that she did not retain some power. As the bearer of a womb that had been sanctified she became a moral symbol, in a sense a kind of purgative agent, a cleansing counterpoint to the lascivious Eve. Her purity expunged the primal sin of Eden from the masculine mind. In the faint self-deprecation of her downward glance, the coyly lidded eye, we see in the shy, retiring, Virgin with her child the vanishing after-image of a much more radiant and commanding power, Ishtar, sparkling in her jewels and stamping in the blood of mutilated men, Inanna alight with lunar fire, Artemis of Ephesus for whom holocausts of live animals were once corralled and burned. It is but the wan and ghostly hand of such goddesses that in Mary's fond embrace still clings to the Christian myth. In Mary we reach the end of the goddess story or so it might have seemed until the discoveries at Nag Hammadi.

In December 1945 an Arab peasant unearthed fifty-two texts that had lain concealed for hundreds of years at Nag Hammadi in Upper Egypt. The writings were Coptic translations of Greek originals. The papyrus and its Coptic script was dated to somewhere around the fourth century A.D. The originals, it was generally agreed, went back much earlier, to the first century at least. Some were perhaps even older than the writings of the New Testament, older, some said, than the first gospel Mark. They were truly a motley collection of texts, poems, myths, secret gospels, cosmogonies and works on magical and mystical practice.

From the asseverations of the early Church fathers we know that a number of these texts were considered heretical by the Church. In fact, some had been systematically rooted out and burned at the time. Hence the importance of the find, for the writers of these scripts did not see themselves as heretics at all. They believed they had the true 'knowledge', 'gnosis' in Greek, which is why today they are called Gnostics from the Greek word. Although they may not have seen themselves as heretics, this was certainly the opinion held of them by the Church which is why until the discoveries at Nag Hammadi most of what we know of their movement came from orthodox attacks upon it. In point of fact, some of their writings had already come to light prior to Nag Hammadi although their true significance had not been grasped. The most important of these earlier finds was made at Cairo in 1896. A German Egyptologist bought a manuscript that contained, to his surprise, a Gospel of Mary featuring Mary Magdalene and three additional texts. One of these other texts, the *Apocrypha of John*, was found in triplicate at Nag Hammadi. Clearly such writings circulated widely in the Ancient World.

The Gnostic movement which produced the scripts at Nag Hammadi was probably at its strongest about a hundred years after the birth of Christianity. It appeared first in Syria.[15] From there it spread south to Samaria and the borders of Judaea. Around the time of the Emperor Hadrian (A.D. 110-38) it developed a powerful following in Egypt. Not long after that it reached its apogee. At its height there were Gnostic communities dotted around the entire Mediterranean. It was a movement in which a number of influences were mixed, Platonism from the Greeks, mysticism from the East, and a smattering of theology from the Hebrew Bible. It is its attitude to the Old Testament which helps us to locate it in the religious context of the times. Christianity, we saw, tended to recruit the Old Testament in support of its doctrines.

The Gnostics also quoted the Hebrew Bible but with greater ambivalence, almost in an attitude of rebellion against it.[16] It looks as if they were in fact marginalised members of Jewish communities or Gentiles living on the fringes of Jewish life in the cities of the Middle East. The knowledge of the Old Testament revealed in Gnostic texts is not very deep yet their authors felt threatened enough to want to diminish the prestige of the Jewish god by presenting an alternative. Psychologically, this is an important factor to bear in mind when examining Gnostic texts for in creating their alternative Theology many Gnostics turned back to the image of the goddess.

There was never really a Gnostic Church, nothing to compare with the centralising power of the Christian organisation. From its beginning to its end the movement was little more than a loose collection of fissiparous sects, some ascetic, others orgiastic, many cloaked in mystery whose tenets are unknown to this day. Vows of secrecy leave us dependent on hearsay. Sadly for the Gnostics' case, the hearsay comes from the pens of their triumphant Christian enemies. It is possible these may have exaggerated the composite nature of Gnostic beliefs. Such is the nature of polemics. Yet, diverse though the texts undoubtedly were and deep their doctrinal difference, we can still manage to extract a common kernel of beliefs.

The 'knowledge' the Gnostics claimed was not of sin and repentance but enlightenment. In this, however, they were as much a victim as Christianity of the transcendence of the divine that had occurred by this time throughout the Ancient World. Like the Christians at their most extreme, the Gnostics yearned for release from a godless, corrupting material world. The difference lay in the stratagems they chose to free themselves. For these they found justification in their myths. Man, they agreed with the Christians, had a spirit self, a soul. In the Gnostic imagination it was like a spark of divine light. Aeons ago, they believed, it had been caught and trapped in matter.

The perpetrators of this entrapment were the malevolent powers of darkness. By guile and cunning these demonic powers had managed to lull mankind into a sleep of the soul that had left it drifting like a somnambulist on earth, unconscious of its lost spirit self. For the Gnostics the tragedy for mankind lay not in its sinful but in its sleeping state. Only gnosis, the knowledge of its formerly enlightened state, could reawaken the sleeper and return him to the consciousness of his divine origin. Such consciousness could never come from another's sacrifices for it had somehow to be awakened within the self. Yet sacrifice of a kind there was from on high. To liberate mankind a succession of emanations flowed down to earth from the ethereal world of light. The last of these emanations to try to shake mankind from its dormant state was Wisdom.

Wisdom we have met before in the Old Testament and we have noted her powerful goddess features. We have also observed the tension she created there in close proximity to the male god. To a degree the same tension afflicted Gnosticism. We can see this as soon as we explore their cosmogony. In the beginning, the Gnostics believed was Light, eternal, infinite, incorruptible. To this principle of light was opposed one of Darkness. Out of their eternal battle was to emerge mankind's tragic fate. The supreme embodiment of light was the primordial father, unbegotten, imaginable only as a glittering sea of light. Out of him came a thought, the celestial mother, the first woman, the Holy Spirit some said.

This archetypal feminine principle became his co-creator. So prominent was she in the work of creation that some Gnostics believed she may have been from the beginning co-existent with him. Together they created the Primordial Son, Adam, the Archetype of man, followed by aeons, ages or orders of the universe in space and time. The last of these was Wisdom. Wisdom, or Eve as she was sometimes called, gave birth out of herself unseeded, unaware she had usurped the prerogative of the primordial father. Her offspring was a misbegotten power, the Demi-Urge, and ultimately also the lower world of demonic principalities and powers. The lowest of all these worlds was the base material world of Man. But Man has from his remote origins a spark of her divine light which gnosis 'knowledge' can awaken if it can escape the thrall of the demonic powers. To awaken him and bring back the light, the emanations then descend from on high until finally a repentant Wisdom herself goes down. Unfortunately she too finds herself mired in the world of matter. To free her, the Primordial God of Light must descend himself or send his son and in the process liberate mankind too from the grip of matter and the domination of the lower power.

No outline of Gnostic mythology could be anything more than a generalisation from a diversity of different texts. Nor in the conditions of the time, could any theory of the beginnings of things avoid the vexed issue of the role of gender. In confronting this issue Gnostic writers faced the same dilemma as the authors of the Old Testament but they sought to resolve it in a far less patriarchal way. To begin with at least, their description of a god of light in counterpoise to the forces of darkness could be slid with ease between the lines of the first chapter of Genesis. Where the two myths begin to diverge is at the point when the feminine principle surfaces in the Gnostic text. Not only is this much earlier in the Gnostic version but it is with a considerably more elevated role and status. In some Gnostic cosmogonies indeed the point of entry is shunted back to make the goddess virtual co-ruler of the universe as member of a dyad.

Whatever her initial status, on one point there is little doubt. To her can be traced the genealogy of man. Old Testament Adam, we recall, was formed by God in the absence of the opposing gender. When that gender finally arrived in the text it did so by a weird peripheral trajectory from Adam's rib. In Gnostic myth by contrast, the origins of terrestrial man are traced to a usurping act of parthogenesis. The perpetrator of this act of self impregnation is feminine Wisdom, Eve as she was called in some texts, herself descended from the Celestial Mother. Thus two generations of heavenly women separate Gnostic man from the kind of birth that Adam had. These feminine origins tended to survive even after Gnosticism started to become more christianised. In the Gnostic Gospel of Thomas for example Jesus refers to the Holy Spirit as his divine in contrast to his earthly mother.[17]

Parthogenetic birth harks back to the oldest of our matriarchal myths. Equally derivative from a goddess source was the descent of Wisdom. We witnessed the descent of Wisdom in the Old Testament but the descent of Gnostic Wisdom is refined to a point of far greater dramatic significance. Trapped by demonic powers, she is condemned to wander the material world. The motif recalls Inanna's three nights beneath the earth but with the difference that, in these transcendent times, the material world has taken the place of the Mesopotamian underworld as the dreaded place of no return. What we see in the Gnostic myth is what we suspected lay behind the allusions in the Old Testament, an unbroken narrative tradition stretching back through Inanna's descent to matriarchal times.

In the case of Inanna her rescue required the intervention of the gods, of one, in fact, Enki, significantly the Sumerian god of Wisdom. In Gnostic myth redemption is at the hands of the awakener who must bring Wisdom and mankind back to consciousness of their origins in the world of light. In the earliest Gnostic texts the Celestial Mother is sometimes the awakener. Later this role is often played by the Archetypal Man, the son of the Primordial god. Later still, Wisdom herself is replaced by this divine man, who descends into matter perhaps on the distant analogy of the dying son/lover of the still surviving fertility cults. As Gnosticism became christianised, the figure of Jesus slipped easily into this role of redeemer. Earlier we saw how in his biography two descents were effectively collapsed into one. This device rendered Jesus Christ, in Gnostic terms, both the redeemer and the descending Wisdom figure. What he redeems in this dual form is a fallen world. He is to that extent a second Adam sent to right the primal sin committed by the first.

Gnostic Christs too came down to earth aplenty to redeem mankind not from sin, however, but from the captivity of matter. At the end of his mission the Gospel Christ returned to his heavenly father. In this he was merely following Wisdom's path although here again Gnosticism showed greater fidelity to the old goddess myth. Inanna and Ishtar had had to descend and return through the seven gates of the underworld. In Gnosticism these gates had become the seven zones between earth and the world of light each ruled by its own archon or planetary power. As the goddesses on their way down had had to divest themselves of part of their regalia at each of the gates, so Wisdom on her ascent had to remove in seven stages the material encumbrances of her earthly past.

Wherever we look in Gnostic literature we find a greater tendency than in Christianity to embrace the image of the divinely feminine and introduce its symbolism into the text. If we see Gnosticism as a reaction to Judaism, then the motive for this is partly explained. It was an attempt to counterbalance the extreme patriarchal slant of the Old Testament. In the Gnostics, we might almost say, the old goddess cult fought its last stubborn rearguard before retreating underground. A perfect illustration of this counter-revolutionary bias can be found in one of the texts unearthed at Nag Hammadi. This tells the story of the Garden of Eden through the serpent's eyes.[18] Nothing could be more diametrically opposed to the vision of the Old Testament scribes. For the Gnostics the serpent was the symbol of wisdom and in much of their literature Eve emerges as Adam's teacher and spiritual guide. In one of their texts, the Hypostasis of the Archons, it is she who embodies the spirituality which alone can raise Adam from his benighted entrapment in the material world.[19] As for the Lord who drove her form Eden, who could that have been but the Demi-urge, his bible a ruse to trick mankind, its authors those very demonic powers that delight in obscuring all vision of the source of light?

Given these tendencies, it would have been remarkable if women had not been prominent in Gnosticism. Indeed we find them mentioned frequently among its worshippers. Early Christianity appears to have been no different in this respect. Women are certainly in the foreground of the early Gospel narratives. Whether this reflected a real prominence in the primitive Church or merely a thematic prominence in the fertility myths from which Gospel writers took their images it is difficult to say. Lists of women's names, notably the famous Maries, doubtless figured among their sources. What we can say with certainty is that whatever prominence they may have enjoyed was not long in being suppressed by the later Church.

A number of commentators have pointed the finger at Saint Paul in much of this. A confirmed misogynist, his epistles betray a willingness, wherever possible, to separate women from the mainstream of religious life. In this respect, however, his attitude was perhaps no more than symptomatic of the age. On this point the suggestion has been made that women may have been attracted to the Gnostic sects for the precise reason that they contained elements which had been abandoned by the orthodox Christian Church. The positions they sometimes acquired in those sects deeply concerned the leaders of the Church.

Among the Marcusians, quasi-christian followers of a certain Marcus, women, it was said, were allowed to officiate at the Eucharist. If this was disturbing, more worrying still was the encouragement they received to preach and prophesy. There is plenty of evidence of the existence of prophetesses in the Gnostic texts, like Maximilla and Priscilla of the Montanists and Marcellina of the Carpocratians. Marcellina managed to gather around herself an entire religious community in Rome. Wherever women came to the fore like her, they raised the old male ascetics' terror of sex. In the eyes of the venerable Church fathers her group was a particularly lascivious sect.

Regrettably for the Gnostics, most of what we know of them, apart from their own texts, comes from the pens of their orthodox foes. Much of this is highly charged and polemical, although unquestionably there was a kernel of truth in a lot that was said. Tales about how they smeared semen on themselves after holding it glistening in the light or, worse, ate it mixed in cakes cannot necessarily be dismissed as Church propaganda. Semen as the source of life carried the divine light and could not therefore, in the dogma of some sects, be consigned to matter in the sexual act. Reproduction was pointless. It could only serve to perpetuate entrapment in the material world. Much better to preserve the light by returning the precious semen to the self. In believing this, the Gnostics were as much victims as the orthodox Christians they despised of the patriarchal rise to divine transcendence that had left mankind alienated from the material world.

Yet, despite its limitations, had Gnosticism survived as an influence it might well have left us with a Christianity more oriented to the Goddess. With the benefit of hindsight we can see now why the Church fathers were so keen to persecute the Gnostic sects. They were simply too matriarchal, too fatalistic, too geared to the cyclical and, above all, too worrisomely schismatic for a patriarchal Church heading towards a unified ethical system of sin, free will and guilt. The urgency of the patristic attack is also understandable in the conditions of the time. It used to be thought that Gnosticism was a Christian off-shoot that turned heretical. After the findings at Nag Hammadi that interpretation had to be modified.

It now looks as if Gnosticism was not only contemporary with early Christianity, it may even in some areas have pre-dated it. It was once believed that Christianity supplied the gnostics with their core beliefs. Perhaps the stream of influence should be reversed. One gospel at least, John, is heavily gnostic in a lot of its imagery. We know that at the time there were gnostic gospels in circulation. Together with the themes from the fertility cults and the Old Testament prophetic tradition, Gnostic literature may have constituted the third and final strand in Gospel source material. In the presence of so many Gnostic sects dotted around the Mediterranean this dependence at source would have presented the early Church with the problem of what modern marketers call brand definition. In its struggle to survive in the bustling religious marketplace of the Classical World with its many competing religions and sects the Church had to define a message that would enable its scattered communities to coalesce. Critical to this was the creation of a biography for its founder, a symbol to unite believers and prevent the spread of separate sects. We can imagine there were also many Gnostic candidates for the role of redeemer, potential Gnostic Christs in fact. Fear that any one of such claimants could steal the show may have been the trigger for the production of the first Gospel of Mark.

The anxiety would have been increased by the sight of unofficial gospels going the rounds of the more Christianised Gnostic sects. The objective behind Mark would have been to get the accredited story out so as to scotch the rumours circulating of these other Christs. A number of commentators have pointed to the often crude narrative linkages in Mark. At times the text gives the impression of having been put together in haste and under pressure. Doubtless the same urgency added to the hostility to the Gnostics and their later persecution by the Church. An example of the threat the Church saw can be seen in the career of Simon Magus.

Simon Magus is the only recognised Gnostic leader to get a mention in the New Testament. Although the description of him there is curt and dismissive, we know of him also from accounts elsewhere. Indeed, the size of the following he attracted is attested by the vicious attacks on him by the fathers of the early Church, notably Justin and Irenaeus of Lyons. From their inevitably prejudiced reports of this man and his followers we get a rather lurid picture of their brand of Gnosticism which is more or less confirmed by the New Testament account. It is in the Acts of the Apostles that Simon gets his walk-on part. We find him there operating in the region of Samaria. Now Samaria belonged to the world of Judaism but it was notoriously schismatic, actually pagan in parts. So sinister was its reputation in this regard that orthodox Jews travelling south to Jerusalem would often travel along the far bank of the Jordan river rather than taint themselves by passing through it. Simon, we gather from Acts, had been there for some time and the strength of the movement he had built can be gauged by the extremity of the accusation levelled against it. Simon, we are told, had 'bewitched' the people of Samaria:

'Giving out that himself was some great one: To whom they all gave heed, from the least to the greatest, saying, This man is the great power of God.'[20]

The phrasing of this, it has been suggested, lets slip the attempt by the author to alter his sources.[21] What Simon's followers are more likely to have called him is simply 'the great power', in the original Greek, a claim to divinity the significance of which we shall shortly see. Evidently we are meant to take the accusation of bewitchment of the people quite literally for in the very next verse we read,

'And to him they had regard, because that of long time he had bewitched them with sorceries.'[22]

This also bears out what we are told elsewhere. The Simonians, as they were called, had acquired a reputation for magic and witchcraft.[23]

The allegation lays the ground for a smear a few verses later which has left Simon with an infamous reputation in the annals of the Church. In the lead-up to this carefully prepared aspersion we see Simon, overcome by the power of Philip the Evangelist leading a mission to Samaria, suddenly deciding to abandon his past and become converted and baptised. Immediately he is drawn within the inner circle of the mission's leader. This is odd in itself. It could suggest there was an attempt to incorporate

173

Simonian Gnosticism by the Church in Samaria. Anyway, whatever the reason, Simon soon manages to overreach himself. His 'faux pas' is to offer to buy the secrets of what he believes to be the apostles' magic repertoire. For this he is vehemently condemned by Peter who has just come up from Jerusalem to help Philip's mission. The condemnation is obviously the whole point of the tale for with it Simon vanishes from the text. The sleaziness of the incident reflects the hostility to Simon which was widely felt among the leadership of the early Church.

Simon Magus clearly represented an important threat to the nascent Christian Church. According to Hippolytus, who, admittedly, lived long after these events (he died in A.D. 235), one of the titles assumed by Simon was that of 'Christ'. A Gnostic redeemer, however was not, as we have seen, quite the same as a Christian one. He was the Archetypal man, the primordial son, the last emissary sent to free Wisdom from the imprisonment of matter. Such divine origins would have fitted well with Simon's reference to himself as 'the great power'. According to Clement of Alexandria Simon also referred to himself as 'the Standing One', possibly originally 'the pillar'.[24] The name brings to mind Peter the 'rock' or 'pillar' of the early Church. The conflict between these two figures which we saw engineered in Acts was part of the propaganda of the Church and may well have spread further afield for, if we are to believe Justin, a Church father native to Samaria, Simon had a powerful following in Rome by the time of the Emperor Claudius. A number of stories circulated about the conflict between Simon and Peter in Rome. As a rule, these stories border on the fantastic, virtually a clash of magicians in fact, and omit to give a clear account of the doctrinal matters in dispute. For these we need to turn to the other city with which Simon's name was linked. This was the city of Tyre.

Tyre on the Mediterranean coast to the north west of Israel had been one of the centres of the goddess cult which the Old Testament prophets had found so threatening. To them it was an urban sink of iniquity, a sewer of corruption. The moral aberrations of the city drew upon it a long and bitter tirade from the prophet Ezekiel:

'Behold therefore I will bring strangers upon thee, the terrible of the nations: and they shall draw their swords against the beauty of thy wisdom, and they shall defile they brightness. They shall bring thee down to the pit, and thou shalt die the deaths of them that are slain in the midst of the seas.'[25]

The fact that it is as the personification of wisdom that Tyre is doomed to descend into the pit is interesting because the city was suggested as the source of the idea that enabled Simon to achieve such a hold over his followers. This idea was embodied in the figure of a woman whom, according to Justin, our earliest source for this story, Simon had rescued from a brothel in Tyre. Her rescue from this state of degradation he had effected in the belief, it was said, that she was the incarnation of Gnostic Wisdom. This was merely the last in a succession of incarnations on earth, each one more degrading than the last, until eventually she had ended up in the brothel in Tyre where Simon claimed to have found her.

It was the powers of darkness, the Simonians believed, who had forced Wisdom to suffer this cycle of humiliation. Such was her shame that the supreme God had come down himself to free her in the incarnate shape of Simon. He was not trapped, of course, for he was not a man. He had merely assumed the characteristics of a man to conceal his divine essence from the demonic powers the better to effect her escape. Such trickery was a common motif in Gnostic myth. Through his descent he would free not only her but anyone who chose to join her. Ordinary mortals would thus be shown how to escape from the prison of earthly existence and return with her to the light from which they had come.

Thus far, what the Simonians believed appears not unlike the doctrine of other Gnostic movements at the time. According to Valentinus, a Christian Gnostic of the second century, the fate of Wisdom was likewise the axis upon which the destiny of mankind would turn. It was her fall, he believed, which had trapped mankind in the charnel house of matter. Like her mankind must be redeemed and for the Valentinians as for the Simonians redemption would come by the grace of a male divine saviour. There was nothing very original in this. The concept of a Gnostic redeemer had been around for some time and may indeed have been influenced by what the Gnostics read in the orthodox Gospel accounts of the life of Christ.

What was original, if the Church fathers are to be believed, was that the Simonians chose to extend the myth by presenting the incarnate symbol of Simon as a part of its embodiment. In other words, they were doing, in effect, what the Church was attempting through the Gospel narratives. They were historicising their myth by presenting their redeemer in a biographical form. Not only Simon but Wisdom herself had had a human form. According to the Church fathers, who presumably on this point took the Simonians at their word, the two of them had travelled around together. We cannot be sure that two such figures ever really existed any more than we can be certain of the historical reality of Jesus Christ. But that is not the point. The crux of the matter and the point at issue between the Simonians and the Church was that they like it had a historical myth. Hence the particular hostility to them of the leaders of the Church.

Of less interest to us than Simon at this point is the incarnation of the Wisdom he espoused. She was called, the Church fathers tell us, 'the first Ennoia', or first thought. The name recalls the myth of the celestial mother emerging as a thought of the Gnostic god. More intriguing, however, was her earthly name. This was Helen. In view of her connection with the goddess-worshipping city of Tyre it seems a significant choice. It reminds us of the Hanged Helen of our dying goddess myth, the alter ego of Artemis and like her linked to the moon. As an aspect of the moon goddess, Helen like Artemis, Kore and Ishtar would have been worshipped at Tyre as she was throughout the Eastern Mediterranean well into the Christian era.

Could the Simonians have been the last lineal inheritors of the dying goddess myth? The idea is not so fanciful as at first it seems. Helen was above all a symbol of lunar wisdom.[26] So the conceptual link with Gnostic Wisdom is patently clear. The descent to entrapment is another theme shared. The 'Helen' symbol may go back, in fact, to the very origins of the Simonians. The teacher of Simon himself, it was said, was a certain

Dositheus, whose sect had thirty disciples and one woman Helene, whom the group identified with Selene, another goddess of the moon.[27]

The lunar goddess, the 'Helen' of the primal myth had descended to the underworld. Her destination was the axis mundi, the tree of life and knowledge in the orchard of paradise. Mythologically, trees were formalised as pillars. Pillars became icons of the goddess throughout the Ancient World. We are reminded of Simon's other title: 'the pillar' 'the standing one', an ascription also applied to Dositheus, his teacher, who was known as 'the upright one'. The symbol travelled into Christianity in the description of Peter, in fact, his very name in Greek, the 'rock' or 'stone'. For the Gnostics, we know, the journey to the pillar became a journey to salvation from a degraded material world. Have we in the doctrines of the Simonians the final abstraction of our lunar myth?

According to Justin, Simon Magus was the founder of the entire Gnostic heresy in Samaria, creating there a movement which later spread throughout the known world. Writing much later, Justin could not have known Simon Magus if indeed he ever existed. What Justin knew was what had been handed down by tradition in his native Samaria. That tradition gave Simon a Samarian birthplace in the village of Gitta. Not far from there was the city of Sebaste, a Roman colony in Christian times. In the ruins of this city a temple has been found which we can almost certainly attribute to the goddess Persephone.[28] Sebaste was only a few miles from the city of Samaria whose inhabitants, Acts tells us, had been bewitched by Simon Magus. Persephone in myth was, as we saw, the 'Helen' of the underworld, the lunar goddess beneath the earth. Was it from her cult that the Simonians took their own symbol of Wisdom, their own 'Helen'?

There is a parallel to Helen in the Gospels. This is the figure of Mary Magdalene. We have already noted her primacy at key points in the Gospel narrative. Like Helen there are dark undertones in her past life. There is a similar reference to enthralment by demonic powers. From her, we recollect, were cast out seven devils. The image brings to mind the seven archons or demonic powers of Gnostic myth. We are left with the suspicion that Jesus was her exorcist,[29] in other words, her redeemer, the Simon to her Helen. If the redemption was part of Church tradition then we can only presume it has been carefully removed from the text. Not so easily effaced was her role as chief witness of the Resurrection. This must have been so deeply bedded into early Christian tradition that it could not be so easily extruded from the text. In Mark she is very definitely the first witness.[30] Her solitary testimony is the only evidence at first. John, although much later, keeps faith with this tradition although its author has Peter and another disciple at least see the empty tomb before Mary actually witnesses the risen Christ. Matthew retains her as the first witness but this time not alone. Another Mary alongside her also sees Christ.[31] The accompaniment represents a subtle downgrading of her individual testimony. What Matthew has begun is completed in Luke in which Mary is allowed only to see the empty tomb, and then in the company of other women, but not the resurrected Christ.[32]

That Mary Magdalene once enjoyed a much more elevated status is affirmed by Gnostic Christian texts. In the Gospel of Philip uncovered at Nag Hammadi she is presented as Jesus' most intimate companion.[33] Their relationship has a flavour almost of the amorous. Jesus, we are told, would kiss her often on the lips, much to the dismay of his disciples. So entrenched is the position of Gnostic Mary in the circle of Jesus's confidantes that in another text, the Pistis Sophia, she provokes the wrath of the apostle Peter. His outburst earns him a rebuke from Jesus. Above all, it is in the Gospel of Mary that we get the best glimpse of the role Mary Magdalene may have played in the early Christian story.

As the gospel opens, we find the disciples huddled together, frightened and depressed after Jesus's death. Mary, it seems, is the only one who can raise the morale of the group which she does by pointing to the constant spiritual presence of Christ in their lives. It is she then who is asked, significantly by Peter, for some uplifting recollection of Jesus's words. She responds not by recalling some event from the past but tells them instead of a vision of the saviour she has seen. Her recital leaves the tearful Mary the object of ridicule in the group. Evidently in Gnostic

Christian circles such trance-like visions of the saviour's return were already giving way to what would eventually become the orthodox account of an actual physical resurrection.

We are led to wonder whether this kind of material figured in the source material used by the Gospel writers. Its presence there would certainly account for the ubiquity of Mary in the Resurrection scenes. We have observed the Gospel writers attempts to diminish the significance of her testimony by tinkering with the text. Their motives are not difficult to understand. The concept of the Resurrection was the pivot of the Christian myth. Upon its acceptance all else turned. It was crucial therefore that the leadership of the early Church should have some tradition of special cognizance of this event, a testimony of its truth belonging to themselves. What better justification for their temporal power? Already in Matthew we see clear signs that the leadership would be that of Peter, the 'rock' on which the Church would build.[34] To writers keen to push his claims the presence of Mary as the first witness of the Resurrection must have been embarrassing. Hence their attempt to push her to the wings while simultaneously bringing Peter closer to the centre of the stage.

The texts unearthed at Nag Hammadi are, many of them, already christianised. The question emerges whether even they give us a realistic idea of just what kind of Gnostic material lay in the sources of the orthodox Gospel accounts. One thing we can be sure of. That source material was heavily doctored prior to insertion in the Gospel narratives we read today. Our evidence for this is what we see the different Gospels doing to each other as they go about the task of creating their narratives. As we pass from Gospel to Gospel we see how, for example, Matthew and Luke are quite prepared to alter the story line in Mark if it suits their objectives. Can we expect the author of Mark to have been any less cavalier with his own sources?

And what of Matthew, Luke and John's non-Markan sources? Would they have shown them any more respect than what they read in Mark's own, to them, orthodox account? Now if all four, against the grain of their prejudice, are reluctant to remove Mary

Magdalene from the scene of the Resurrection, we are entitled to wonder whether her status in their sources was even more elevated than their narratives admit. The stubbornness with which she holds her own as a witness despite all attempts to shift her to the wings leads us to suspect she might once have had a far more central role in this event. Here the comparison with the Simon and Helen story is instructive. Could there have been a similar Jesus and Mary myth? Could Jesus have had Simon's and Mary Helen's role in a far more Gnostic resurrection? Could Mary herself once have been redeemed like Helen form a fallen world? Did she too once enjoy an ascent to heaven returning with her saviour Jesus to her celestial mother in the source of light? Was it on this ascent that she found release from her devils as she travelled through the seven zones of the planetary powers to a Gnostic heaven? Could this be why her shade hovers so persistently around the last days of Christ?

Strip away the overlay of the dying vegetation god and we have in John's Mary Magdalene weeping in the garden by the empty tomb the closest image we shall ever meet to Gnostic wisdom, trapped Helen, bemoaning her tragic fate. Have we in Mary Magdalene the last goddess to ascend, the final Christian testimony to our primal myth?

1 Judges ch. 11 v. 1.
2 Judges ch. 11 v. 2.
3 Judges ch. 11 v. 34.
4 Judges ch. 11 v. 37-38.
5 Judges ch. 11 v. 40.
6 Judges ch. 19 v. 25.
7 Proverbs ch. 1 v. 20-21.
8 Proverbs ch. 8 v. 23-32.
9 Proverbs ch. 1 v. 26.
10 Proverbs ch. 3 v. 18.
11 Proverbs ch. 8 v. 2-3.
12 Proverbs ch. 9 v. 3.
13 Mark ch. 1 v. 10.
14 John ch. 1 v. 14.
15 Doresse J. The Secret Books of the Egyptian Gnostics. Inner

Traditions International Ltd. Rochester Vermont, 1986 p. 12.

16 Maccoby H. Paul and Hellenism SCM Press London. 1991 p. 8.

17 Pagels E. The Gnostic Gospels. Penguin Books, Harmondsworth 1980 p. 74.

18 Pagel E. ibid p. 16.

19 Pagel E. ibid p. 51.

20 Acts ch. 8 v. 9-10.

21 Black M. The Scrolls and Christian Origins. Thomas Nelson and Sons. London 1961 p. 64.

22 Acts ch. 8 v. 11.

23 Doresse J. ibid 1986 p. 16.

24 Quoted in Gouldner M. 'The Two Roots of Christian Myth' in Hicks J. (ed.) 'The Myth of God Incarnate' SCM Press London 1977 p. 72.

25 Ezekiel ch. 28 v. 7-8.

26 Young G. M. 1993

27 Doresse J. ibid p. 15.

28 Vincent O. P. Le Culte d'Hélène ... Samarie. Revue Biblique 1936 pp. 221-232.

29 Luke ch. 8 v. 2.

30 Mark ch. 16 v. 9.

31 Matthew ch. 28 v. 1-10.

32 Luke ch. 24 v. 10.

33 Pagels E. ibid p. 84.

34 Matthew ch. 16 v. 13-19.

Chapter 7

The Loss of the Goddess Myth

Mary Magdalene sitting, weeping by the empty tomb of her Jesus, is not what she seems. So much so far is clear. She is no mere 'fallen' woman. Nor is she just the greatest of Jesus's female disciples, elevated though that title might appear to modern Christians. Rather she is, in company with her 'better' half, the Virgin Mary, the last of the great goddess archetypes of the Mediterranean and the Middle East. Of course, we now know that 'fallen' woman and 'virgin' mother were once the same, the amorous mother lover of the vegetation god. We also know that once it was not him or his Christ-like replica but her daughter, the maiden, her Kore that hung on a tree. So much had changed in the masculinisation of the old myths. Indeed, if we follow the outline of Mary back through the long shadowy line of her predecessors, passing each of them in turn as she appears, Gnostic Helen, Helen of Rhodes, Artemis, Ariadne, Persephone, Ishtar, Inanna, we come to the originating source of them all and a world very different not only from our own but even from that in which the Gospels were written.

The concept of this source we have met before. As for her name, let us call her Tiâmat, for that was the name under which she met her end at the hands of Marduk. It was in Tiâmat or, more precisely, in her belly, that it all began. A dim remembrance of her inclusive power survived in the Bible in the story of Jonah and the great fish. Jonah was swallowed by what is now generally assumed to be a whale and spent three days and three nights cowering in its belly.[1] The significance of the length of his sojourn we now all too readily recognise. It is another reflex of

182

our lunar myth. 'Out of the belly of hell' Jonah prayed for deliverance from his affliction.[2] The Lord heard his prayer and spoke to the whale, which promptly vomited him up from the depths of the sea. To Jonah, no doubt, the world inside a whale's innards was a stark and dismal place. Once, however, the belly of the whale had been the belly of Tiâmat, the goddess of the celestial sea, and the world it enclosed was a warm, inviting place to be.

The world inside the belly of Tiâmat was a world in which all phenomenon, all matter and psyche, were contained and bound within an indissoluble unity. The source of this unity was the goddess herself, conceived as a Great Mother encompassing heaven and earth and embracing all space and all time. As a universal unifying force she was inherent in all nature, in every aspect of its birth, efflorescence, maturation and decline. It was a conception of the divine and the numinous very different from that which produced the later patriarchal gods. This goddess did not hover above this world. It was not her artifact. Instead, she was this world. In all its aspects her identity was manifest. All life was lived out in her embrace. She was the source of all becoming, all change, all multiplicity in phenomena. She was the latent and the manifest. We can imagine such a multi-faceted goddess had many faces, cherishing in the womb, menacing in the tomb, inscrutable beyond imagining in the after-life. How her many representations in the world were conceived we do not know. Eventually she separated out into many goddesses but the idea of her oneness, her indivisible and unitary power, never entirely died out.

From the perceived unity of the goddess, the boundedness of her containment, flowed certain principles of reasoning, a kind of primitive associative logic. As the goddess was immanent in nature, all the phenomena of the natural world, stone, plant, animal or man, were seen to flow together in the same numinous stream. In essence they were the same and could become one another. Ever ready to take the charge of energy from the life force, a stone or a tree could acquire a spirit as easily as a man. The modern wasteland of inert matter did not exist. The material world was not an 'it' but a 'thou'. The active imperium of the human subject, logically and grammatically, had yet to emerge. Its converse, the passive focus of its energy, the object, the grammatical accusative had yet to arrive. In this world of process, of endless becoming, the perceived boundaries between phenomena were infinitely permeable. The fluidity of phenomena created a sensibility which, at the extreme, might have thwarted the needs of human survival. To cut into the bark of a tree was to slice the very flesh of the goddess. To kill an animal was to put at risk her totems in the tribe. Any recklessly destructive act could transgress the sacred unity enshrined in the lore of the goddess.

In the horror of such acts lay the motive springs of expiatory sacrifice. The entire universe was a semiotic system. All phenomena, down to the humblest blade of grass were potential indicators of the mood of the goddess. If all that was manifest in the natural world shared in this macrocosmic pattern then the law of 'pars pro toto' operated. The macrocosm was replicated in every phenomenon as if the vastness of it could be caught prismatically in the mirroring of its own reflected light. The concept was not mechanistic. This was no Newtonian universe moving in measured steps to abstract laws. Rather the organic, the animate lay at the heart of it. All physiological and psychic life, all that we call the material world, was a manifestation of the goddess's own corporeal being, no more capable of an autonomous life than the whorls and arches on her finger tips.

A world of endlessly shifting and transmutable forms allows only the most indefinite concept of space and time. Where process is dominant to this extent the human actor, or rather the human manifestation of the ceaseless becoming, is denied the detachment, the disembodiment, to freeze the frame and develop a conception of time as a linearity beyond the time span of the enveloping process. Time is process, a matter of sequence, a succession of events capable of answering only one question: what happens next? The world of Tiâmat's belly had no beginning, no end. In that partly lay its fatalism for from the infinitude of becoming there could be no release. The energy of the goddess was boundless. The boundedness lay in the finite limits of her encompassing shell. The arc of becoming had constantly to describe the environing contours of her belly. In that constraint lay an inexorable fate. This was why when Marduk peered in he saw Destiny written in the belly.

Energy forced to go the rounds of its receptacle, to retrace its steps, inevitably conveys the image of the cyclical. Processes return and are recognisable as much the same. In an organic universe of this kind the constant iteration suggests a unitary life force eternally restoring and replenishing itself in natural cycles. How these cycles reproduced themselves was a mystery. Physiologically, the biological mechanics of reproduction, the precise connection between ovulation and the sperm, was to remain a mystery until mapped out microscopically in modern times.

In the world of the goddess, as we have observed, ignorance of this process went to the point of excluding entirely the role of the male. Men were simply omitted from the biological equation. In fact, there was no equation, only a unity again. Conception was a mystery of women as unique to them as menstruation, gestation, lactation and birth itself. Women somehow managed to produce life out of themselves just like the renewal of plant and animal life on the earth. In so doing they seemed to replicate the role of the goddess herself making manifest what was latent in the natural world.

The latency was the power source of a goddess immanent in nature. To express itself, the language of immanence is heavily dependent on metaphor. A metaphor in turn is an implied simile. When the ancients pounded an image of the deity with mortar and pestle or carried it in a winnowing fan, the message they were implicitly conveying was that the death of the deity was in some mysterious way like the death of the corn. All similes, all 'likes', can be traced to some partial identification between the things compared. In a world of interchangeable forms that identification was almost complete.

Erizu, the Sumarian corn goddess was the corn in the sense that she was what inspirited its presence from the flowing fields to the cut grain. Identities this permeable are a fertile ground for simile. In the world of the goddess one simile, or rather a triad of similes, was paramount. Earth, moon and woman formed a triad with characteristics so conjoint that they seemed each a mere aspect of the goddess linked in their life cycles by a triple loop of eternal recurrence. Women like the earth gave birth to life, returned like the moon to the underworld and yet lived on, their life force reappearing in the wombs of their daughters. The association gave rise to a complex metaphor visible to all in the night sky, of the moon daughter of earth perpetually returning to her mother to be re-born.

Metaphors are the building blocks of myths. Myths have a story structure. The truth of the story told lies within the mythic structure not beyond it. That is partly why there is no irony in myth. Irony presupposes a perspective detached from the narrative, a perspective that conceals an alternative truth related to the world outside it. The absence of that perspective lends myth an emotional simplicity, a naive, almost child-like engagement with the truth of its message, the truth of a world complete in itself. Not all myths are the same in the degree of seriousness they are intended to elicit. Some are fairly tales. These may contain some nugget of wisdom, even some commentary on the human condition but that is all and their insouciance in this respect allows them to travel freely across time spans and culture zones. In marked contrast are sacred myths. They tell a particular community what it is important for it to know to make sense of the universe. They are thus charged with a special seriousness, a sombre attitude of moral concern.

Myths are related to each other in a mythology. Before the development of historicism mythologies formed much of the history of a culture that enabled it to preserve its memory of its own identity through space and time. That they achieved by providing some intuitive understanding of how the life cycles of the collective were patterned with the cosmic order. In the ancient culture of the goddess worshippers the intuition was embodied in the primal myth of parthogenesis. In the vision of that myth the goddess gave birth out of her own self in the shape of the mound that rose out of the encircling belly of her celestial sea. From the umbilicus, the world tree that connected the mound to the sea in the sky above, rose the moon, daughter of earth, to begin her nightly navigation back to rest in the branches of the same tree mirrored in the counterheaven of the celestial sea beneath the earth before once more rising again from the womb of her mother.

We may call such a myth a cosmogony, an explanation in mythic terms of how the universe began, but it would perhaps be a mistake to imagine it expressing an absolute beginning in the sense conveyed by the biblical myth of how God made heaven and earth in seven days. In a world of process, of endless becoming, in which the perceptual stream has yet to be frozen into a concept of being, of what 'is', the idea of beginnings, and of endings also, tends to be obscured by the interminable round of cyclical recurrence. To the imagination of the goddess worshippers life must have seemed like a convoluting spiral of cycles without end. The cycles may have appeared as events, as happenings, but these events had no autonomy in themselves. They were only mirror images, cyclical repetitions of the events enshrined in myth. What the primal myth presented was not a beginning but an archetype, the cycle of all cycles in the world of myth.

No culture can entirely avoid the fleeting perception that the universe is never as stable as it seems but, instead, an entity in a state of perilous equilibrium. When widely shared, the perception can lead to collective panic. From the trigger of such fears spring sacred rites, the dramatic repetition of obsessional patterns which, if spontaneous within an individual, might be deemed psychotic. Yet it is the same pathology operating in both cases, a forced repetition of what is seized upon as axial to prevent the universe toppling into chaos. The image of chaos in the goddess culture was, it was earlier suggested, the appearance of the lunar eclipse, a phenomenon whose patterning was beyond the measurement capacity of the culture at the time and seemed therefore to violate the laws of the cyclical. No doubt other motives too called out for the dramatisation of the archetypal cycle.

So-called primitive societies are probably as vulnerable as our own to the loss of consciousness of the numinous in the world around them, the routine disinheritance that is an inevitable consequence of the daily struggle for survival. For any culture with a concept of the divine it is essential to incorporate the lives of individuals into the drama of the gods, to ground what is mundane and trivial into the grander archetypes of the collective unconscious. Most threatening of all in robbing life of significance is the palpable finiteness of individual lives. Even in a world of the cyclical all must die and all therefore require some notion of extension of life beyond the grave, a vision of the after-life. To reaffirm the numinous of the divine requires some counterpoint to the routine drudgery of daily life, an interval of sacred space and time in which the ideal can be celebrated in safety from the effects of the profane. This is the function of sacred ritual and for it more dramatic narratives are called for. These narratives we call 'cultic myth'.

The cultic myth of the goddess world, the myth that figured in its most sacred rites, was one of death and resurrection. It was based on the metaphor of the moon as the messenger of eternal renewal and the analogy between its cyclicality and the life cycle of women. Like women the moon filled with fiery menstrual blood and decanted on the full. For the moon, however, the decanting had its tragic aspect. The moon daughter of earth began to die at her menarche, waning to a thin sliver in the sky until finally descending for three moonless nights beneath the earth only to rise again transformed on the fourth night. Only at the eclipse was this reassuring pattern broken and it was the trauma of this destabilising phenomenon that lay at the root of the rites. At the appointed time on the lunar calendar the incarnation of the moon daughter of earth, possibly her effigy, hung on the 'axis mundi', the sacred tree is the tribal centre. From it the shade of the lunar maiden descended to the underworld. The journey took her through the labyrinth beneath the earth. Along it she passed through seven gates. At each her only passport was an item of her sacred regalia. Like the waning moon she was successively divested of her clothes until finally she arrived crouching and naked at the end of the tunnel in the underworld. There she bowed before the goddess, her mother as crone goddess of wisdom, in the shade of the world tree of paradise, the tree of life and knowledge in whose branches coiled the snake, another symbol of eternal recurrence.

188

Up above on earth the lamentations began. In her grief Mother Earth wandered in search of her lost daughter, in fact, her own vanished half swallowed by the crone aspect of herself. Deprived of its fertilising lunar dew, the earth itself began to wither. Only a supreme act of supplication could reverse the return of all life to the primal abyss. An appeal was made to the crone goddess by the priestesses at the rites. She would have to release the maiden from the underworld or all the living would be consigned before their time to the world of the dead. The crone at first demurred but then agreed. On the fourth night the lunar goddess was allowed to ascend. Returning through the underworld gates she was re-invested at each one with her lost regalia. As the new moon, the moon daughter of earth was re-born with the wisdom of the crone. As Earth held her in her arms, there was wild rejoicing. The exaltation soon turned to melancholy. There was a heavy price to pay for the deliverance. The maiden had eaten of the fruit of the underworld tree, a pomegranate, the fruit that was the symbol of the wisdom she had gained. The same fruit would now be her perpetual passport to the underworld. The price of wisdom would be her own endlessly recurring return to the world of the crone.

Myths like this may contain their truths to a degree within themselves but they cannot entirely avoid the constraints of the real world. There must be some verisimilitude, however slender, with the patterned world of nature or the message they bear will cease to be functional for human survival. The power of the old goddess myths to explain the nature of the universe received a shattering blow with the discovery of the role of the male in procreation. The effect was to open a gap in the closed loop of the feminine through which the divinely masculine could enter in. The process by which this occurred has already been charted. The impact was by no means immediate but the end result was everywhere the same.

The diminishing status of a Mother goddess immanent in nature was matched by the rise to transcendence of the male god. His ascent took place in successive stages from water to vegetation god, to god of the air and then of the moon, the sun and the sky. In advancing through these stages the god first seized the starring role in the lunar myth of death and resurrection, then freeing himself from the obligation to descend, went on to take over the heavenly role of supreme creator. At the extreme end of this development was Yahweh or Jehovah, the god of the monotheistic Israelites, a god without women, without even any familial ties. If this was the extreme, then not everywhere did the process of masculinisation run to completion. The Greek poets, Homer and Hesiod, through the fame of their epic tales, froze the Olympian pantheon when the sexes in it were still more or less equally divided. Had they not written when they did, we can imagine Zeus, the Greek father god, would sooner or later have swallowed up the last remaining goddesses around him. Similar circumstances elsewhere may have conspired to create other deviations from the patriarchal path. Thus, somehow, the Egyptians ended up with an earth god, Geb, and the Japanese with a sun goddess not a sun god.

The male god sought transcendence to escape from the thrall of earth with whose resident goddess, so full of fertility, he could never on her terrain ever hope to achieve true equality of status. The struggle to break free from her clutches led the god to abandon the world of becoming, the natural world with its dark, dissolving flow of life returning to the earth, for an immutable world of being, light and soul, a world imperceptible to the senses which only thought could divine. It was perhaps inevitable that his rise should take the form of a release from the tyranny of nature for the natural world was so powerfully associated with the goddess that she could never really be driven from its domain. Also inevitable in a world in which male gods sought the light transcendent was the demonisation of nature as goddess after goddess, driven from the skies, descended to the earth and turned malevolent. Not just nature, but matter in the abstract, acquired dark and potentially chaotic properties, a perception that bore strange fruit in the phantasmagoria of the Gnostics. Mired in this dark world, the body itself became a dangerous source of moral pollution. Hence the concept of the soul arose to free man to join his creator in the heavens. From the beginning the soul belonged to the transcendent world and to this world it naturally wished to return.

We saw how at first the god was forced to adapt to the pattern of the lunar myth and descend to Mother Earth to be resuscitated as a dying vegetation god while at the same time replenishing her vigour with his seed. This phase did not last, of course, but the idea of the descending male did survive in a form far less passive and yielding than this. It assumed the character, in fact, of the underworld quest, a search for light, for eternal life, in the subterranean darkness. In the epic of Gilgamesh the theme is tinged with melancholy, the tragic consciousness of the ultimate fatality of human life, the impossibility of escape from the finite. Barbarised by the Greeks, it turned into an invasion of the underworld. Semi-divine invaders like Theseus and Heracles followed the footsteps of the Mesopotamian Nergal on expeditions to plunder the goddess in her last remaining refuge in the earth. It left the Greeks with the ideal of the hero.

Ortega y Gasset once remarked that ancient man took one step back into the past before contemplating action. In the past lay the blueprints for action, the heroic archetypes. When rationalism destroyed these archetypes, the hero was left in a morally chaotic universe. To the dilemma created by this can be traced the often noted instability of the ego of the Ancient Greeks, an inheritance passed on to the modern West. Heroism of the Greek kind was alien to the emotional climate of the Jewish Old Testament. The nearest to the heroic ideal there was the Messiah, the long-awaited anointed warrior king whose arrival on the world scene would usher in the Last Days. The inheritor of this ideal was the New Testament Christ. In him divergent traditions which patriarchy had produced in its rise were combined and the tensions between them resolved. His career was marked by two trajectories into the world of the divine; one chthonic, followed hero, vegetation god and lunar maiden into the earth and out again, the other, transcendent, returned him to his father in the sky. The inter-weaving of so many archetypes must surely have been part of the source of his emotional appeal to the masses at the time.

As the pantheons of the old goddess religion were masculinised, patriarchal theology began to seek for its new master of the universe the ultimate status of a creator god. At this point, however, it encountered problems in finding a replacement for the matriarchal myth of creation. A god who had risen so far was no longer 'in' the world but 'above' it and could not therefore produce organically out of himself a material world of an entirely inferior status. The dilemma was compounded by his womblessness. Creation thus had to become an act of will with some effluent of himself as a hopeful creative agent. We have seen the lengths to which Egyptian priests went in mimicking the goddess myth by having their gods exploit their spit, vomit, semen, breath and words as agents of creation. Almost every orifice imaginable was brought into action to fill the gap.

In fact, Egyptian gods did everything but excrete the universe into life. A universe so formed could be said to reflect the will of its creator. Were he to retain an interest in his artifact and intervene to re-fashion it at times it might even be seen to manifest his state of mind. Any indication of this, however, was heavily dependent on the intuitive powers of his worshippers. The divine order that had chosen to create this world remained forever superior to nature and even to human consciousness itself. Its realm was a realm of ideas inaccessible to the world of the senses, explorable only by the soul, the conscience, the 'inner ear' of the seeker. Later the soul would give way to the intellect floating free from the body in pursuit of divine reason. Whatever the engagement sought, the divine order was always separate from and superior to the world of nature.

The patriarchal god was compelled perforce to create the universe in this mechanistic way. Yet mechanistic theories of creation evaded the crucial issue of what was to be done with the original creatrix. A goddess immanent in nature still posed a threat. She could be demonised, of course, as a dark force that had somehow managed to outwit the god and survive in monstrous form in the depths of his own creation. As such we find her in the Old Testament in the hideous shape of Behemoth and Leviathan or Jonah's whale. The demonology only served to underscore the power she had once possessed. This power was everywhere still manifest in the world of the Old Testament scribes from the wooded shrines in the countryside to the names of the constellations wheeling overhead. How could any god re-create the universe without in some way destroying her? It was this dilemma which the god Marduk alone chose to confront. His 'final solution' we have had occasion to describe. The new world order was hewn from the goddess by the sword. Its overarching edifice was plastered together from her butchered parts.

There was a price to pay for this violent release from a goddess immanent in nature. We saw how in Egypt the uninterrupted rise to pre-eminence of the masculine divine had ended in a sun god who was still visibly a part of nature even if only discernible in the burning outline of the solar disc. In contrast, Marduk's coup d'état deracinated the divine. Cut from its roots by its own blade, the divinely masculine lifted off into the stratosphere of theological speculation. What Marduk accomplished was a revolution in the skies. As such it was a triumph of the will. In the last resort Marduk alone of all the gods had had the courage to confront the awesome power of the goddess and bring her down. His victory had the finite and determinable shape of a motivated action in mythic space and time. It was a once and for all time event that defied the cyclical. Thus it was a challenge to fatalism. This was the significance of the many myths it spawned of monstrous serpents murdered by male gods. The serpents that died in these heroic encounters were the ancient symbols of eternal recurrence linked to the tree of life. Henceforth the cyclical might re-emerge as a pleasing abstraction in schools of philosophic thought but it had lost forever its value as a reassuring vision of the world.

A universe created as a mechanism, the artifact of a god, a composite of spare parts, is prey to the finite in another sense. It has a beginning, a point of manufacture. Like a perceptible dot on an unending line, it appears at a point in mythic time within the infinite life span of its creator. By the same token it can end at any moment. The cosmic mechanism may cease to function either of its own accord or through the derelict indifference of its creator. Cosmic beginnings and endings give added status to their heavenly creator who seems all the more impalpable by comparison with such finite limitations. Eventually no iconography is fit to express the image of his power. Not only would it be too far beyond the powers of the human imagination to devise. The very thought of creating icons of such a god begins to seem a fearful impertinence. How could anything that emerged by human hand or eye out of his own finite and inferior creation have any hope of embodying his infinite and exalted power?

A universe that could one day come to an end of its own accord or through the malevolence or wilful neglect of its creator is potentially a very unstable place. The more unstable the universe, the more inscrutable seems the will of its creator. Trying to understand the intentions of such a god is like attempting to decode a message from a scrambled signalling system. Now the goddess too had her chaotic side which revealed itself in the horror of the lunar eclipse. The difference was that the apparent chaos of the eclipse was a reflection of herself, a dark aspect of her personality seen through the transparency of nature. It was not a chaos that could separate off and career like a juggernaut along its own crazed path.

Yet this was exactly the scenario most feared from the universe that Marduk created. It left his Mesopotamian worshippers in a nightmare world of demonic forces that had to be appeased by endless rituals. It also left them clinging to the fiction that he might at least impart some tolerable stability to his own creation by returning annually at the New Year Festival to determine the destiny of all things for the coming year. The problem for his worshippers was how to read the fates Marduk had decreed. Their only hope was to find some patterning, some ordered reflection of his will, in the bewildering complexity of the world of nature. The search for this patterning led to the growth of astrology, a primitive empiricism of which the Mesopotamians naturally became the most adept practitioners in the Ancient World.

The elevation of the male creator god not only destabilised the world. It also plunged it into darkness. In the old goddess cult light was a reflection of the presence of the goddess in the here and now of the natural world. The identification of the god with light and his subsequent rise to the ethereal regions beyond the world of the senses deprived the earthly world of its ownership of light, which was now seen as a mysterious property of the

194

godhead that somehow managed to trickle down from him to the murky depths of matter he had left behind. It was an easy step, then, for male theologians to equate matter, chaos and darkness and to complete the equation by the demonisation of the ancient feminine powers of earth. The effect of this equation was to give light a moral quality it had not before possessed. Moralising the light that was the essence of the divine, making it the focus of a system of ethics, helped to hold stable the image of the creator in an otherwise unstable world. It created a point of connection, a pathway to the intentionality of the god. By moralising his god and then by incorporating the system of ethics, the worshipper could also feel himself to be swelling his soul with ethical light, building up enough ballast, as it were, to enable him eventually to float up to the divine source of light itself. There an eternal state of grace awaited him in the company of his creator. This was the dilemma then, either to rise above nature to the celestial source of light or sink into the dark, sinful, feminine chaos of the material world, and it explains so much of the asceticism, the punitive self-abnegation of masculine religion, so alien to the psychology of the goddess cult.

We have emphasised the importance of the image of the cyclical in the goddess cult. The concept of the cyclical is in some ways antithetical to morality as we understand it. The nearest it offers is a kind of 'natural' morality. Life seems most ordered, most harmonious in such a vision of the world when lived with sensitivity and compassion, in attunement to the ever-recurring cycles that govern it. Very different is the morality that follows when the cyclical universe is replaced by one with an absolute beginning and a conceivable end, one, moreover, created by a 'moral' god as a kind of test of his own inscrutable intentionality, a deliberately baffling experience for its human incumbents. Then, inevitably, the pressure is away from the cyclical and towards the linear.

The motives, the 'morality' of the creator function like a set of coordinates which the human soul must track and follow in order to survive and reach its goal. The linearity of this conception is apparent in the metaphors we use to speak about the moral life. We talk of 'keeping to the straight and narrow', 'toeing the line', 'not wandering from the path' and so on. Moral reckoning of this kind implies some notion of progress. The search for some sort of resolution of the inner tension it creates offers the distant hope that the resolution sought may one day be achieved. We have seen the importance of the people of Israel as path-finders at this stage of patriarchal development. The Bible offers us the illusion of a dialectical progression. Not only does it have an absolute beginning but it also prophesies an end, a day of disaster for the heathen and the Israelite unfaithful, a day of deliverance for the righteous among the chosen people. The idea pervades the Old Testament. The Christians were its direct inheritors. There is little doubt that the early Church confidently expected an immediate end to the world with the second coming of the Messiah. Nor did the idea end there. It has had a radical effect on the social and political ideas of the West. From it, in fact, derive, all our modern concepts of evolutionary progress. Whether Marxist or Capitalist, they are merely the materialisation of that original end-state of heavenly grace so long the gift of the patriarchal god.

The world of the cyclical is a world not of will but of necessity. The more cyclical the world seems, the more everything seems to recur in a pattern of return, the greater the fatalism the vision bestows. At a certain point the notion of an unconditioned will, the very source of activism, begins to seem absurd. A fruitful and fulfilling life can only be lived in a state of constant awareness of the endless return. Such may have been the natural attitude, the taken for granted reality of life lived according to the precepts of the lunar myth. If so, Marduk's revolution would have caused a fateful breach. It opened up the untrammelled will of the creator for future generations to behold.

By example it also set a blueprint for the conduct of life on earth. The free will exercised by the creator god extended the compass of the human psyche which, reflecting the divine, also caught a glint from the voluntarism of the creator. Henceforth, men, too, could ape their god and subject the world of nature to their will. The conviction of free will also hollowed out the human psyche by turning it into a battleground of competing motives. The two effects were linked for it is only the emptiest souls which seek to fill themselves by ingesting those they have subjected to their will. Here the experience of the people of Israel is once more instructive. Combining the monotheism of Aten with the wilfulness of the Mesopotamian creator god, they forged the image of a particularly intrusive and volatile god. The result was, as we have witnessed, a massive and unstable interiority of guilt, conscience and sin which they could only control by a constant search for some clue as to the mood and motives of their god.

What the people of Israel created was a kind of ethical empiricism, a march for spiritual truth in their collective experience as a people. Vulnerable to much the same stresses of life in a patriarchal universe, the Ancient Greeks, however, tried to resolve them in a slightly different way. Their creator god was Zeus. His name recalls the ancestry of the Greeks. It comes from the same stem as the Sanskrit 'dyaus', 'the bright sky'. The name thus identifies the most primitive conception of this deity as a weather god who later came to embrace the sky and all its phenomena. As such, he came to be worshipped everywhere on mountain tops, most notably that of Mount Olympus. The pattern is one we have noted many times before.

The Greeks identified their Zeus with the planet Jupiter. This was also the planet of Marduk. Zeus shed the wilful character of his predecessor but not his violent path to power. Fragments of the battle with Tiâmat did survive in Greek myth. We find them in the Greek Gaia who produced a monstrous brood of rebels in her attempt to unseat Zeus. The terrible Titans were among the brood. So was the giant Typhon. Their role was similar to that of Kingu in the Mesopotamian myth. The Python, too, belonged to her although its destruction was the work not of Zeus but of Apollo. The fragments litter the landscape of Greek myth but without the connecting coherence of the old story line. What the Greeks had learnt of the destruction of Tiâmat they had clearly either re-interpreted or forgotten. Moreover, the original savage principle of the tale had been civilised and softened. It had acquired more moderate and relaxed motifs. It was not by the sword that Zeus consolidated his domain but by trickery and dalliance. Where Marduk hacked the world out of the belly of the goddess, Zeus consummated his victory in the marriage bed.

Powerful though Zeus became, he never quite attained the lofty eminence of the God of Israel. There was one important limitation on his power. This was the noisy, quarrelsome family pantheon that followed in his train. The checks and balances built into this divine assemblage may have preserved the Greeks form the trauma of having to cope with the single, uncontrolled will of a totally autonomous creator god. The confusion created by this half-way house along the patriarchal path can be seen in the Greeks' attitude to fate. They never quite resolved the question of its relationship to Zeus. Unlike Marduk, the head of their pantheon was not really a creator god. He had not therefore the same power to control the destiny of the universe. At times Zeus seems to be subordinate to fate. What the Greeks meant by fate was certain eternally fixed bounds that no-one, not even the gods, could overstep. The concept was the echo of the lost harmonic of the goddess religion, an ordering that followed from some mysterious self-regulating principle in nature.

The theology of the Greeks also differed from that of the people of Israel in another significant respect. Their poets, we earlier observed, wrote down their myths at a stage when their pantheon still contained a numerical equality of the sexes. This was not the only reflex of the goddess cult to survive in Greek religious thought. We have recorded already a number of fragments of the goddess myths that lingered on in folk tales and religious cult and literature. In fact, women's cults and festivals persisted as a feature of Greek religious life until the rise of Christianity. In this respect the Greeks resembled the Canaanites rather than the Israelites. Yet the mainstream of Greek life was nonetheless patriarchal for that. It was the fate of the Greeks, said Friedrich Nietzsche, to subdue the woman in the man and it has justly been said that Greek women lived out their lives in the shadows of the patriarchal world. Not surprisingly, for despite all the relics of the goddess cult that still endured, its over-arching myth had been irrevocably lost.

The loss of this myth left the Greeks as much as the people of Israel searching for some element of permanence in an unstable world. Their search, however, took them along quite different paths. The divergence between their two quests can also be traced in part to the different images they had inherited of the divine. From their past the Israelites had derived the image of a solitary patriarchal god with an omnipotent will. To control this god they had 'moralised' his preoccupation with their fate and then tied his hands by subjecting themselves to what they took to be his ethical demands. The consequence, we have seen, was the ideal of the righteous sufferer who by fulfilling his part of the contract could call upon his divine creditor to release him from his debt of suffering at the end of time. Such a strategy was denied to the Greeks by the very nature of the pantheon their poets had enshrined. Not only was it difficult to 'moralise' so many gods, all with their different personalities, but the personalities themselves left much to be desired. The inheritance of a more barbarous age, the all-too-human characteristics of their gods were not the stuff of which morality could be made. Humourous, vengeful, lustful, they lacked the sombre dignity of 'moral' gods. The philosopher Plato was even loth to allow their tales to be read in his ideal Utopia in case their obvious immorality should prove infectious. Naturally, when men like him sought some moral order in the universe they were forced to dismiss the candidature of such gods in favour of a less humane, more abstract concept.

Deprived of an emotional relationship with a personal god, the Greeks were compelled to intellectualise their task. In the process they virtually invented mathematics, science, philosophy and history. In fact, once set upon this path, they began to speculate about the nature of the universe with a vigour and determination not seen before or since. The list of their philosophers, Thales, Anaximander, Anaximenes, Pythagoras, Heraclitus, Parmenides, Empedocles, Anaxagoras, Leucippus, Democritus, Protagoras, Socrates, Plato and Aristotle, reads like a roll-call of the major seminal thinkers of the West. Yet the search remained throughout the same, the pursuit of some concept of order, of pattern, of lawfulness to replace the lost harmonic of the old goddess myth. The approach may have been different but the focus of these aspirations were the same as in the Old Testament: a relationship to deity that could give some hope of immortality to humankind. All elements in this relationship were intellectualised. The deity, who for the Israelites had been a projection of their emotions, became in the imagination of the Greeks an intellect purged of feelings, the celestial personification of Reason. As a patterned reflection of this Mind, the soul of man acquired a divine intelligence too. The logical capacity of thought could then, it was hoped, uncover the will of the creator. True knowledge would then come from a meeting of minds, of the divine mind, in fact, with the divinely intelligent soul of man.

Unfortunately there was an obvious impediment to this celestial assignation. If there was such an embodiment of absolute truth in the world of the divine then presumably this absolute was imperishably fixed and timeless. Yet when the Greeks looked around them they saw only the very perishable and impermanent material world apparent to their senses. Knowledge of the eternal truth they were seeking, they concluded therefore, could not be derived from the senses. It could only be achieved by the intellect managing somehow to surmount the world of sense-impression. What appeared to the Greeks to be superior to the impressions of the senses was the concepts they used to describe them. These alone in the world they knew appeared to have the timeless quality they sought. In fact, if these concepts were those the creator had given them through his own conceptualisation of the universe then his perfection could be deduced from them as a self-evident truth.

These concepts were embodied in the words and phrases of the language the Greeks spoke. So they ended up worshipping the forms of their own language as a manifestation of their god. Language, however, is imperfect. Its meanings often obscure and evanescent and sometimes contradictory in use. The Greeks soon realised that a more abstract, more perfect language was needed as a vehicle for eternal truths. This they found in mathematics, particularly geometry, which appeared to offer the possibility of formulaic thought totally free from the imperfections of the world of the senses. If the world of the senses did not always fit the model mathematics imposed then, sadly, so much the worse for the world.

Caught in a similar dilemma to that of the Old Testament prophets, the dilemma caused by the death of the goddess, the prophets of the Greeks, their philosophers and sophists, could only reach a resolution through extreme, sometimes absurd, forms of rationality. Their rationalism created a very different kind of world from that of the goddess worshippers. The mythology of the goddess had deified nature. Its light was a reflection of her luminescence. It is surely no accident that the images that have come down to us from Minoan Crete, the only ancient matriarchal culture of which we have much archaeological evidence, seem to present us with a world that trips along on the surface of life, in an innocent and joyful apprehension of the senses. Luminous may have been the eternal truths of the Greeks but there is no doubt that they cast a shadow on the world of the senses. After all, that was the world they rejected in favour of an ethereal world of pure thought.[3] The rejection of the world of the senses, in fact, was taken to extremes. Putting all their faith in the invisible power of a transcendent god, they condemned the visible world as a sinister illusion, a murky and deceptive medium which obscured the heavenly light of the divine intelligence which might otherwise have come percolating down to them.

Why such a benign god chose to create this obfuscating world of the senses was a question the Greeks were not, any more than the prophets of Israel, willing sincerely to confront. Such a question could not easily be accommodated by the attitude they developed towards their god, that strange mixture of admiration for the forms of logic and emotional attachment to eternal truths, that combination of theology and mathematics that was the Greeks' ominous legacy to the culture of the West. The Greeks, of course, would have seen that legacy differently. For men like Socrates and Plato the world of nature was beyond redemption. They could think of no greater aspiration than to leave their bodies at death and drift up to the world of absolute truths so long concealed in life by the unillumined depths of matter, where they could at last, freed from the tyranny of their bodily flesh, live in transcendent bliss in the company of their god. The consequence of this was a dichotomy of thought, between reality and appearance, reason and sense, mind and matter, soul and body, the rational and the mystical, that has afflicted the West ever since.

When Socrates died, it is said that his last words were 'Crito, I owe a cock to Asclepius: will you remember to pay the debt?' It was a tradition for men to give a cock to the Greek god of healing on recovering from a sickness. The inference many have drawn from this dying remark is that in death Socrates felt himself cured from the sickness of life. It was inevitable, perhaps, that the belief in a heavenly truth hidden from men by the obstruction of matter should have led to such a despairing attitude to the world of the senses. From this time on, a strain of world-weariness was always apparent in the Ancient World. At its root lay the debilitating belief in the existence of a trans-cendent god, an abstract embodiment of Reason, so abstract as to seem indifferent, unaware even, of the trivial material affairs of men.

In some ways the people of Israel were less obviously cheated by their prophets of the joys of this world. Their god had, after all, for good or ill, created this world. He had also for some obscure reason elected to take a particular interest in a part of it, namely, the career of his chosen people. The whole idea of the elect implied a creator who, although partial, was at least concerned. The resurrection of the righteous of past ages that would occur on the Day of Judgement was also generally conceived in physical terms. The attitudes of Judaism were thus less rejecting of the material world. The idea of a concerned creator passed on to Christianity with an added ingredient. The Christian god was so concerned that he sent his own son down to earth to redeem his creation through his death.

The life of Christ could be said, in a sense, to have redeemed and, by redeeming, justified the world of the senses. It is interesting in this respect that the biography of Christ in the Gospels has him enjoying a bohemian, some would say in the conditions of the time, libertine existence, enjoying his food and drink, mixing with publicans and sinners, keeping noted prostitutes at less than arm's length. There were Christians of another kind of course, obsessive ascetics like Saint Paul, but the argument that could justify the material world was always there.

The ultimate beneficiaries of this argument were the scientists that first began to appear in the West in the seventeenth century.

Christianity, like Judaism, offered its adherents an emotional truth, a message of salvation. In the Middle Ages that followed the end of Classical civilisation the emotionality of the message took a particularly sombre form, one which tended to excoriate the material world in the manner of Saint Paul. The wars of religion of the sixteenth century, if anything, intensified this attitude. When the wars had run their course, however, and the emotional climate had settled down, men turned once more to the search for a rational truth but this time one focused on a material world justified now as the creation of the Christian god.

The old dilemma of whether a perfect creator could have created an evil world was silently resolved. Aware of his own goodness, God, it was answered, could only have created the best of all possible words. Its complexity, its opacity, its contrariariety at times, was only in semblance an evil and would ultimately prove benign. The universe, in other words, was worth knowing. In this curious way some of the benevolence of the goddess mythology returned in the new myths of science although with consequences that were rather less benign.

With Western science the attempt began to understand creation not in spite of but through the experience of the senses. What was true was what corresponded with the pattern of nature now seen as the reflection of the divine reason of its creator. Truth for the Ancient Greeks had lain in the inner consistency of their logical arguments which always led them circularly back to the self-evident truths of their premises. Truth for the Western scientist lay, in contrast, in the consistency of the patterning it claimed to find in the world of nature. But it was also more than that. The new science was based less on what someone believed than on how and why they believed. All Greek reasoning had gone back to the ordered perfection of God which they claimed to know by intuition. Scientists too had their premises. These were their hypotheses about the nature of the world. The hypotheses, however, were confirmed or disconfirmed not by intuition but by the nature of the material evidence considered relevant to their truth. It is thus with science that we get something we do not find to any great extent among the Greeks, the patient and controlled collection of facts in pursuit of that truth.

The scientist assumes two modes of perceiving the world he investigates. One is accidental. This is the image we innocently form of the world in the daily round. The goddess worshippers assumed that the moon sank into the earth on the nights when it was not visible in the sky. Empirically, their perception did not fit the facts as we know them but it was sufficient for the ordering of their lives. That ordering was metaphorical and ultimately explicable to them in terms of an explanatory myth. The ideal of science, however, is to achieve a perception beyond the realm of metaphor by pursuing truth in accordance with the canons of the community of science.

Yet in formulating his pursuit of truth the scientist must also take refuge in metaphor. When Newton, the greatest scientist of the seventeenth, some would say of any, century propounded his law of universal gravitation, namely, that every body attacks every other body with a force directly proportional to the product of their masses and inversely proportional to the square of the distance between them, he was exploiting a metaphor, not only in using the word 'attack' but in expressing the relation in the form of a 'law' anyway. Laws, as Newton knew them in their original sense, governed the affairs of men. It is easy to forget at this distance of time that after a thousand years of Christianity the opinion was generally held that such secular laws were not even human in conception. They reflected the divine reason of the male creator in his heaven. It was thus but a short and satisfying step to imagine that a concept that governed the relations of god and men could be extrapolated to the world of nature. Was nature, after all, not simply a manifestation of the same divine Reason that regulated the activities of men?

The reign of laws, divinely ordained, thus established its hold on the scientific imagination. But it was based on ultimate premises no more testable than that of the goddess myth. Science could not advance beyond the quantitative to the 'why' of creation. We can imagine that to a goddess worshipper the 'why' would have seemed a pointless question. The goddess had given birth to the earth unaided out of herself. Its hills were her breasts; its rivers her veins. It was her eternal self. Life on earth involved a fatalistic acceptance of her enduring mystery. The 'why' of it only arose after the male creator god was separated out from the product of his own creation and then only after centuries of rationalism had taught men that everything must have a reasoned explanation. Newton was truly the heir of Marduk in this respect. When pondering how his law-governed mechanistic universe got moving in the first place, he assumed that the whole contraption had somehow been hurled into motion by the hand of god. Once this prime mover had done his work, the machine proceeded to function on its own well-oiled way without further divine intervention. But the 'why' of it, the motive of the creator, remained the conundrum it has always been.

That the prime mover was a male god was never doubted by the heirs of Marduk. This god had risen to transcendence to escape the suffocating embrace of a feminine nature. To the early patriarchs what he had escaped was dark, chaotic, demonic even. It could never be in their eyes an embodiment of the masculine divine. The tendency to see nature not as dark and sinister but as a reflection of the ordering intelligence that created it to some extent reversed this attitude but as a trend in thought it was doomed to a limited span of life. A transcendent god who had risen above the world of the senses could not successfully be explored in the patterns of that world for there could never be any certainty in the course of an investigation that the transcendent had actually been made manifest to the experience of the senses. A god who cannot be apprehended by the senses must become in the course of time an illusion to the experimental scientist in search of experiential proof of his existence. Science eventually destroys the patriarchal god, in fact, all gods, because it demonstrates the futility of mysticism and the impossibility of a rational metaphysics. Hence the truth of Nietesche's conclusion, that God is dead and it is the West's restless search for truth that has killed him.

The goddess had given a unity to nature. To her worshippers the world they inhabited was her corporeal being. Her death always threatened to leave the natural world in chaos with the present-iment of chaos. To the Greek philosophers nature was just that, a disabling inscrutable phenomenon that clouded their vision of the transcendent truth beyond it. The scientist accepted the inscrutability but only as a surface phenomenon. Beyond its apparent randomness the universe was governed by laws to the nth degree. This was the myth of science and it contained a curious non-sequitur often perceived by mystics from the East. If the universe is so lawful why bother with empirical investigation? Why not simply intuit it deductively in the first place. In other words, accept it as a fact from the start. It then became the object of awe and meditation. Such a critique, however, misses the point of science as a movement. The purpose of its quest for truth is less the 'why' than the how of it. It is the mode of delivering the truth rather than the nature of the truth itself that defines the role of the scientist. The character of the quest, how it is conducted, is the justification for the quest itself. In other words, not the end of the quest but that there is a quest and that it conforms to the canons of that quest is the raison d'être of science. In this sense the scientists are the heirs not just of Marduk but of Gilgamesh on his underworld quest.

The apparent randomness of the universe is a stimulus to the the scientist in another way. In a random universe there are no restraints on free will. This widens the scope of the investigator by giving him the latitude to travel unrestrained through the world of his data. The free will of the disembodied mind to work its own way to some understanding of the universe is yet another myth essential to the enterprise of science. The quest of this free-floating mind is a lawful quest to the extent that it searches for a law-governed universe in conformity to the canons of science but it has within its approach tendencies that carry it with each step further from the harmonic unity of the goddess.

We see these tendencies most clearly when we contrast the modern scientist with the philosophers of Ancient Greece. The latter deduced their truths from premises they thought self-evident. The scientist, however, induces truth from the sum of the parts of his experience of the material world. Seen in another light, the world he explores is a mechanism and as in all mechanisms the parts can be partially understood before they are fitted to comprise the whole. This is why the advance of science is by a piecemeal and cumulative classification of the world, a piling up of 'little truths' that may one day come together to make a total edifice. This is the implicit ideal but the effect of science is generally the reverse. By tentatively classifying and then sub-classifying the material world, by challenging every category but the canons of the quest, its momentum is always towards the fragmentation of the universe. A unified theory, the scientist's answer to the goddess myth, has beckoned tantalisingly for centuries but always to disappoint.

Science ends by killing the creator god the vision of whom had originally invoked its search for truth. It also destroys the other element in the patriarchal spiritual equation: the immortal soul. The soul becomes a victim of its emphasis on the evidence of the senses. As all truth is in the course of time reduced to the test of sense experience, consciousness itself becomes merely a function of the coordinator of that experience, the human brain. The soul, once the most elevated form of consciousness, so elevated it could survive out of the body after death, is demoted to being a reflex of stimulus-response connections, of neural impulses in the brain. As the soul dies, the self, the shell that contained it, suffers the loss of its inner hold and starts to collapse out into innumerable fragments.

It is doubtful if the world of the goddess cult had a concept of the self in the modern sense or any individual psychology of any depth. Its orientation was outward to the inspirited world around it not inward to a self. It was religions like Judaism and Christianity which hollowed out the self as a battleground of motive. To the scientist the significance of the self was that of a perceptor that refracted the experiences of the senses. It was not long however before science turned from the source of that experience to the perceptor itself. With that, psychology, in fact, all the psychologies of modern life were born, bringing to the self the fragmentation already inflicted on the outer world. Thus the true spiritual descendant of the Old Testament prophets relaxes now on the psychotherapist's couch.

It is surely no coincidence that the rise of science has gone hand in hand with the spread of an increasingly unbridled egoism in the West. The ego is the power-house of the self. Paradoxically, it becomes more self-seeking in the absence of a coherent concept of the self. Nothing feeds the intolerant aggrandisement of the ego more than the anxiety of a disintegrating self to survive in a morally chaotic universe. Science gave distant encouragement to this development for it needed the free-floating unconditioned self to fulfil its quest.

For centuries Judaism and Christianity had circumscribed the self and channelled its egoism through an ethical creed. Any hope that this moral enterprise might offer succour to modern man has not survived the arrival of the scientist on the scene. When Adam was driven from Eden he found himself in a degraded world but one that made him very much the centre of the universe. Not only was he the focus of his creator's moral concern but the earth he tilled was happily the axis on which the constellations turned and he was divinely ordained to do with it what he willed. For Jew and Greek alike, man was the measure of the universe.

The foundations of this unquestioned assumption were corroded away by the investigations of the scientist into the 'true' nature of the material world. When in the sixteenth century Kepler and Copernicus confirmed the heliocentric model of the solar system they only asserted what knowledgeable men had long suspected but the effect of their work was to tip the earth off its axis and send it spinning round the sun. The uniqueness of the patriarchal inheritance was further confounded by the discoveries of Galileo. Other planets had satellites, it seemed, moons like that of earth. To a disbelieving Church the astronomer offered the evidence visible through the lens of his telescope, the evidence, in other words, of the senses. Newton admittedly brought some order to this vision. His universe was a mechanism that ran in harmony with laws elegantly expressible in mathematical terms but the earth was only a part of the mechanism, a cog in the wheel of infinitude.

The scientists of the sixteenth and seventeenth century destroyed the space of patriarchal myth by stretching it to unimaginable lengths. The god of the Old Testament created time when he set the universe in motion. That 'historical' time was predicted to end on the Day of Judgement with the salvation of the elect. Many have been the attempts of biblical fundamentalists to estimate the life span of the universe to their own day by totalling up the biographies of biblical characters back to the day of creation. In the nineteenth century, however, Darwin showed not only that life on earth pre-dated the biblical creation but that man, the measure of it, was merely one point, a stage of development on an evolutionary scale of inconceivable length.

Even at this stage some idealism still remained. Man could at least admire the sublime in the universe by passive contemplation, perhaps imagine a new, still more inscrutable, creator god, an architect of complexity for its own sake, less morally concerned, until, that is, Marx asserted that man could never be a passive receptor, but was always an organism engaged with the environment, his perceptions simply a reflex of his activities in the material world. In Marx's materialism man's entire apparatus of perception was finally absorbed into the blind locomotion of the dialectic of material change. Finally, with Einstein, matter itself became an illusion of energy. The faster a thing moves, he demonstrated, the more its mass increases. Time, in addition, had no absolute meaning but was affected by gravity. With acceleration through space, time slows down. Everything, therefore, is relative and the basis of his theory of relativity was that space and time are not separate, as previously thought, but inextricably connected.

Einstein's theory of relativity seemed absurd when first proposed for it appeared to contradict the deepest assumptions of patriarchal thought. Yet the consequences of its popularisation have been profound. It has deposited relativism on an unsuspecting world. Truth now cannot be absolute but must always be a matter of perspective. The problem of the relativist is how to prevent himself becoming a victim of his own relativism. If the observer is from another perspective only another observed then how, by the canons of science, can he avoid extending his own observation to include himself. Patriarchy is nothing without its absolute truths for these were ultimately only the self-evident truths of its own transcendental creator and generations of western philosophers laboured to affirm this connection. In a sense what Einstein did was to distil in an equation a lethal concoction that had long been brewing in the heart of western culture. The curious combination of rationalism and materialism in science was always going to end by destroying the transcendental creator and wrecking the patriarchal value system.

Science has not had it all its own way. It has had at times a battle to survive. Not surprisingly, it has provoked hostile reactions. There has been a great deal of hostility from the Church which foresaw the consequences of the untrammelled search for a truth it had, in origin at least, partly helped to create. Another was from the Romantic movement in western thought which began in the eighteenth century. The Romantics turned against the rule of reason. Also, where science appeared to diminish the individual by robbing him of his soul they reaffirmed the inner self by freeing it from the last fetters of the patriarchal value system. As an antidote to its conventions they counselled a return to nature.

But from the nature to which they wished to return the goddess had already fled. Nature had ceased to be inspirited. Centuries of rationalism had seen to that. Attempts to re-inspirit it were vain for who could now seriously believe in a goddess, or, indeed, any gods. Nature could only be admired as a landscape for art. Wild and craggily precipitous might be its wonders but spiritually they were dead, inert, fit only for aesthetic contemplation at best. Romanticism, moreover, gave a final savage twist to the egoism of the West. By exalting the individual at the expense of all social convention, it prepared the way for the war of all against all so characteristic a feature of modern life. Its fateful legacy is with us today in the killing zones of our cities.

'Knowledge is power', said Francis Bacon, the leading theoretician of seventeenth century science. The power he sought was to give mankind mastery over the forces of nature by the results of scientific discovery. Unconsciously, he was calling on science to fulfil the old biblical mandate to go forth and subdue the earth. In all analysis, there is a hint of cruelty. In the endless classification of the scientist there is a failure somehow to accept the phenomenon aesthetically in itself and be at peace with it. In a bizarre way, Bacon's own death, at least the manner of it, exemplifies the truth of this. He died of a chill caught one night when he got out of bed to strangle a chicken and stuff it full of snow. He had intended it to be an experiment on refrigeration. When analysis is turned into a technology the angst at the heart of it, the restlessness, converts into a power drive that breaks down the phenomenon, the thing in itself, and transforms it into something more malleable to human ends.

It is no surprise, therefore, to find technology condemned by the aesthetic defenders of the earth. The earth, we have seen, was once the embodiment of the goddess. Her mythology placed mankind in symbiotic relation with a nature steeped in sacredness. To her worshippers nature was not an 'it' but a 'thou'. The bark of a tree was her sacred skin, its resin her menstrual blood, its wood her flesh, its roots ran through the mouths of the skulls of the dead to her very womb itself. No doubt some of this attitude lingered on into the patriarchal period. 'Even in Classical times the Ancient Greeks as a people still lived in a divinely inspirited nature.

The spirit within, however, could not for all time survive the death of the goddess. In the modern world matter has been desacralised. Shorn of the goddess, it has long since lost its link with its transcendental male creator. Worse than that, it has been left unprotected to face the technology, the power-drive of the West. God made a contract with Noah to succour his seed but nature, sadly, was not part of it. Her protecting contract had lain hidden in the goddess myths. With those gone, there was no protection left. The consequences we see in the world around us, a landscape forged by technology from resources mercilessly drilled from the womb of Mother Earth.

What was it, then, that we lost when we lost the mythology of the goddess? What was the vision of those, women we presume, who sculpted the figurine at Catal Hüyük with mother and daughter enclasped like Siamese twins? It was a vision of a world in which above and below, inner and outer, world and self were an indissoluble unity, a world conceived as a Great Mother with her daughter, the moon goddess, returning eternally like the whole of humankind to her earthy embrace. This was the message of those many dying heroines and goddesses that have come down to us in myth. The world they illumined we can probably never resurrect. Even if we could, we would no doubt find it too chthonic, too accepting of the cyclical, perhaps too fatalistic for our tastes. It is hard, too, for us to accept that life is a mystery, its truth forever veiled, its understanding a matter of mystical attunement to the whole rather than analytical assessment of its parts. The Christian West has had its mystics, men and women who strove to see the harmony through the creator's eye, but, if not condemned as heretical, they were generally kept apart from the mainstream of the Church's life. Philosophically, it is the East that has inherited most of the legacy of mysticism not the Christian West.

The mystic attempts to capture in a vision the unity behind the multiplicity of phenomena. A visionary orientation to the harmony of the whole runs counter to the measuring and classifying approach to the material world which has come to predominate in Western science. It is in the East, where the analytical attitude has been less developed, that the mystical tradition has been refined to the greatest extent. The assumption from which all Eastern mystical religions begin is that the multitude of phenomenon perceived by the senses are merely different manifestations of one all-embracing reality. The supreme goal of their followers is to become aware of this ultimate unity and achieve a kind of visionary identification with it. The acquisition of this awareness, known as 'enlightenment', involves, inevitably, the dissolution of the ego. The unified vision is of a reality dynamic and organic in which spirit and matter are intertwined. Significantly, the concept is frequently expressed in maternal terms. In the words of the Taoist sage, Lao Tzu:

'There was something complete and nebulous
Which existed before the Heaven and the Earth
Silent, invisible
Unchanging, standing as One.
Unceasing, ever-revolving
Able to be the Mother of the World
I do not knows its name and call it Tao.'[4]

The Tao in question is the 'path' or the way of enlightenment, the natural order or flow of the universe, harmony with which is essential for a happy and spontaneous life. Yet, in describing it, Lao Tzu conjures up our goddess in all but name.

The goddess of the ancient matriarchal culture was inherent in nature. More than just a blind force, we could almost say she was a personality, a principle of intelligence and creativity that pervaded it. Much of this notion, too, was retained in the East. Where the West saw the creative principle directing its creation from above, the East conceived it as working to assemble its manifestations from within. The dynamics of the goddess's creative power were cyclical. What she gave returned eternally to herself to be released once more in her own life force. That idea, too, was preserved in the East. We find it in Buddhism, in the 'samsara' 'the cosmic wheel of existence, in Hinduism, in the notion of 'Karma', the cycle of consequence that connects successive lives, in the innumerable cycles of Jainism, in the Chinese conception of the Tao, the cosmic way along which 'ch'i', the life force, flows, forever returning to its source.

It is interesting to speculate as to why the East managed to hold onto so many features of the old cosmology that were lost in the West. India had a flourishing urban civilisation as early as the third millennium B.C. At one of its sites, Harappa, a large number of pottery figurines of pregnant females have been found which look very much like the Venus figurines we noted further to the west. These and other evidence point to the presence of a Mother Goddess as powerful as the goddesses of the Mediterranean and the Middle East. This whole region was also hit by an invasion of patriarchal sky god worshippers similar to those that led to the rise of Marduk in the west.

In India, however, the density of patriarchal settlement was always strongest in the north. For centuries the mass of the people in the south were scarcely touched and it is there that we find an unbroken line of goddess worship right up to the present day. It is no surprise that a mother goddess does not figure much in the earliest literature of the patriarchal invaders. Gradually, however, she does appear and begins to make her way into the

Hinduism of the Brahmans, the descendants of the patriarchal invaders, during the Middle Ages. It is likely therefore that the wholistic, mystical and cyclical features of Indian religion also percolated through over the centuries from the same matriarchal source.

Yet, strong though this undercurrent remained, when compared with the West, it could only percolate upwards through the filters of the dominant patriarchal culture imposed by the invaders. The logic of patriarchal religious development continued to hold sway, giving to Eastern theology an impetus and a direction not unlike that we have observed in the West. Male gods came to the fore in the pantheon. Goddesses lost a lot of their ancient status. Moreover, the concepts of the old religion were radically transformed in the process of acceptance and much of their former meaning and significance was lost. The creative principle may have been seen operating within the world and not above it but it was masculinised and abstracted just as in the West.

Very little remains in Eastern mysticism of the primitive animism of the old cult, the idea of the goddess as a persona inherent in nature. Furthermore, the cyclicality of her creative force, once a source of exaltation to worshippers, who saw in it the spiral pathway to the after-life, has been transformed by patriarchal theologians into a cause of pessimism and withdrawal. The Hindu mystic seeks to free himself from the yoke of karma. On this point Hindu sacred literature is very clear. The Buddhist struggles to transcend the vicious cycle of samsara, to see through the veil of Maya, the distracting illusions of the phenomenal world, and reach a total state of liberation called Nirvana. The attitude enjoined is always one of disengagement from the world of the senses to get to the transcendent unity behind the shroud.

Such a mentality of ascetic withdrawal seems alien to what we know of Minoan Crete, the only ancient matriarchal culture of which much is known. There life seems to have a vivacity, a joy in the multiplicity of the phenomenal world, a patina of high-spiritedness that still lingers playfully on the images of it that have come down to us. Of all the Oriental mystical traditions, only Taoism, the most feminine of them all, appears to have retained some notion of this joyful immersion in the world of the senses. Spontaneity is the principle of the Taoist, spontaneity modelled on the flow of the Tao. A spontaneous life is one lived in harmony with nature but a nature seen from more of a feminine aspect than in the West. In achieving this harmony it is the feminine aspect of ourselves the Taoist emphasises. By displaying the yielding and intuitive qualities in our own natures, we can merge with the flow of the Tao and enjoy a perfectly balanced yet sensuous existence on the ever-shifting surface of the world of the senses. That, for the Taoist, is the state of perfect unity.

Taoism is less a religion more a set of prescriptions for the good life. We search in vain in its texts for any trace of the mythology of the goddess. If there was ever a Taoist hanged goddess, she is no longer there. Her tree, though, can still be found in other Chinese texts. A book from the time of the Chou dynasty tells of an eastern Valley of Light. There grew a tree known as the Fu-sang, a hundred miles high, it was in the branches of this tree that the sun rested before beginning its daily crossing of the sky. Leaving the tree, the sun made its daily transit till it reached the mountain of Yen-tzu in the extreme west. There, where it set, grew the Jo tree whose flowers shone with a reddish glow.[5]

The Fu-sang was, in actual fact, the mulberry tree, a tree almost universally sacred not to the sun but to the moon. The myth is clearly a solarisation of an earlier lunar myth and the significance of that myth we already know. The tree is the world tree, the umbilicus of earth, the tree of life and knowledge. Strange, far to the East, it has managed to survive in this quaint myth. Perhaps not so strange, for we find it again, more abstract now, as the Tree of Enlightenment, the 'bodhi', under which the Buddha sat and meditated upon eternal truth. He was tempted there, say Buddhists, by Mara, the Evil One, but we now know who she once was, the guardian spirit of the tree itself. Far to the north and west it was the same tree from which a far less civilised Viking god swung for nine days and nights for a vision of destiny and a knowledge of the fates. Deprived of its life-giving properties, it became the tree of knowledge whose baleful fruit the seductive Eve passed on to Adam. To this same spot, perhaps same tree, popular church tradition believed, Christ returned to hang upon the cross. He was not the first, of course, to return to this fateful spot. Many had been there before him, a line of goddesses, in fact, and a maiden who had hung there turning, twisting, turning, for a dying vision of the after-life.

1 Jonah ch. 1 v. 17.
2 Jonah ch. 2 v. 1-10.
3 Russell E, *History of Western Philosophy*. George Allen and Unwin London 1946 p. 93.
4 Quoted in Chang Chung Yuan: *Creativity and Taoism*. Wildwood House, London 1963 pp 34-35.
5 Bodde D. *'Myths of Ancient China'* in Kramer S. N. (ed.) Mythologies of the Ancient World, Anchor Books. New York 1961 pp 367-408.

FREE DETAILED CATALOGUE

Capall Bann is owned and run by people actively involved in many of the areas in which we publish. A detailed illustrated catalogue is available on request, SAE or International Postal Coupon appreciated. **Titles can be ordered direct from Capall Bann, post free in the UK** (cheque or PO with order) or from good bookshops and specialist outlets. Do contact us for details on the latest releases at: **Capall Bann Publishing, Freshfields, Chieveley, Berks, RG20 8TF.** Titles include:

A Breath Behind Time, Terri Hector
Angels and Goddesses - Celtic Christianity & Paganism, M. Howard
Arthur - The Legend Unveiled, C Johnson & E Lung
Astrology The Inner Eye - A Guide in Everyday Language, E Smith
Auguries and Omens - The Magical Lore of Birds, Yvonne Aburrow
Asyniur - Womens Mysteries in the Northern Tradition, S McGrath
Begonnings - Geomancy, Builder's Rites & Electional Astrology in the
    European Tradition, Nigel Pennick Between Earth and Sky, Julia Day
Book of the Veil , Peter Paddon
Caer Sidhe - Celtic Astrology and Astronomy, Vol 1, Michael Bayley
Caer Sidhe - Celtic Astrology and Astronomy, Vol 2 M Bayley
Call of the Horned Piper, Nigel Jackson
Cat's Company, Ann Walker
Celtic Faery Shamanism, Catrin James
Celtic Faery Shamanism - The Wisdom of the Otherworld, Catrin James
Celtic Lore & Druidic Ritual, Rhiannon Ryall
Celtic Sacifice - Pre Christian Ritual & Religion, Marion Pearce
Celtic Saints and the Glastonbury Zodiac, Mary Caine
Circle and the Square, Jack Gale
Compleat Vampyre - The Vampyre Shaman, Nigel Jackson
Creating Form From the Mist - The Wisdom of Women in Celtic Myth and
    Culture, Lynne Sinclair-Wood
Crystal Clear - A Guide to Quartz Crystal, Jennifer Dent
Crystal Doorways, Simon & Sue Lilly
Crossing the Borderlines - Guising, Masking & Ritual Animal Disguise in the
    European Tradition, Nigel Pennick
Dragons of the West, Nigel Pennick

Earth Dance - A Year of Pagan Rituals, Jan Brodie
Earth Harmony - Places of Power, Holiness & Healing, Nigel Pennick
Earth Magic, Margaret McArthur
Eildon Tree (The) Romany Language & Lore, Michael Hoadley
Enchanted Forest - The Magical Lore of Trees, Yvonne Aburrow
Eternal Priestess, Sage Weston
Eternally Yours Faithfully, Roy Radford & Evelyn Gregory
Everything You Always Wanted To Know About Your Body, But So Far
    Nobody's Been Able To Tell You, Chris Thomas & D Baker
Face of the Deep - Healing Body & Soul, Penny Allen
Fairies in the Irish Tradition, Molly Gowen
Familiars - Animal Powers of Britain, Anna Franklin
Fool's First Steps, (The) Chris Thomas
Forest Paths - Tree Divination, Brian Harrison, Ill. S. Rouse
From Past to Future Life, Dr Roger Webber
God Year, The, Nigel Pennick & Helen Field
Goddess on the Cross, Dr George Young
Goddess Year, The, Nigel Pennick & Helen Field
Goddesses, Guardians & Groves, Jack Gale
Handbook For Pagan Healers, Liz Joan
Handbook of Fairies, Ronan Coghlan
Healing Book, The, Chris Thomas and Diane Baker
Healing Homes, Jennifer Dent
Healing Journeys, Paul Williamson
Healing Stones, Sue Philips
Herb Craft - Shamanic & Ritual Use of Herbs, Lavender & Franklin
Hidden Heritage - Exploring Ancient Essex, Terry Johnson
Hub of the Wheel, Skytoucher
In Search of Herne the Hunter, Eric Fitch
Inner Celtia, Alan Richardson & David Annwn
Inner Mysteries of the Goths, Nigel Pennick
Inner Space Workbook - Develop Thru Tarot, C Summers & J Vayne
Intuitive Journey, Ann Walker
Isis - African Queen, Akkadia Ford
Journey Home, The, Chris Thomas
Kecks, Keddles & Kesh - Celtic Lang & The Cog Almanac, Bayley
Language of the Psycards, Berenice
Legend of Robin Hood, The, Richard Rutherford-Moore
Lid Off the Cauldron, Patricia Crowther
Light From the Shadows - Modern Traditional Witchcraft, Gwyn
Living Tarot, Ann Walker
Lore of the Sacred Horse, Marion Davies

Lost Lands & Sunken Cities (2nd ed.), Nigel Pennick
Magic of Herbs - A Complete Home Herbal, Rhiannon Ryall
Magical Guardians - Exploring the Spirit and Nature of Trees, Philip Heselton
Magical History of the Horse, Janet Farrar & Virginia Russell
Magical Lore of Animals, Yvonne Aburrow
Magical Lore of Cats, Marion Davies
Magical Lore of Herbs, Marion Davies
Magick Without Peers, Ariadne Rainbird & David Rankine
Masks of Misrule - Horned God & His Cult in Europe, Nigel Jackson
Medicine For The Coming Age, Lisa Sand MD
Medium Rare - Reminiscences of a Clairvoyant, Muriel Renard
Menopause and the Emotions, Kathleen I Macpherson
Mind Massage - 60 Creative Visualisations, Marlene Maundrill
Mirrors of Magic - Evoking the Spirit of the Dewponds, P Heselton
Moon Mysteries, Jan Brodie
Mysteries of the Runes, Michael Howard
Mystic Life of Animals, Ann Walker
New Celtic Oracle The, Nigel Pennick & Nigel Jackson
Oracle of Geomancy, Nigel Pennick
Pagan Feasts - Seasonal Food for the 8 Festivals, Franklin & Phillips
Patchwork of Magic - Living in a Pagan World, Julia Day
Pathworking - A Practical Book of Guided Meditations, Pete Jennings
Personal Power, Anna Franklin
Pickingill Papers - The Origins of Gardnerian Wicca, Bill Liddell
Pillars of Tubal Cain, Nigel Jackson
Places of Pilgrimage and Healing, Adrian Cooper
Practical Divining, Richard Foord
Practical Meditation, Steve Hounsome
Practical Spirituality, Steve Hounsome
Psychic Self Defence - Real Solutions, Jan Brodie
Real Fairies, David Tame
Reality - How It Works & Why It Mostly Doesn't, Rik Dent
Romany Tapestry, Michael Houghton
Runic Astrology, Nigel Pennick
Sacred Animals, Gordon MacLellan
Sacred Celtic Animals, Marion Davies, Ill. Simon Rouse
Sacred Dorset - On the Path of the Dragon, Peter Knight
Sacred Grove - The Mysteries of the Forest, Yvonne Aburrow
Sacred Geometry, Nigel Pennick
Sacred Nature, Ancient Wisdom & Modern Meanings, A Cooper
Sacred Ring - Pagan Origins of British Folk Festivals, M. Howard
Season of Sorcery - On Becoming a Wisewoman, Poppy Palin

Seasonal Magic - Diary of a Village Witch, Paddy Slade
Secret Places of the Goddess, Philip Heselton
Secret Signs & Sigils, Nigel Pennick
Self Enlightenment, Mayan O'Brien
Shamanica, Martine Ashe
Spirits of the Air, Jaq D Hawkins
Spirits of the Earth, Jaq D Hawkins
Spirits of the Earth, Jaq D Hawkins
Stony Gaze, Investigating Celtic Heads John Billingsley
Stumbling Through the Undergrowth , Mark Kirwan-Heyhoe
Subterranean Kingdom, The, revised 2nd ed, Nigel Pennick
Symbols of Ancient Gods, Rhiannon Ryall
Talking to the Earth, Gordon MacLellan
Taming the Wolf - Full Moon Meditations, Steve Hounsome
Teachings of the Wisewomen, Rhiannon Ryall
The Other Kingdoms Speak, Helena Hawley
Tree: Essence of Healing, Simon & Sue Lilly
Tree: Essence, Spirit & Teacher, Simon & Sue Lilly
Through the Veil, Peter Paddon
Torch and the Spear, Patrick Regan
Understanding Chaos Magic, Jaq D Hawkins
Vortex - The End of History, Mary Russell
Warp and Weft - In Search of the I-Ching, William de Fancourt
Warriors at the Edge of Time, Jan Fry
Water Witches, Tony Steele
Way of the Magus, Michael Howard
Weaving a Web of Magic, Rhiannon Ryall
West Country Wicca, Rhiannon Ryall
Wildwitch - The Craft of the Natural Psychic, Poppy Palin
Wildwood King , Philip Kane
Witches of Oz, Matthew & Julia Philips
Wondrous Land - The Faery Faith of Ireland by Dr Kay Mullin
Working With the Merlin, Geoff Hughes
Your Talking Pet, Ann Walker
Menopausal Woman on the Run, Jaki da Costa

Environmental
Gardening For Wildlife Ron Wilson

Capall Bann Publishing
Julia & Jon Day
Auton Farm, Milverton
Somerset, TA4 1NE
Tel 01823 401528
Fax 01823 401529
www.capallbann.co.uk